CA 8/08

Cricket's
GREAT
ALL-ROUNDERS

First published in Australia in 2008 by
New Holland Publishers Australia Pty Ltd
Sydney • Auckland • London • Cape Town

1/66 Gibbes Street Chatswood NSW 2067 Australia
218 Lake Road Northcote Auckland New Zealand
86 Edgware Road London W2 2EA United Kingdom
80 McKenzie Street Cape Town 8001 South Africa

A record of this book is held at the National Library
of Australia.

ISBN: 9781741106428

Publisher: Fiona Schultz
Publishing Manager: Lliane Clarke
Editor: Terry Johnston
Project Editor: Jenny Scepanovic
Designer: Natasha Hayles
Production Manager: Linda Bottari
Production Assistant: Liz Malcolm
Printer: Power Printing (China)

10 9 8 7 6 5 4 3 2 1

Cricket's GREAT ALL-ROUNDERS

THE GREATEST ACROSS THREE CENTURIES AND NINE COUNTRIES

NEW HOLLAND

KERSI MEHER-HOMJI

Dedicated to the memory of
my friend Michael Nemeruck,
whose every sentence included a
reference to cricketing all-rounders.

Acknowledgements

This book would not have been finished at all but for the encouragement from Carl Harrison-Ford, Jason Ford and statistical help from Rajesh Kumar. These days so many books are written on cricket that mostly only those written/ghost written by cricketing celebrities see the light of day. But Carl and Jason egged me on as I tried to finish the last 15 kilometres of the marathon *Cricket's Great All-Rounders* without a publisher in sight.

So thank you Martin Ford and Diane Ward of New Holland Publishers for accepting this book, the first book on international cricket all-rounders, spanning three centuries and nine countries and not forgetting the gloved all-rounders.

My grateful thanks to Alan Davidson, Australia's great Test all-rounder, who wrote a terrific foreword for my book. I also thank him for spending time with me on the definition of the term cricketing all-rounder.

Warwick Franks has been an inspiration and made valuable suggestions and I acknowledge the help of Colin Clowes and Bob Brenner from NSW Cricket Association Library.

Thank you, Rajesh Kumar, India's top statistician and friend, for answering all my statistical queries quicker than a century from Viv Richards or Adam Gilchrist. Also I thank another friend C. Keshava Murthy for his statistical suggestions.

The books and magazines referred to in writing this book have been listed in the Bibliography. But I must especially thank the *Cricinfo* website, many editions of *Wisden Cricketers' Almanack*, *World Cricketers* by Christopher Martin-Jenkins and *The Wisden Book of Test Cricket, Volumes I and II* compiled and edited by Bill Frindall.

Every effort has been made to contact the holders of copyright.

Finally, my thanks go to the late Vinoo Mankad, the great Indian all-rounder of 1940s and 50s, and Andrew Flintoff of this millennium to inspire me to write this book.

Foreword

by Alan Davidson

ricket has probably produced more literature than all other sports put together. The variety of topics is amazing. Not for Kersi Meher-Homji a humdrum biography or a tour book full of controversies. He specialises in off-beat themes not touched by other authors.

The titles of some of his previous 11 books: *Out for a Duck, Nervous Nineties, Six Appeal, Hat-Tricks, Famous Cricketing Families, Dramatic Debuts and Swan Songs* prove what I mean. Who else would dare to write a book on cricketers making ducks?

Being an all-rounder myself, I often wondered as to when a comprehensive book on cricket all-rounders would ever be published. And lo 'n behold, Kersi Meher-Homji—a cricket-lover I have known for three decades—sent me his manuscript on this very topic. I found it an interesting read.

Like his previous books, *Cricket's Great All-Rounders* has international flavour. It includes versatile cricketers from nine countries spanning three centuries. Although focusing on Test all-rounders from George Giffen, Monty Noble, Keith Miller and Richie Benaud to Garry Sobers, Ian Botham, Imran Khan, Richard Hadlee, Kapil Dev and Andrew Flintoff, he also covers one-day international all-rounders from the mentally tough Steve Waugh to the six-smashers Shahid Afridi, Andrew Symonds and Sanath Jayasuriya. He also features the much-neglected wicketkeeper-batsmen all-rounders from Les Ames, Godfrey Evans, Jeff Dujon and Alan Knott to Rod Marsh, Ian Healy, Mark Boucher and Adam Gilchrist.

Being a research scientist by profession and a noted cricket statistician, Kersi is well equipped to put together a book encompassing all-round excellence in proper perspective, using statistics judiciously.

Although the book is rich in facts and figures, Kersi writes with insight and humour. A few examples:

'Bowling was Kapil Dev's 'wife', his life, his 10 to 6 job. Batting was his 'mistress', his indulgence. He seldom strayed when bowling and hardly batted with a straight bat, his cross-bat flings giving spectators almost orgasmic delight.'

'If facing the Windies pace like fire in 1980s was like walking on burning coal, keeping wickets to them was like placing a burning ember on your tongue. Ask Jeff Dujon!'

The book also includes less-known facts, namely Garry Sobers was born with 12 fingers. Also one of Andrew Flintoff's sixes almost landed in his Dad Colin's palm in the upper tier of a Stand during the 2004 Birmingham Test. But Dad 'dropped' it for which he was roasted by Andrew during the post-match press interview!

Kersi's book made me feel nostalgic, thinking of 'Nugget' Miller and my mate Richie Benaud. To me 'Nugget', Garry Sobers and Ian Botham were the greatest all-rounders.

Kersi has brought their and other all-rounders' mighty deeds to life. As David McNicoll wrote in *The Bulletin* in 1994, 'Move over *Wisden*. If you have not heard of Kersi Meher-Homji, let me tell you he has given me more enjoyment with his cricket book [*Out for a Duck*] than some of the turgid tomes produced by various of our Test cricketers … This chap Homji is the first person I've encountered who can make a cricket book interesting for a non-cricket fan. Quite an achievement.'

I wish Kersi all the best for his engrossing and entertaining *Cricket's Great All-Rounders*. I am deeply honoured to be associated in a small way with this magnificent publication.

Alan Davidson

Maurice Tate, page 44

Contents

Foreword by Alan Davidson — 8

Introduction — 14

The Golden Age of All-Rounders — 21

1 TOP TEST ALL-ROUNDERS — 24

George Giffen Australia — 26

Monty Noble Australia — 31

Aubrey Faulkner South Africa — 37

Jack Gregory Australia — 40

Maurice Tate England — 45

Wally Hammond England — 53

Mark Boucher, page 236

Keith Miller Australia   **61**

Vinoo Mankad India   **68**

Trevor Bailey England   **74**

Richie Benaud Australia   **78**

Alan Davidson Australia   **87**

John Reid New Zealand   **94**

Trevor Goddard South Africa   **99**

Garry Sobers West Indies   **103**

Tony Greig England   **109**

Ian Botham England   **114**

Imran Khan Pakistan   **120**

Kapil Dev India   **126**

Richard Hadlee New Zealand   **133**

Contents

Wasim Akram Pakistan   **140**

Chris Cairns New Zealand   **148**

Shaun Pollock South Africa   **155**

Jacques Kallis South Africa   **160**

Daniel Vettori New Zealand   **168**

Andrew Flintoff England   **173**

2 WICKETKEEPING TEST ALL-ROUNDERS   **180**

Les Ames England   **182**

Godfrey Evans England   **186**

Farokh Engineer India   **189**

James M Parks England   **193**

Alec Stewart England   **195**

John Waite South Africa   **198**

Alan Knott England   **201**

Syed Kirmani India   **205**

Jeffrey Dujon West Indies   **209**

Rod Marsh Australia   **212**

Ian Healy Australia   **217**

Andy Flower Zimbabwe   **222**

Adam Gilchrist Australia   **228**

Mark Boucher South Africa   **235**

Kumar Sangakkara Sri Lanka   **238**

3 **ONE-DAY INTERNATIONAL ALL-ROUNDERS**   **242**

Steve Waugh Australia   **244**

Michael Bevan Australia   **249**

Lance Klusener South Africa   **252**

Chris Harris New Zealand   **256**

Sanath Jayasuriya Sri Lanka   **259**

Shahid Afridi Pakistan   **264**

Abdul Razzaq Pakistan   **267**

Chris Gayle West Indies   **270**

Andrew Symonds Australia   **273**

Snippets   279

Statistics   287

Bibliography   304

Index   307

Introduction

Sobers or Imran, Tarzan or Gorilla, Beno or Davo, Hadlee or Freddie—take your pick.

Before the emergence of South Africa's Jacques Kallis and England's Andrew 'Freddie' Flintoff on the Test scene, it seemed that Test all-rounders had become a dying race. Where are the Giffens, Nobles and Faulkners of pre-World War II era, the Millers, Mankads, Benauds, Davidsons, Reids and Goddards of 1950s and 1960s, the Sobers, Greigs, Bothams, Imrans, Hadlees, Kapils and Wasim Akrams of more recent times?

The enigmatic Carl Hooper of the West Indies, the adventurous Chris Cairns of New Zealand and the steadfast South Africans Shaun Pollock and Kallis showed potential as 20th century turned to 21st.

Then came the fantastic 2005 Ashes series in England when England's 27-year-old charismatic Flintoff effected vital breakthroughs while bowling and hit runs and sixes with wild abandon as England retained the Ashes after 16 years.

He was then hailed as the next Ian Botham. The 193cm tall 'Freddie' weighing 101kg has the potential to be a destructive batsman who can spray sixes like confetti, a fiery fast bowler with a mean bouncer and a brilliant close-in fielder, making him a three-in-one match winner. But injuries have inhibited his progress in subsequent years.

The shortage of all-rounders is keenly felt in Australia. Despite their almost non-stop successes over a decade, they have not produced a genuine all-rounder since Richie Benaud retired in 1963. Australia had produced two of the first genuine all-rounders in George Giffen 1881–1896 and Monty Noble

1897–1909. The early post-World War II period was dominated by Australian all-rounders Keith Miller, Benaud and Alan Davidson. Suddenly, and for a prolonged period, it was a case of 'and then there were none down under'. The last four decades have produced only limited-overs all-rounders, useful but not brilliant, in Gary Gilmour, Steve Waugh, Michael Bevan, Ian Harvey, Darren Lehmann, Andrew Symonds and Shane Watson. Symonds has had a good run with both bat and ball in recent years. His acrobatic fielding has added a zing to the current Australian side. He promises to become the Test all-rounder Australia has been chasing for the last few decades.

Still Australia is doing extremely well in Tests and limited-overs internationals. That makes one ponder: In these days of specialisation, are all-rounders necessary at Test level? Trevor Bailey, a capable all-rounder himself, wrote in his biography of Garry Sobers titled *Sir Gary*, 'Every sport needs balance and this is what the all-rounder provides in cricket'.

An all-rounder adds a third or fourth dimension to cricket but what is the definition of a great all-rounder? On many pages, this book poses this question. For instance, can we consider Shane Warne an all-rounder as he scored 3154 runs and took 708 wickets, a record till November 2007 in Test cricket? To experts he is an outstanding bowler but only a useful batsman who has scored over 3000 runs because he played 145 Tests.

As ace all-rounder Alan Davidson who retired in 1962 said, 'When I started playing state cricket at 20 and Richie [Benaud] at 19, we were encouraged to be both bowlers and batsmen. These days, cricketers are categorised as batsmen or bowlers as they start their career. This could explain why there are fewer all-rounders now than in our days. I think the selectors are currently on the right track but should also be looking at players in the Australian Under-19s. In the meantime we just need to be patient. People like Andrew Flintoff take years to develop. He's done a lot of hard work and had a lot of expert coaching. That's the difference between the superstars and the others.'.

In Andrew Symonds and Shane Watson, Australia currently have two potential all-rounders but the players are sometimes thrust into this role in the longer format of the game. 'That's a very difficult thing to achieve', added Davidson, 78, a former national selector. 'There are prospects, but nobody who shows enormous potential. I think Watson's a very fine young batsman but he's got an awful lot to learn about bowling.'

Davidson added that a true all-rounder should be able to take five wickets in an innings and hit 70 or 80 when the situation demanded it. 'In my view our last real all-rounder was Gary Gilmour, but he had specialists like Dennis Lillee and Greg Chappell around him who were great, and there wasn't so much need for an all-rounder … Neither Symonds nor Watson has contributed much with the ball, despite bowling first change, and they should play as batsmen. I must add that Symonds is a magnificent fielder.

'A bowling all-rounder is superior to a batting all-rounder because in majority of cases bowlers win matches and batsmen save them. To me the greatest all-rounder of all time was Keith Miller who could change the complexion of a match in a couple of overs. And of course there were Sobers, Botham, Hadlee, Kapil, Imran, Wasim Akram, Benaud … all in the highest class.'

A genuine two-in-one among Australians today is Adam Gilchrist, a wicketkeeping all-rounder who is following the padded footsteps of Rod Marsh and Ian Healy. Although there is a chapter on wicketkeeping all-rounders keepers who can also win a match with the bat, the book is mostly about cricketers who were match winners as batsmen and bowlers.

The evolution of one-day cricket has also forced more bowlers to bat till the end in the new millennium. This flows in at Test level to a certain extent. In an article 'A sting in the tail' from *Inside Cricket*, Louis White wrote, 'Australian cricket currently boasts a group of fast bowlers who are more than handy with the bat'. He cites the example of 'prize rabbit' Glenn McGrath scoring 61 in the Test against New Zealand in Brisbane in 2004–05, adding 114 runs with Jason Gillespie (54 not out) for the 10th wicket. Gillespie, picked in the Australian team as a fast bowler, scored an unbeaten double century against Bangladesh at Chittagong in March 2006. He also scored a century for South Australia in October 2007.

'I remember when I first turned up at state training in early 1990s I didn't even bother to take my batting gear because I was there to bowl', Gillespie told White. Now the emphasis on batting by tail-enders is more apparent. McGrath provided six instances of helping batsmen reach Test centuries by defending at the other end. Other Australian fast bowlers like Andy Bichel, Michael Kasprowicz, Brett Lee, Matthew Nicholson and Ashley Noffke, among others, have scored well at first-class level. Shorter boundaries and protective equipment have also encouraged the lower-order batsmen to perform better.

But these quickies cannot be termed all-rounders as their batting successes have been few and far between.

At Test level genuine all-rounders have also been few and far between, apart from perhaps South Africa's Jacques Kallis and Shaun Pollock and England's Flintoff. Son of Peter Pollock, a fiery fast bowler of 1960s and nephew of Graeme Pollock, a magnificent batsman from any era, Shaun has inherited talent from both even if the gene pool has been diluted. In 2004 Shaun joined Ian Botham, Imran Khan, Richard Hadlee and Kapil Dev in the exclusive group to have recorded the Test double of 3000 runs 300 wickets.

Many yardsticks have been used to assess cricket's great all-rounders: the attainment of unique Test doubles: 8000 runs and 200 wickets only by

Introduction

Garry Sobers and Jacques Kallis, 5000 runs and 400 wickets only by Kapil Dev, and scoring a century in a Test innings and capturing 13 wickets in that Test by Botham alone. However, just as one cannot judge a book by its cover design, one cannot rank an all-rounder as great on figures alone. The personalities of the players and their ability to swing a match from sure defeat to an incredible victory in a short but fiery spell with bat and ball are equally important.

The immediate inspiration to write this book came with the emergence of England's new hope Flintoff in 2005. However, all-round excellence in crises has fascinated me ever since I was a little boy in India, listening on radio, late at night, the Lord's Test between England and India in June 1952. India lost by eight wickets but not without a valiant one-man show. Opening India's innings, Vinoo Mankad scored 72 and 184 out of India's modest totals against Alec Bedser and a rookie tornado named Fred Trueman. Mankad then bowled 97 overs (36 maidens) in the match, taking 5 for 196 in the first innings. The match is remembered as Mankad's Test even after more than 55 years. History of cricket is full of such matches, Faulkner's Test, Tate's Test, Miller's Test, Benaud's Test, Davidson's Test, Umrigar's Test, Botham's Tests (there were two), Hadlee's Test, Akram's Test, Kallis's Test and others named after such 'solo flyers' who outshone 21 also-rans in that match.

On figures alone, Sir Ian Botham, nicknamed 'Both', 'Beefy' and 'Guy the Gorilla', perhaps emerges as the top all-rounder in 130 years of Test cricket. But according to some experts, the Supremo title should go to Keith Miller who played significantly fewer Tests than cricketers after 1970. As English author Gerald Brodribb wrote, 'Spectators saw in Miller the fine Tarzan-like physique they would all like to possess, the devil-may-care attitude to bowlers and statistics they would all like to adopt and the daring and powerful style of play they would all like to call their own.'

My vote goes for the left-handed genius of Sobers. As a batsman he was supreme, an automatic choice for any Test team of any period, any World XI. As a bowler he was three-in-one; bowling fast medium, orthodox spin and wrist spin with equal skill. 'I have never known anyone else adopt three contrasting methods in first-class cricket, let alone in Test matches', opined Bailey in *Sir Gary*. Also Sobers was a superb fielder anywhere.

Sobers or Imran, 'Tarzan' or 'Gorilla', 'Beno' or 'Davo', Mankad or Kapil, Hadlee or Wasim Akram, Kallis or Flintoff … have your pick as the book takes a kaleidoscopic view of all-round excellence from Australia's George Giffen and Monty Noble, South Africa's Aubrey Faulkner and England's Maurice Tate before WWII to Cairns, Pollock, Kallis and Flintoff at the turn of the millennium. The all-rounders appear to be back in business as Flintoff and Kallis lifted the Sir Garry Sobers Trophy in October 2005 as the ICC Cricketers of 2005.

To quote John Arlott from *Cricket: The Great All-Rounders* (1969), 'The truly great all-rounder probably is the rarest of all cricketers. The batsman who can bowl or the bowler who can bat will not do: the truly great all-rounder is of Test match quality as both batsman and bowler.'

It was interesting to discuss the greatness of Test all-rounders with former captain of England Tony Greig, now a television commentator on Australia's Channel 9 for over thirty years. He suggested an unusual criterion to judge the greatest all-rounder.

'There is one little statistic that I do enjoy,' he said. How many all-rounders have averaged over 40 with the bat and fewer than 35 with the ball? Perhaps the best all-rounders should be those who have the largest margin between their batting average and their bowling average. I have never been happy with the media's formula for judging all-rounders but I do know that the 2000 runs, 200 wickets or 3000 runs, 100 wickets comparison are definitely not the way to go. Number of runs and wickets is proportional to games played and if I were one of the great players of yesteryear I would feel let down by the infatuation with runs and wicket milestones. There has to be a better way and it's up to us to find it.'

On this harsh criterion only four qualify, South Africa's Kallis and Audrey Faulkner, the West Indies legend Sobers and Greig himself (qualification being minimum 20 Tests played). Kallis comes on top with a batting average minus bowling average differential of 26.87 followed by Sobers with 23.75, Faulkner 14.21 and Greig 8.23.

Although cricketers shining out as both batsmen and bowlers at Test level form the bulk of the book, those all-rounders excelling in one-day internationals are also profiled. And there is a chapter on outstanding wicket-keeper batsmen in Test cricket to showcase all-round excellence. Call it symbolism but the two inductees in the Hall of Fame during the Allan Border Medal presentation night in February 2008 were George Giffen, the first great all-rounder in the game's history and Ian Healy, a wicket-keeper batsman all-rounder.

Note: All statistics are as at 21 March 2008.

The Golden Age of All-Rounders

*'The golden age never was
the present age'*—Jean de la Fontaine

History, like distance, lends enchantment and imparts golden haloes—mostly real but at times imaginary. According to old-timers, the success of Australian teams under Mark Taylor, Steve Waugh and now Ricky Ponting can never match the feats of Bradman's 1948 Invincibles. Don Bradman is an exception, the numero uno among batsmen with a Test average of 99.94 and a century every 1.8 Tests. Yet there were critics in his time who would not acknowledge his number one status among Australians, let alone in the world. To some, Australian legend Vic Trumper was the greatest batsman, England's Ranjitsinhji and Wally Hammond more elegant and Jack Hobbs the real master on all pitches.

However, few can deny that the golden age for all-rounders was as recent as the 1980s. And for once this was acknowledged in the 1980s. It was the decade of intimidating fast bowling by Jeff Thomson, Andy Roberts, Michael Holding, Malcolm Marshall, Joel Garner, Curtly Ambrose, Dennis Lillee… and prolific run-scoring from Clive Lloyd, Viv Richards, Greg Chappell, Sunil Gavaskar, Gordon Greenidge, Allan Border, David Gower, Javed Miandad, Gundappa Viswanath… The Fabulous Four, Ian Botham, Richard Hadlee, Imran Khan, and Kapil Dev, BHIK to coin an acronym, were fast-medium bowlers and attacking batsmen. They had to encounter assaults from both ends and triumphed so splendidly that each scored over 3000 runs and captured over 300 wickets in Test arena. No one before them and only Shaun

Pollock and Shane Warne after them have reached this exclusive double although Wasim Akram came close in 2001.

From the time Imran Khan made his debut in 1971 till Kapil Dev retired in 1993, the BHIK quartet scored 17,379 runs at an average of 32.18 and took 1610 wickets at 25.85 and 251 catches in 407 Tests. Between them, they hit 30 Test centuries and captured 5 wickets in a Test innings 109 times. They played concurrently for their respective countries and often against each other from 1978 to 1990, a total of 13 years.

This is a record for all-rounders shining out concurrently. Keith Miller, Vinoo Mankad and Trevor Bailey played at the same time from 1949 to 1956—a Test span of eight years. Richie Benaud, Alan Davidson, Trevor Goddard and Garry Sobers also played concurrently for eight years, from 1955 to 1962.

Botham, Kapil, Imran and Hadlee figure prominently in the list of the players who have achieved the Test double of 2000 runs and 150 wickets, as shown in the Statistical Section.

However, BHIK were more than just record breakers. They had positive personalities that enlivened many matches. One could hear the hush as they walked to the middle. Imran Khan, the Lion of Pakistan, was glamorous and a sex symbol. He led his country with distinction including the 1992 World Cup triumph in front of over 70,000 in Melbourne. He aspires to be the President of Pakistan. He certainly has demonstrated leadership but political commentators think he is too forthright and inflexible to be a successful politician.

Sir Richard Hadlee became the first cricketer to take 400 Test wickets. His haul of 431 scalps was a Test record until eclipsed by another all-rounder, Kapil Dev and then by Courtney Walsh, Shane Warne, Muttiah Muralitharan, Glenn McGrath and Anil Kumble. Hadlee also held the record for most 5 wickets in a Test innings 36 times and 10 wickets in a Test nine times until broken by the controversial Muralitharan. Hadlee was not probably as charismatic as Imran or Botham but he did have that certain presence, a menacing presence. He cold bloodedly studied weaknesses in batsmen's techniques 'in the manner of a surgeon studying x-rays before probing for the source of the problem', to quote Don Mosey in *Wisden* 1991. His most probing 'surgery' was during the Brisbane Test of November 1985 against Australia when he took 9 for 52 and 6 for 71 and scored 54 runs as New Zealand won by an innings. It was New Zealand's first victory over their 'big brother' on Australian soil and is remembered as Hadlee's Test.

Sir Ian Terrence Botham arrived on the scene with a swagger and made his presence felt with his six appeal. He was a man in a hurry and reached the Test double of 1000 runs and 100 wickets in least number of Tests, 21, and in shortest time, 25 months after his debut. He achieved the unique double of a century and 13 wickets in the same Test in Mumbai in February 1980. He will be remembered for the Headingley Test a year later for an astounding performance. He took 6–95 and scored 50 in the first innings and when England was forced to follow on 227 runs behind, he smashed an unbeaten 149 and incredibly England won. These matches are recognised as Botham's Tests.

India's pride and joy Kapil Dev from Haryana, Punjab is nicknamed the 'Haryana Express'. The first all-rounder to play 100 Tests, he is the only one to achieve the Test double of 5000 runs and 400 wickets. Under him little fancied India won her only World Cup in 1983, defeating the mighty Windies in the final at Lord's. A magnificent all-rounder, bowling was his life, his wife, his 10 to 6 job, his bread and butter. Batting was his mistress, his indulgence. He seldom strayed when bowling and hardly batted with a straight bat, his cross-bat flings giving spectators almost orgasmic delight.

Individually, these four were world-beaters. Collectively, they ushered in the golden age of all-rounders.

1 TOP TEST ALL-ROUNDERS

Who were the greatest Test all-rounders? The selection is based on match-winning performances and is guided by statistics, not governed by them.

Selecting cricket's top Test all-rounders is like selecting a World XI. It is impossible to satisfy every one including oneself; too many ifs and buts and what-ifs. If one were to use statistics as the sole yardstick, for instance, including those who have completed the Test double of 2000 runs and 200 wickets, specialist bowlers like Australia's Shane Warne 3154 runs and 708 wickets, Sri Lanka's Chaminda Vaas 2815 runs and 331 wickets and India's Anil Kumble 2419 runs and 604 wickets would get in. And no one, not even these players themselves, would call them genuine all-rounders.

Besides by this criterion, internationally reputed pre-World War II all-rounders George Giffen, Monty Noble, Aubrey Faulkner and Wally Hammond would miss out because they played comparatively fewer Tests. Even some of the post-WWII cricketers like Australia's colourful Keith Miller and Alan Davidson and India's Vinoo Mankad would have to be excluded.

The mushrooming of Test matches after 1970s has made it easier for recent players to reach these statistical milestones. Thus in this book, numbers are crunched only when they throw light rather than when the light they emit is so bright that it blinds us. In other words the selection of all-rounders in this book has been guided by statistics but not governed by them.

So who is a genuine all-rounder? One definition is that he should be so versatile that he gets selected as a bowler alone or as a batsman alone. But this would be too restrictive. For instance, would Maurice Tate, Alan Davidson, Richard Hadlee, Daniel Vettori and Shaun Pollock get selected in a Test team for their batting alone? By the same token, would Wally Hammond and Jacques Kallis be picked only for their bowling? One can debate on this issue forever. But here is my list of the Top Test all-rounders who have played a minimum of 20 Tests based on their personalities, match-winning performances and statistics.

So far no-one has written an all-encompassing book on international all-rounders' diverse deeds. A personal selection of 25 Test all-rounders is featured in this chapter in chronological order, starting with Giffen, the first genuine all-rounder.

The all-rounders featured are among the greatest in 130 years of Test cricket. Well, that is a personal opinion and hence subjective after delving in many reference books and consulting historians but I do not expect universal approval. Many among these will be popular choices viz. Giffen, Noble, Faulkner, Miller, Mankad, Benaud, Davidson, Sobers, Botham, Imran Khan, Hadlee and Kapil Dev. Kallis and Flintoff are on the verge.

There will be question marks on others: Why Maurice Tate and Jack Gregory and why not Warwick Armstrong and Learie Constantine, why Wally Hammond and not W.G. Grace, Wilfred Rhodes and Frank Woolley, why Trevor Bailey and Wasim Akram and not Ray Illingworth, Polly Umrigar and Rusi Surti, why John Reid, Chris Cairns and Daniel Vettori and not Mushtaq Mohammad, Carl Hooper, Ravi Shastri and Bapoo Nadkarni, why Trevor Goddard and not his team-mates Eddie Barlow and Mike Procter ... ?

So many whys and why nots!

Test figures of all 25 Test all-rounders in this chapter are given in the Statistical Section at the end of the book in chronological order.

GEORGE GIFFEN

Australia

Although dead more than 80 years ago, the name of George Giffen lives on. A story circulated in early 1900s that Adelaide parents taught their children to say, 'God bless Mummy and Daddy and George Giffen.'

George Giffen and Merv Hughes had many similarities although they came from different eras. Both were heavily moustached and possessed enormous wrists and both completed the Test double of 1000 runs and 100 wickets, although Hughes could hardly be described as an all-rounder. Each took five wickets in a Test innings seven times and 10 wickets in a Test once. They had similar bowling average at Test level, 27 for Giffen, 28 for Hughes and accepted almost the same number of Test catches, 24 for Giffen, 23 for Hughes. Both were crowd pleasers and enjoyed a drink. There the similarities end.

While Merv Hughes huffed and puffed as he bowled—especially towards the end of his career, George Giffen was like a well-oiled machine without a squeak, even at 50. 'Nothing on two legs could undo him [Giffen] for stamina, not even a marathon Olympic runner from Kenya', wrote Ray Robinson in *On Top Down Under*. 'He was strong as a scrub bull, worked like a horse and developed thirst like a camel.'

The third son of a carpenter, George was born on 27 March 1859. He worked in a post office in South Australia as a letter sorter, just as he sorted out opposing batsmens' weaknesses in Australia and England. His rise to fame was rapid and remained steady for many seasons. At 17 he was selected to represent South Australia against England and for many years he was 'Mr South Australia' personified; batting, bowling and fielding

George Giffen was the world's first great Test all-rounder. Here he is seated, third from left, in Australia's team to England in 1893. Note that 13 out of 15 players had a moustache!

like a man possessed. He made his Test debut in 1881–82 when 22 and continued playing until 1896 when he was 37, losing neither his enthusiasm nor his penetration. In 31 Tests, all against England, he scored 1238 runs at 23.35, hitting a century (161 vs England in Sydney in 1894–95), captured 103 wickets at 27.09, taking 7 wickets in an innings twice and took 24 catches. He was the first cricketer to achieve the Test double of 1000 runs and 100 wickets.

He toured England in 1882, 1884, 1886, 1893 and 1896 and subsequently visited USA, Canada and New Zealand. George was a gifted all-rounder—being a reliable batsman, a crafty off-spinner and a safe fielder anywhere.

Top Test All-Rounders

His feats for his state and country were staggering. Among Australians he remains the only player to total over 10,000 runs and capture over 100 wickets in first-class matches. He captured 16 wickets in a match an incredible five times and five wickets in an innings an astonishing 48 times. He bagged all 10 wickets for 66 runs for an Australian XI against the Rest in Sydney in 1883–84. It remained a unique feat in first-class cricket in Australia for 49 years until Tim Wall, also of South Australia, took 10 for 36 against New South Wales in Sydney in 1932–33.

George puzzled batsmen by hiding his arm during his eight-step run-up. He mixed up his off-breaks with cutters by varying his pace and flighted the ball cleverly. He remains the only cricketer to make a double century and take 16 wickets in a match. For South Australia against Victoria in Adelaide in 1891–92, he scored 271 and captured 9 for 96 and 7 for 70. This made England's cricket historian Harry Altham comment that it was 'surely the greatest all-round performance in recorded cricket history of any class'.

Giffen remains the only cricketer to make a double century and take 16 wickets in a match.

In January 1891, George scored 237 runs and pouched 12 wickets (5 for 89 and 7 for 103) for South Australia against Victoria in Melbourne. Victoria must have been his favourite foe as in 1885–86 in Adelaide he grabbed 17 for 201, the first Australian to take 17 wickets in a match. After him only two Australians have emulated this feat: 17 for 50 by Charles 'Terror' Turner in 1888 and 17 for 54 by Bill Howell in 1902–03.

During his 1884 tour of England he became the first player to score a century and take a hat-trick in the same match. This was for the Australians against Lancashire at Manchester. W.G. Grace had achieved such a feat for MCC vs Kent at Canterbury in 1874 but it was a 12-a-side fixture and hence rated non first-class. No other Australian has performed this double. Twelve of his 16 centuries were scored in Australia, four of which were double hundreds. His 203 against G.F. Warner's England XI at the Adelaide Oval in December 1888 was the first double century against a touring team.

George was a dominant figure during his tours to England. He headed both the batting and bowling aggregates in 1886, amassing 1424 runs and 154 wickets. He achieved the 1000 runs, 100 wickets double twice during subsequent tours to England in 1893 and 1896. Warwick Armstrong remains the only other Australian to achieve this double three times during tours to England in 1905, 1909 and 1921.

George had happy memories of Sydney. In the 1891–92 Sydney Test, he bagged 4 for 88 and 6 for 72. His second innings spree bundled out England for 157 when they needed 230 to win. He made his only Test century, 161, in the Sydney Test of 1894–95 and added 171 runs with Frank Iredale and 139 with Syd Gregory. He considered this innings as his best. This was also his best series as he scored most runs 474 at 52.77 and captured most wickets 34 at 24.11. He led Australia in the last four Tests, winning two and losing two. He was never asked to captain Australia again as 'he bowled himself too much', according to Sir Pelham Warner. Jack Pollard added, tongue-in-cheek, 'A change of bowling only meant changing ends for George!'

George retired from first-class matches at 42 but was recalled for a match between South Australia and Victoria. He had lost none of his skills or zeal as he scored 178 for once out and captured 15 wickets. His career spanning 26 years 1877 to 1903 was outstanding: 11,758 runs at 29.54 and 1023 wickets at 21.29 apiece. In one 12 year period he scored one-third of the runs and five-eighths of the wickets for his teams.

'While Giffen was wheeling along 46,355 balls for his wickets, his moustache was the only thing that drooped', wrote Robinson in *On Top Down Under*. George was blunt but warm-hearted and respected cricket's enduring virtues. He was so popular that once, after a match, spectators donated 400 sovereigns—a tidy sum then. He coached after retirement from his post office job and bowled immaculately even at 61. In a 'Hit one stump while bowling' competition at Belair National Park in South Australia he struck the solitary stump nine times out of nine—coming straight from the pub after a few quick ones! The next best score was two hits out of nine.

When he died in 1927 aged 66, Australian greats Joe Darling and Clem Hill eulogised him for his all-round excellence. In the Members' Stand in Adelaide named after George Giffen hangs his portrait by May Grigg, a noted artist. A plaque underneath recognises his lifelong service to cricket. Historian Harry Altham insisted in late 1890s that George was Australia's greatest all-rounder of his time.

At the Allan Border Medal presentation night in February 2008 in Melbourne, Giffen was inducted in the Hall of Fame.

MONTY NOBLE
Australia

When Monty was born on 28 January 1873 in Chinatown's Dixon Street in Sydney, his mother Maria predicted that her son would become famous. She said it because a military band played outside her home when Monty poked his head out! And he did not let her down as he is still well known to cricket lovers 67 years after his death. Her only regret was to give him the initials MA when she later realised that fans were calling him Mary Ann after these initials!

Montague Alfred Noble (1873–1940), known to his friends and fans as Monty or Alf and nicknamed 'Mary Ann' (for his initials) and 'Boots' (for his size 10½ feet), was a genuine all-rounder. He batted with patience and aggression depending on the state of the match, mixed off-spin with clever flight at medium pace on occasions employing a mystery juggling delivery to puzzle the best and was a safe fielder and a successful captain to whom discipline came first.

Noted coach Eric Barbour ranked him as the best all-rounder in the first third of the 20th century. In his book *On Top Down Under*, Australia's perceptive writer Ray Robinson describes Noble as 'the most accomplished player Australia produced as bowler, batsman, captain and fielder in the pre-1954 era'. He achieved the 1000 runs, 100 wickets double in only 27 Tests, the quickest Test double then and improved by only England's Ian Botham in 21 Tests, by India's Vinoo Mankad and Kapil Dev in 23 and 25 Tests respectively, and South Africa's Shaun Pollock in 26. (England's Andrew Flintoff took as many as 41 Tests to complete this double.)

'Monty' Noble is ready to face another delivery.

Monty learned his cricket playing with his brothers on the streets of Paddington in Sydney where his father managed a pub. When 20, Monty scored an unbeaten 152 for XVIII Colts of NSW against England. His batting style impressed the legendary Vic Trumper and he was soon promoted to the NSW team in the Sheffield Shield and selected in the Test team when 24.

The selection in the Australian team was not an unmixed blessing. He had to resign as a bank clerk because he could not get leave. The positive side was that he took up a course in dentistry and became a respected dentist by profession. He was tall and stately, 185cm (6 foot 1 inch) tall and weighed 83kg (13 stone) but remained agile and unsurpassed in his time when fielding at point. However, cartoonists had a field day, concentrating on his big boots.

In between extracting teeth and filling cavities, he played 42 Tests, scoring 1997 runs at 30.25 (one century and 16 fifties, highest score 133), took 121 wickets at 25.00 (best being 7 for 17) and 26 catches. He won eight of the 15 Tests he captained.

In 248 first-class matches from 1893 to 1919 he scored 13,975 runs at 40.74 with 37 centuries and 66 fifties (highest score 284) and captured 624 wickets at 23.14 (best 8 for 48) and 187 catches.

He was a cricketer of unwavering confidence in his own ability and inspired his teammates to give of their best. They had no choice as he was a lovable martinet. Playing beach cricket in his early years gave him tremendous stamina. On voyages to England in ships, he was the team's tandem-skipping champion. It involved each player holding a giggling girl by the elbows as the pair cleared a twisting pole. This brought merriment and got the team together. These days it would be called bonding. One can well imagine screaming headlines in the media today!

Monty learnt his unusual bowling style from a US baseball team. Holding the ball between his thumb and forefinger, he took 15 wickets in his first two Tests in 1897–98, (1 for 31 and 6 for 49 on debut on the Melbourne Cricket Ground and 3 for 78 and 5 for 84 in Adelaide). Thus he started his Test career as a bowler who could bat. When his medium-pace, spin swerve delivery had England's Archie Jackson caught, the batsman exclaimed, 'Hang it, a batsman can't play jugglery'. Jackson was disgusted with himself; he had changed his stroke twice and was out playing the third.

Such deceptive deliveries combined with a well-concealed faster one and a penetrating off-cutter on a moist pitch were the reasons why the great Ranjitsinhji rated him among the six best medium pacers he had faced.

Monty had a memorable inaugural tour of England in 1899. He started off in a blaze of glory, an unbeaten 116 in 210 minutes against South of England at Crystal Palace. But he was so disappointed with himself after a 'pair' in the Leeds Test that absentmindedly he walked away in the wrong direction. Teasingly, his colleagues presented him with a 5cm long silver duck. Being superstitious, he always carried that duck in his pocket when batting.

He defended heroically in the subsequent Manchester Test to save Australia from a certain defeat. In the first innings, with his country on life support system at 7 for 57 against England's 372, he stonewalled for 190 minutes for his 60 and 320 minutes for his 89 in the second. At one stage he remained run-less for 45 minutes and the spectators started intoning *The Dead March* and an anonymous donor presented him a leather medal inscribed: 'To M.A. Noble, the greatest Australian cricketer, 1000 runs in 1000 years!' Noble later apologised to the crowd for his funereal run-rate.

It was as a bowler that he shone out in the 1902 New Year Test in Melbourne. He captured 7 for 17 off 7.4 overs in the first innings, 13 for 77 in the match as England was shot out for 61 and did just as badly in the second innings, 175, and Australia won by an innings and 229 runs. Fourteen of his 32 wickets in the series were wrapped up by wicketkeeper Jim Kelly, 11 caught and three stumped.

Although a disciplinarian who warned his team against late night drinking, he was well liked.

Monty was appointed as Australia's captain in his 23rd Test when he was 32 in 1903. Captaincy seemed to agree with his batting as he scored 133, his sole Test ton, to rescue his country from a disastrous start in Sydney. Although a disciplinarian who warned his team against late night drinking, he was well liked. He was an inspiring leader and a master at setting fields, and kept bowlers fresh by not over bowling them. The knowledgeable English great C.B. Fry nominated him as Earth's captain against Mars.

Although he scored only one Test century, he hit seven double centuries at first-class level, his highest being 284 for touring Australians against Sussex at Hove in 1902. During this innings he was associated in a 428 run partnership with Warwick Armstrong for the sixth wicket. Monty was engaged in three other triple century stands. Perhaps his best all-round feat was at Hove in England in 1905 when he hit 267 runs against Sussex and took 6 for 39. Recalling the 'double', Francis Collingwood commented in *The Cricketer*, 'What a performance! What a M.A.N.!'

What about Monty Noble as a man? He was popular wherever he played and it was his dexterity as a dentist that won him a bride. One of his patients was the famous scorer and baggage man Bill Ferguson. When Bill sent his sister Ellen to him for dental treatment, romance developed and Monty, 40, married Ellen, 24. They had a happy marriage that produced four children. He died aged 67 in 1940, Ellen passed away 25 years later.

Although careful with his diet, eating mostly fruits for lunch, he was a smoker, puffing a pipe to relax. But he would stop smoking and imbibing alcohol the night before a match and advised his team to do likewise. His baritone voice was heard in the Sydney Choral Society chorus, singing Handel's *Messiah* at the Town Hall.

To help cricket back after World War I, Monty appeared on the field aged 46. He had not lost his all-round excellence as he scored 10 and 52 runs and took 5 for 58 and 2 for 23 for NSW against Victoria in Melbourne in 1918–19.

A grandstand at the SCG is named after him. He wrote books on cricket and was involved in early 'ghost' broadcasts of the Tests from England on radio in 1920s.

Monty Noble's Benefit Match brought in £2000, a tidy amount in early 1900s. To mark the occasion, S.C. Coy wrote the following verse in *Sydney Mail*:

Top Test All-Rounders

When old England's at the creases
And our bowling's gone to pieces
And we fancy all the records will be broken by our foes,
Then the eyes of all observers
Are just fixed on Noble's swervers
As he sends along a beauty and a batsman homeward goes…
When the wicket's sticky
And treacherous and tricky
And we want a bat who'll stay there till the evening shadows fall,
You're glad the strain has ended
And you go home feeling splendid
When you've witnessed Monty Noble with his back against the wall.

AUBREY FAULKNER

South Africa

In this galaxy of all-round stars, some cricketers with a Test double of 2000 runs and 200 wickets have failed to make our Top 25 list. Therefore the inclusion of South Africa's Major George Aubrey Faulkner (1754 runs and 82 wickets at Test level) needs an explanation. Firstly, he played only 25 Tests in a career spanning from 1905 to 1924. These days a cricketer chalks up 25 Tests in about three years. Secondly, statistic is not the only criterion used in the selection process.

Aubrey Faulkner (1881–1930) was a versatile character, an army Major with a distinguished record in World War I who was awarded the DSO, a gifted cricketer who shone out in batting, bowling, fielding and coaching (he opened his famous School of Cricket in England after retiring from active cricket) and died tragically by his own hand. A dominant figure in South African cricket, he formed a famous googly trio with fellow Springboks Reggie Schwarz and Bert Vogler at the beginning of the 20th century. Faulkner captured 449 wickets in first-class matches with his medium-paced googlies at an astonishing average of 17.42, scored 6366 runs at 36.58 (hitting 13 centuries) and took 94 catches.

He was the first batsman to make 200 runs and take eight wickets in the same Test. This was in the first Test against England in Johannesburg in January 1910 when he scored 78 and 123 and bagged 5 for 120 and 3 for 40, thus contributing richly to South Africa's narrow 19 run victory. He took 2 for 51 and 6 for 87 and scored 47 in the first innings enabling his country to win the second Test in Durban. He contributed with both bat and ball as

Top Test All-Rounders

South Africa won the exciting series 3–2, Aubrey chiming in with a bitter sweet 99 in the final Test in Cape Town.

Faulkner's Test debut in the Johannesburg Test of January 1906 coincided with South Africa's first ever Test victory. Coincidentally, the googly-trio of Faulkner, Schwarz and Vogler made their combined Test debut in this historic Test, capturing 12 wickets between them. Opening the attack, Faulkner took 2 for 35 and 4 for 26 as South Africans won the thrilling Test by one wicket. Retaining the same XI in all five Tests, South Africa won the series 4–1.

On the tour to England in 1907, he headed the batting aggregate with 1163 runs at 29.82 and took 64 wickets at 15.82. In the Leeds Test of July 1907, he captured 6 for 17 as England collapsed for 76 and 3 for 58.

He had a marvellous home series against England in 1909–10 when he topped the batting with 548 runs at 60.55 in five Tests and sharing most wickets with Vogler, Faulkner snaring 29 wickets at 21.89.

Aubrey Faulkner was at his peak against Australia down under in 1910–11 when he amassed 1651 runs (with four centuries) at 61.14 and took 49 wickets at 27.06. He was at his best in the Tests, scoring a monumental 732 runs at 73.20, creating a series aggregate record at Test level. He also became the first South African to score a Test double century, 204 in the second Test in Melbourne.

Here is how he tormented the Aussie bowlers that summer in five Tests: 62 and 43 in the first Test in Sydney, 204 and 8 in Melbourne, 56 and 115 in Adelaide, 20 and 80 (as South Africa gained their first victory over Australia despite the legendary Vic Trumper's unbeaten 214), 20 and 80 in Melbourne and 52 and 92 in Sydney. But with his mediocre form with the ball (only 10 wickets in the series against batting maestros Trumper, Clem Hill, Warren Bardsley, Charlie Macartney and Warwick Armstrong), South Africa lost the series 1–4.

In the Triangular series against England and Australia in 1912, he scored 122 not out in the Manchester Test against Australia and took 7 for 48 at The Oval, his best bowling figures in 25 Tests, against England. He achieved the double of 1075 runs (at 23.88) and 165 wickets (at 15.42) in first-class matches on that tour.

He will also be remembered as a coach who unearthed talent at the Aubrey Faulkner School of Cricket in England, the most prominent being England's tall leg-spinner Ian Peebles. Despite all his success with the bat and ball and as a coach, Aubrey Faulkner was subject to melancholia and sadly took his life on 10 September 1930. He was only 48.

Aubrey Faulkner returning to the pavilion.

JACK GREGORY

Australia

'In terms of dynamism and impact in batting, bowling and fielding, Jack Gregory has to be included as a great all-rounder', commented cricket historian Warwick Franks, the former editor of Wisden Australia.

The Gregorys produced cricket's earliest cricketing family. Their story starts with Edward William Gregory, the father of Australia's first Test captain, Dave. He played in Sydney's Hyde Park in the 1820s, little imagining that his grandson Jack would be hitting headlines in three continents a century later. Of Edward's 13 children, seven were boys. Five of them played cricket for New South Wales. Twenty of his grandsons represented the State in various sports—cricket, sailing, athletics or football. The four sons who represented NSW in cricket were Edward Jnr (Ned), Dave, Charlie and Arthur. Edward Jnr (Ned) and Dave played together for Australia in the first-ever Test in 1877 in Melbourne.

Dave Gregory won the first toss in Test history and also his team won that Test.

Edward Gregory Jnr, nicknamed 'Ned the Lionheart', was six years Dave's senior. Ned will be remembered for the laying out of the area that became the SCG. It was also Ned who designed the SCG scoreboard. He had two cricket-playing sons, Syd and Charles.

Syd became the first son in Test history to follow his father's footsteps leading to Test fame. And, like his father, he scored a duck in his first Test innings! Syd's cousin Jack also scored nought in his Test baptism!

Jack Gregory, the only all-rounder in the family, was a superstar in his own right. Less classical than Syd, Jack was more versatile and eye-catching. He was acknowledged as a great all-rounder when he retired in 1928. To quote the great Australian author Ray Robinson: 'Like a fiery comet that flares into view every 70-odd years, a cricketer as spectacular as Jack Gregory is a rare sight for the world. Tests had been played more than 40 years before such an eye-catching all-rounder bounded on the scene. Soon he was the most feared express bowler before [Harold] Larwood, a record-making slip catcher with fly-paper fingers and scorer of the fastest 100 in Test history.'

'Gelignite' Jack, according to Moyes, had 'little rhythm in his approach but abundant vigour and venom; all thunder and lightning like an electric storm'. Very little was known of Jack Gregory when the Australian Imperial Forces (AIF) selectors gave

Jack Gregory's bowling action was described as a towering inferno. He was 'a fiery comet that flares into view every 70-odd years.'

this lanky artilleryman—'all arms and legs'—a chance after World War I.

In a rare interview given to *The Cricketer* (England) a few months before he died near Sydney in August 1973 at the age of nearly 78, Jack modestly recalled to David Frith: 'Plum Warner gave me my chance. It was the name that did it. He found out I was Syd's cousin.'

Top Test All-Rounders

Three accidents helped Australian cricket enormously. When Jack injured his finger in the outfield, AIF skipper Herbie Collins brought him in to a slips position—a precious chance discovery because Jack subsequently became a wizard in that position. His acrobatic anticipation is still remembered by old-timers.

When AIF's regular bowler Cyril Docker strained his back, a desperate captain gave Jack a bowl. His bowling action was clumsy, but the speed he generated was phenomenal. One of his deliveries gashed keeper Ted Long's face. Another keeper had to be located in a hurry and thus was pitchforked shy, little Bert Oldfield into the AIF XI. He went on to become one of the greatest stumpers of all time.

Jack captured 131 wickets and took 44 slip catches in 25 matches—thus becoming the only Australian to take over 100 wickets in his opening first-class season. In his first match at Melbourne, Jack bagged 7 for 22. He had a dramatic debut on the Sydney Cricket Ground. For AIF vs NSW, he scored 122 and 102 and took eight wickets in the match. In the Melbourne Test of 1921, he reached his hundred in 135 minutes and took 7 for 69.

His most destructive spell was taking three wickets without conceding a run in the 1921 Trent Bridge Test. With the stylish Ted McDonald, Jack Gregory formed the first double-edged pace attack. Like later partners in pace, Larwood and Voce, Lindwall and Miller, Trueman, Tyson and Statham, Hall and Griffith, Lillee and Thomson, Roberts and Holding, these two (McDonald and Gregory) were perfect foils for each other.

Against the grace and rhythm of McDonald, Jack, 193cm, looked awkward. He took 12 outsize steps of which the ninth one was a kangaroo leap on the right foot. Jack's towering inferno action created by his hefty figure and fearsome expression, terrified the batsmen before he even bowled.

The legendary Walter Hammond, when 18 years old, had a baptism of fire facing Gregory and later wrote: 'Jack Gregory had cultivated a fearsome stare and gave me the treatment. With knees trembling and hands shaking, I was relieved when he bowled me first ball.'

Jack bowled right-handed and batted left-handed. He never bothered to put on a cap, gloves or a groin box. He played in 24 Tests against England and South Africa and totalled 1146 runs with two centuries. His batting average of 36.97 was better than Syd's of 24.53.

Jack's electrifying century in 70 minutes in the Johannesburg Test of 1921–22 is, even today, the fastest Test hundred (in time taken). His most consistent season was 1920–21 against England when he recorded 78, 77, 76 not out, and 93 in consecutive Test innings.

A cartilage operation on his right knee cramped his swashbuckling style and he seemed to be on the decline when touring England in 1926. But the following season he made his highest first-class score, 152 for NSW, having hit a century before lunch.

The first Test of 1928 against England proved historic, being the first Test played in Brisbane and the Test in which Don Bradman made his debut. Unfortunately, it was the last one for Jack Gregory. His knee gave out as he was bowling to Harold Larwood who, as a boy, had hero-worshipped Jack. 'I'm finished boys' was his much-quoted exclamation as he limped from the ground. This was the end of not only Jack's playing days, but of all the Gregorys. His tall son, John, was a pacey left-arm bowler for his college in Sydney, but he did not play for his State.

'I'm finished boys' was his much-quoted exclamation as he limped from the ground.

Jack Gregory's record of 15 catches in a Test series still stands. Bill O'Reilly who played against Hammond and saw other slips-experts like Bob Simpson, Colin Cowdrey and the Chappells, ranked Jack Gregory as the greatest slips fielder he had seen. Scorer Bill Ferguson once said that

Top Test All-Rounders

Jack had arms like an octopus 'only they seemed twice as many and twice as long'.

Jack's best all-round performance was in the Melbourne Test of 1920–21 when he reached his century in 135 minutes and took 7 for 69 and 1 for 32, thus equalling George Giffen's grand double of scoring a century and taking eight wickets in the same Test (against England in Sydney in December 1894).

Group photo including Wally Hammond (fifth from left) and Maurice Tate (extreme right) for MCC v Australians, 1928.

MAURICE TATE
England

More than for his accuracy, penetration and endurance, big Maurice Tate will be remembered for his big smile, big heart and big feet, and for his 'Tateisms'—his mangling of words such as 'stannima' for 'stamina' and saying the most trivial and obvious things with a sombre, secretive face.

Maurice Tate was the famous son of an obscure Test cricketer Fred Tate. Fred had played only one Test in 1902 and was an outstanding failure. A crucial catch dropped by him cost England a Test which they lost by three runs. Full of remorse, he had told team-mate Len Braund after that Test: 'I've got a little kid at home who'll make it up for me.' This has become one of cricket's most touching stories and an accurate prediction.

Maurice grew up to become one of the immortals of the game: the finest of his type and a happy player who infected team-mates and spectators with his bouncing enthusiasm and toothy smile. He went on to play 39 Tests and did the double of 1000 runs (1198) and 100 wickets (155). In first-class cricket he achieved a rare triple of 20,000 runs (21,717), 2000 wickets (2784) and 200 catches (242).

He was one of Fred's 10 children—three sons and seven daughters—and was born on 30 May 1895. Unlike Fred, Maurice's Test debut was positively sensational. Against South Africa at Edgbaston on 16 June 1924, Maurice opened the bowling with his Sussex and England captain, Arthur Gilligan. He took a wicket with the very first ball he bowled in Test cricket. He captured 4 for 12, Gilligan had an amazing haul of 6 for 7 and the Springboks were routed for an all-time low of 30. In that series, Maurice took 27 wickets.

To batsmen, it was terrifying to see Maurice Tate's bowling action, his big arms appearing like a monster spider.

A few months later, in Australia, he had his most successful Test series—capturing 38 wickets at 23. His victims were the cream of Australian batsmen and his triumph came despite dropped catches, near misses and a painful toe.

He was keen on cricket, but had little ability and was found not good enough to represent his school. One of his masters advised him: 'We know your father is a great cricketer, but you'll never be one. You stick to football!'

However, Maurice could not be convinced. After all, to quote him: 'My baby milk was diluted with cricket. I was weaned on it and it was served after every meal!' Was he guided by his father? 'I want to put it on record that I was never coached in bowling. It came to me naturally and must have been inherited from my father', he recalled.

He left school at 14 to become an apprentice fitter with a gas company. The following year, on a request from Sussex County Club, Fred took Maurice to Hove for a fortnight's trial. The committee members were unimpressed by the clumsy, awkward boy with enormous feet and prominent teeth. But, to his surprise and delight, he was engaged in the Sussex nursery. In his first season, his off-breaks earned him 55 wickets. He made his debut for Sussex in 1912, aged 17. At the end of the 1913 season, he played for Haywards Heath and scored 84. The opposition included 46 year-old Fred Tate who scored 65 not out and hit the winning run.

World War I interrupted Maurice's cricket career and he enlisted in the Services. By the end of the war, he had filled out and became a lumbering giant. He had lost his shyness and awkwardness and had become a happy extrovert who enjoyed his game. Cricket resumed in 1919, and Maurice scored his first century on 30 July, 108 runs in 110 minutes against Lancashire at Old Trafford. He also completed 1000 runs during the season—a habit he kept up for 11 years in a row. Against Oxford University, he showed his all-round ability, scoring 90 and 35 and taking 5 for 48 and 6 for 43.

Until 1922, Maurice was an off-spinner—his bowling action so similar to his father's that, according to Arthur Gilligan, 'it was almost uncanny to watch them'. Maurice was then considered more of a batsman with 151 and 47 not out vs Nottinghamshire, 142 in 114 minutes vs Hampshire, 203 in 180 minutes vs Northamptonshire—adding 385 runs with Ted Bowley. After this hitting spree, Maurice was nicknamed 'Boundary Tate'.

In 1922, he was reborn as a fast-medium bowler who could move the ball both ways. His transformation from a rather harmless off-spinner to a speedy terror was one of cricket's happy chance discoveries and had a great impact on Test cricket tactics. There are several versions of Maurice's metamorphosis which are detailed in Brodribb's extremely readable biography *Maurice Tate* published in 1976.

One version is that Maurice was exasperated at being hit all over the place by Philip Mead and, in desperation; he bowled a faster ball which beat a stunned Mead, bowling his leg stump.

Maurice described this as a fluke in his autobiography but Brodribb was not convinced. According to him, other batsmen including his Sussex captain, Gilligan, had been surprised by Maurice's faster balls before the encounter with Mead. Whatever the genesis, Maurice's abandonment of the spin for speed was a stroke of luck for Sussex, England and cricket. In a matter of weeks, he became England's No. 1 bowler and remained so for 10 years until Douglas Jardine introduced bodyline in 1932.

Even at his swiftest, Maurice was not genuinely fast. But after pitching, the ball picked up incredible pace. Soon after this transformation, he played for England against The Rest and wrecked the opposition who crashed from 5 for 202 to 205 all out, Maurice taking the last 5 wickets in 10 balls without conceding a run. And he produced all this fire with a run-up of barely eight paces. After he took 8 for 18 against Worcestershire in 1924, *Wisden* called him 'unplayable'. His short run-up produced problems for the batsmen because it did not give them time to relax.

'One ball had hardly gone when another was on its way like some relentless bowling machine' was the way a county batsman saw Tate. To batsmen it was also terrifying to see his flailing arms and big hands coming at them like a monster spider. He gave the ball a whip with the swing of his body and a flip of the wrist, so that it gathered speed—or so it seemed— off the pitch. To those unaccustomed to his bowling, the ball sounded like a hissing snake.

The seasons 1923, 1924 and 1925 were memorable for him. He topped 200 wickets and scored 1000 runs for three years in a row—a record without parallel. Only two players had achieved this rare *double* before him—Albert Trott twice and Albert Kennedy once. Since 1925 no one has done it even once.

In 1924, he made his never-to-be-forgotten debut against South Africa at Edgbaston (4 for 12). Then, in Australia in 1924–25, he reached the peak of his power.

In England in 1924 he had one precious moment to remember. Playing against Yorkshire, he scored an unbeaten century and, during the innings, he received a telegram informing him of the birth of his first son, Maurice jnr. Oddly, a few minutes previously, Herbert Sutcliffe had also received a telegram about the birth of his daughter. Sutcliffe, too, celebrated the occasion with a century.

Playing against Yorkshire, he scored an unbeaten century and, during the innings, he received a telegram informing him of the birth of his first son, Maurice jnr.

Everything went smoothly for Tate's overseas tour to Australia in 1924–25. Against a strong NSW team, he captured 7 for 74 and among his victims were Charlie Macartney, Tommy Andrews and Alan Kippax— all for ducks. This was the first of his many 'mad moments' on the tour.

Even though Bill Ponsford scored a century in the first Test at Sydney, he was all at sea against Tate, and his captain, Herbert Collins, had to shield him. Tate had a marathon spell of 712 balls in this Test and captured 11 for 228.

He bowled 627 deliveries in the second Test at Melbourne. By the time the third Test started in Adelaide, his toe nail had been pushed back into his flesh and he was in agony. Although he was the Australian batsmen's worst enemy, he was every Australian spectator's best friend. They loved him and they shared his pain. His big toe and big feet made headline news. Once a placard for an evening paper read: TATE'S NEW FOOT, which was—fortunately—only a misprint for Tate's New Boot!

In the final Test in Sydney, interest was centred round his impending record: 'Would he get past Mailey's 36 wickets in a series?' As a climax, he broke Mailey's stumps and record in one ball. Maurice's 38 wickets in a Test series was a record aggregate in Australia until 1978–79 when Rodney Hogg took 41 against England. Skipper Arthur Gilligan commented after the series: 'With ordinary luck, Tate would have taken 58 instead of 38 wickets' referring to the number of dropped catches and near misses which shaved the bails or stumps. Other comments: Collins—'Tate was the best bowler seen in Australia for 25 years and was, in some respects, better than the great Barnes, as he sent down more unplayable balls.' Bert Oldfield—'Of all the bowlers I have faced, slow, fast or medium, I regard Tate as the greatest.'

Fast or medium pace bowlers usually become stale after a tour of Australia, but not Maurice who enjoyed his cricket. He was just as devastating as ever in county cricket for Sussex, taking 7 for 23 and 7 for 35, 8 for 100, 7 for 58 and 5 for 36 within a fortnight.

In the third Test at Leeds, against Australia, he dismissed left-handed opener Warren Bardsley off the very first ball of the Test. In the same over, the great Macartney was dropped and went on to make a masterly hundred. Although Maurice took only 13 wickets in the series, he was still the most feared bowler from either side. In the final Test at The Oval, he took 4 for 52 in 46 overs, an important factor in England regaining the Ashes.

In 1926–27, the MCC toured India. Maurice played in 28 matches and scored 1160 runs at 36, and took 116 wickets at 13.7, to become the only English player to perform the 'double' outside England. At Bombay, Guy Earle and Maurice delighted 45,000 fans by adding 154 runs in 65 minutes. Of the tour, Maurice wrote: 'I don't suppose I shall ever again have such a wonderful trip as I had through India'.

He had a fine sense of humour. Sujoy Gupta narrates a delightful anecdote in *Seventeen Ninety Two, A History of the Calcutta & Football Club*. In a match between MCC and Maharajah of Patiala's XI on that tour in Lahore, he had the Maharajah clearly caught in the slips. But he did not appeal. When asked why, he replied jokingly, 'Don't be a fool. We will be staying at this chap's palace later on and I don't want to be poisoned!'

In the domestic season of 1927, Tate was at his best as an all-rounder, hitting three centuries in a row and also bowling effectively. He was among the first picked to tour Australia in 1928–29. Although he was unable to recapture the fire of 1924–25, he took 17 wickets and was the key figure in England's attack and in retaining the Ashes 4–1.

He scored his only Test century against South Africa in 1929, at Lord's. For a change, his batting saved England when he added 129 with Maurice Leyland in 70 minutes.

When the Australians toured England in 1930, Don Bradman stole the limelight. But when 'the little devil' was not playing in a match against Sussex, Maurice took 6 for 18 before lunch—his victims being Ponsford, McCabe, Jackson, Richardson, Fairfax and a'Beckett.

This was Maurice's final fling against the Aussies. Although he toured Australia for the third time in 1932–33, skipper Jardine had no room for him in his bodyline tactics. Larwood later commented: 'Tate was still good enough to play for England but was too much of a gentleman to express his disappointment.'

When Tate retired from first-class cricket in 1937, he had scored 21,584 runs at 25, with 23 centuries. He had also grabbed 2784 wickets at 18, taking 5 wickets in an innings 195 times and 10 wickets in a match 44 times. He performed the 'double' of 1000 runs and 100 wickets in eight consecutive seasons.

Just as his father had had a memorable batting partnership with Ranjitsinhji, Maurice had a big stand with Ranji's nephew, Duleepsinhji. They put on 205 runs in 105 dazzling minutes; Tate 111 and Duleep 333 in one day.

Maurice's proud moments were when asked to captain Sussex occasionally. It was a rare honour for a professional in those days and he proved a successful and popular leader. After his retirement, he took coaching assignments in Tonbridge School in Kent and it was here that he spotted the talent of young Colin Cowdrey.

Top Test All-Rounders

Just three weeks before Maurice's sudden death of heart failure on 18 May 1956, he had umpired a match between Ian Johnson's Australians and the Duke of Norfolk's XI at Arundel Castle. He was then almost 61.

The day to remember for the Tate family was on 17 May 1958 when the Maurice Tate Memorial Gates at the entrance of the County Ground at Hove, Sussex, were opened by the Duke of Norfolk.

Maurice Tate is considered to be one of the five greatest medium-pacers in cricket history—Syd Barnes, Alec Bedser, Fazal Mahmood and Glenn McGrath being the others. Experts who saw both Tate and Bedser, ranked Tate higher, although it may be fair to point out that Bedser did not get uncovered pitches whereas Tate did. But to balance this, the new lbw rules introduced after 1935 would have helped Tate to trap more victims. So accurate was he that his Sussex keeper said, 'You could keep wicket to Maurice sitting in an easy chair.'

When asked to select the best opening bowlers among his contemporaries, Bradman once said 'Ted McDonald with the wind, Maurice Tate into it'.

There can be doubts about Maurice being considered a Test all-rounder but at first-class level he certainly was among the best. In a letter to Gerald Brodribb, Don Bradman referred to Maurice . . . 'as an opponent he was marvellous, always jovial, and a joy to play against'.

To sum up, I quote John Arlott from *Rothmans Jubilee History of Cricket 1890–1965*: 'A humorous character with a relish for life and a great enthusiasm for the game; Maurice Tate felt that his bowling made some amends for his father's error in the Old Trafford Test of 1902.'

WALLY HAMMOND
England

Although Walter Reginald Hammond is remembered more for his classical style than statistics, his figures are awesome. In 85 Test matches from 1927 to 1947, he scored 7249 runs at an average of 58.45, hitting 22 centuries (highest score being an unbeaten 336 against New Zealand at Auckland in 1932–33) and 24 fifties. His triple century was spiced with 34 fours and 10 sixes, incredibly eight on the off-side! His 7249 runs and 46 innings of over 50 runs constituted records at the time of his retirement.

So you never saw Wally Hammond bat. Nor did I. But being one of my heroes, I have pored over books and articles featuring him, read his biographies, seen his action pictures and have a mental image of one of the most majestic batsmen of all time.

So here is my recipe of drawing an identikit of Hammond. Add the grace of David Gower and Mohammad Azharuddin to the power of Viv Richards and Sachin Tendulkar, garnish these with the on-drive of Greg Chappell, the late outswing of Alec Bedser, the sticky fingers of Mark Taylor and Mark Waugh in the slips and you can have the glimpse of a rare all-rounder.

Deliberately, I have left out his inimitable cover-drive. No batsman before him, or after him, could execute this stroke with his elegance and timing. How do I know? If a picture is worth thousand words, an action photo study of Wally Hammond cover-driving is worth kilograms of epigrams. A life-size photograph of him cover-driving at the Bert Oldfield Sports Shop in Sydney in 1970s made me stop in my track. It was perfection, everything in place, including the handkerchief in his right pocket.

Top Test All-Rounders

Hammond also captured 83 wickets at 37.80 (taking 5 wickets in an innings twice, best being 5–36 in his Test debut in 1927-28) and held 110 catches.

He was the first player to achieve the Test double of 7000 runs and 100 catches. If he was not under bowled by his captains, he could have reached the Test triple of 7000 runs, 100 wickets and 100 catches, a feat achieved only by the West Indies great Garry Sobers and South Africa's Jacques Kallis decades later.

It was in a way unfortunate for Hammond that his Test batting career coincided with Don Bradman's. The latter outshone him in average and sheer killer instinct. But experts rank Hammond higher in poise and grace, if not in thunder and lightning. To quote Ronald Mason, 'Nothing that he [Hammond] did was without grace; nothing that he did was without authority. He was orthodox but he expressed his orthodoxy in rich chorded tones. His on-drive was right out of the book; his off-drive was right out of the world'.

Also there was his expertise in bowling and fielding. In a distinguished first-class career spanning four decades from 1920 to 1951, Hammond amassed 50,551 runs at 56.10 with 167 centuries and 185 fifties, 732 wickets at 30.58, pocketed 819 catches and made three stumpings.

How did it all start? Hammond was born in Kent at Dover, UK on 19 June 1903, the son of a professional soldier. There was no cricket in his family, nor did he have any formal coaching. Soon after his birth, his father was posted to Malta and he followed him there with his mother. He learnt his cricket by chalking a wicket on a door and played with a cut-down bat discarded by the soldiers.

The family returned to England in 1914. He was enrolled in the Cirencester Grammar Boarding School in 1918. A month later he was called to his headmaster's study to be informed about the shattering news of his father's death in action.

Wally Hammond was among the most elegant batsmen in the game's history. Here he is driving in his inimitable style.

The 15-year-old had to bear his grief alone and in the opinion of his biographer Derek Lodge in *The Test Match Career of Walter Hammond* (1990), 'It may well have been at this time that the seeds of his moodiness, that withdrawn air that was to characterise him all his life, were sown.' This incident may also have deepened his resolve to become a professional cricketer, as he did not enjoy his school homework.

Just before his 19th birthday, he was picked for his School XI and outshone other players by scoring over 500 runs and capturing 86 wickets. To play for Gloucestershire was the next step and wrote *Wisden 1924*, 'Irreproachable in style and not as yet 21 years of age, Hammond has all the world before him, and there is no telling how far he may go'.

Prophetic words indeed! The promising lad turned into a polished performer on 25 August 1924. On a rain-affected pitch in Bristol, Gloucestershire was bowled out for 31. Middlesex did little better, 74 all out. Chancing his arm, young Hammond struck 174 sensational runs in less than four hours on a pitch where 20 wickets had tumbled for 105 runs.

> *Chancing his arm, young Hammond struck 174 sensational runs in less than four hours.*

Raved the *Daily Telegraph* (UK) the next morning, 'His gallantry, his confidence, the freedom with which he treated almost unplayable bowling recalled the days of [Gilbert] Jessop with his back to the wall'.

In 1925 he toured the West Indies with MCC and developed a disease that almost killed him. Details remain obscure but it appears that he was stung by a mosquito when on the tour. He returned home with a severe form of blood-poisoning and spent most of the summer of 1926 in a hospital. It seemed for a while that his leg would have to be amputated to save his life.

Fortunately for him and the cricket world, this was not necessary and he made a complete recovery. Next season he was at his best for

Gloucestershire, scoring 99 and a run-a-minute 187 at Old Trafford against Lancashire which made Neville Cardus rhapsodise, 'It was one of the greatest innings ever witnessed on the ground. No other living Englishman could have given us cricket so full of mingled style and power, an innings of strength, bravery, sweetness and light … in his own way, another [Victor] Trumper in the making.'

Hammond went on to score 1000 runs in May that summer, only the second batsman after W.G. Grace to do so 32 years before. Hammond was now ready to represent England. Selected for the tour of South Africa in 1927–28, he made his Test debut in the Johannesburg Test memorable by scoring 51 runs and taking 0–21 and 5–36 as England won by 10 wickets. The newcomer had arrived and was to put his stamp of greatness in the battle for the Ashes in Australia the next summer.

This series saw Wally Hammond at his scintillating best, amassing 905 runs in five Tests at 113.12 with 251 (including 30 fours) as his top score in the Sydney Test of December 1928. He became the first batsman to register double centuries in successive innings when he hit 200 in the Melbourne Test a fortnight later. In the next Test in Adelaide in February 1929, he struck 119 and 177, becoming the fourth batsman to record a century in each Test innings and the second after Herbert Sutcliffe also of England to notch four centuries in a rubber.

Incredibly he had aggregated 779 runs in five innings at 194.75 and included two centuries and two double centuries. However, he was never to dominate an Ashes series again, as Bradman took over the Supreme Conqueror role.

But according to England's prolific opening batsman Len Hutton in *Walter Hammond* by Gerald Howat, 'He [Hammond] was the finest batsman that I have played with or against'. Hutton ranks two innings he saw against Yorkshire on a pitch taking spin as masterpieces. 'I was at Lord's in 1938

Walter Hammond and a large group of fans.

to see his double century against Australia. This elegant, powerful innings stands out for me today [1983] just as clearly as it was played over 40 years ago.'

Everyone who saw Hammond bat has his favourite memorable innings. Whereas Bradman had a weakness on wet pitches, Hammond was at his best when the chips were down and the balls skidded low. To quote Hutton again, 'Hammond could hit the ball as though it had been fired from a gun. He could make spin bowlers on a turning wicket look inept.'

It is beyond the scope of this profile to describe all his masterpieces. But no one can ignore his dazzling 240 against Australia in the Lord's Test. Howard Marshall commented in the *Daily Telegraph* (UK), 'His innings must rank with [Stan] McCabe's as one of the greatest ever played in Test matches'.

World War II broke out soon after this masterly exhibition of strokeplay. He enlisted and became Squadron Leader and was posted to RAF Middle East Headquarters at Cairo from 1940 to 1943. When the war ended and cricket resumed, Hammond was in his forties and not at his best. Severe lumbago added to his decline.

In retrospect, it was unwise for him to tour Australia as captain in 1946–47 aged 43. But his intention was to boost the confidence of war-ravaged England with his experience. He totalled 168 runs at 21.00, did not bowl and took five catches—hardly Hammondesque—and England lost the Ashes 0–3.

He returned to London on 9 April 1947 and got married to Sybil Nees-Harvey, an attractive South African girl, the next day. It was his second marriage. Dorothy Lister was his first wife and that marriage had lasted about 11 years. Dorothy was tired of living the life of a 'cricket widow'. Wally always wanted to be a father and had three children with Sybil, son Roger in 1948 and daughters Carolyn in 1950 and Valerie in 1952.

Hammond continued his car business with Marsham Tyres. He also reported on the Ashes series for the *London Star* in 1948. In March 1950 at the Annual Gloucestershire Dinner, he was presented his portrait, painted by Edward Halliday, and was paid glowing tributes by Sir Pelham Warner and Duke of Beaufort among others. Hammond was overcome with emotion.

The next year he migrated to South Africa and things started going wrong. To set up a business he needed big money which he could not raise and was soon job hunting. A Durban businessman and cricket lover offered him the position of General Manager of Denham Motors. However, by 1959 the demand for cars had declined and Hammond was out of a job.

Things got worse the following year. He was motoring to do some cricket coaching when involved in a crash with a truck. His car rolled over and he was left for dead. Only the timely intervention by a doctor passing by and seeing a motionless body saved the legendary cricketer's life. He was hospitalised for almost a month and was nursed back to health by Sybil. A year later he played club cricket and was later appointed sports administrator and selector of Natal University. Surprisingly and disappointingly, no efforts were made to involve him directly in South African cricket at higher levels.

He appeared a sad and lonely figure when Mike Smith's MCC team was doing net practice before the 1964 Durban Test. The noted British commentator Brian Johnston spotted him and introduced him to the English team. In a touching Foreword in Derek Lodge's biography of Hammond, Johnston wrote, 'From that moment he became part of the MCC team. I shall never forget seeing him that evening in the hotel surrounded by the players who were listening spellbound to the great man.'

Wally Hammond died of a heart attack, aged 62, on July 1, 1965. However, the legend of Wally Hammond lives on four decades after his passing.

Wrote A.E.R. Gilligan in 1940s: 'W.G. Grace drew all England to him and made cricket a national game. Jack Hobbs saved it after the First World War. Walter Hammond has kept the torch brightly burning in these dark and difficult days.'

Gerald Howat concludes the biography *Walter Hammond* with: 'Yet in the end we are left with the image of a man who gave happiness to thousands but who never quite secured a fair share for himself; whose mastery of technique delighted the purists but whose philosophy of life faltered; who amassed runs yet failed to amass the personal assurance which men crave; whose cover-drive was a gift from the gods but whose craftsmanship in the building of relationships showed human frailty. He was a great public figure but a very private person.'

KEITH MILLER

Australia

Ask cricket critics to name 10 greatest all-rounders, 10 most awe-inspiring bowlers, 10 best hitters of sixes, two handsomest cricketers and 10 most charming characters of the game and only one name will be there in all these lists. It would be Keith Miller, universally adored, respected and nicknamed 'Nugget'. Tall and handsome, dashing and debonair with a mane of black hair, Miller in 1940s and 50s exuded sex and six appeal.

He was Australia's most adventurous batsman since World War II and only England's dynamic all-rounder Ian Botham and Australia's Adam Gilchrist could challenge him in consistent high hitting. Yet Miller was not a slogger.

Had he not been asked to concentrate more on bowling fast (he formed a menacing pace-like-fire combination with Ray Lindwall), he would have been remembered as a batsman of class. 'The pedigree of his stroke play rivalled Wally Hammond's', wrote Mihir Bose, his biographer.

After Miller's scintillating batting during the 1945 tour of England with the Australian Services team, C.B. Fry said on BBC, 'Miller has something of the dash and generous abandon that were part of Victor Trumper's charms.'

Miller was more than a six symbol, being a living legend before words like 'legend' and 'icon' became commonplace with the advent of sensation-seeking scribes and computers. His death on 11 October 2004 at the age of 84 made almost as many headlines as did the passing of Sir Don Bradman three years previously. Tributes flew in from all corners. Well-respected

Dynamic Keith Miller exuded sex and six appeal.
Here he is hitting out to bring spectators to their feet.

English writer Christopher Martin-Jenkins penned in his obituary in *The Times*: 'Keith Miller, an Ian Botham or Andrew Flintoff of his day, was a natural champion with a special touch in human relationships'.

'There has never been a more glamorous cricketer than Keith Miller, not even Imran Khan', eulogised historian David Frith in *The Wisden Cricketer*. 'His stride was that of a catwalk. His sleek hair anticipated Elvis [Presley] by some years.'

'Fiery' Fred Trueman, another charismatic character, had recalled in 1979, 'Keith Ross Miller will go down in the history of Test cricket as one of the greatest all-rounders of all time. In my opinion, he will also remain the biggest enigma that Australian cricket ever produced or is likely to. He had the flair, as any cricketer of the highest class must have, to be able to perform great feats that surpass even one's own expectations. He also had a great personality that influenced all he came into contact with him and I do not think anyone could say they knew how he would react to a situation on a cricket field. That was where his greatness lay.'

When writing my book *Six Appeal*, I was lucky to have had a long chat with Miller. He was then recovering from a mild stroke. 'Ask me any question on horse-racing or classical music but not cricket.' Yet within an hour he recalled his extraordinary six-hitting sprees in 3-D effect.

'I'll tell you a funny yarn from the 1945 tour of England. I hit a straight six in the direction of the BBC room. Commentator Rex Alston's description, I'm told, went like this: "Miller has hit the ball in the air, it's coming this way, yes, it's…"—then crash, kaboom as the ball shattered the BBC glass pane.'

Now he was in mid-season form. 'When I toured England in 1953, an English newspaper offered a cash prize of 600 pounds to anyone hitting a ball across river Thames and into an island named Tagga's Island, a carry of 130 yards… I gave the ball a mighty heave-ho and it sailed across, amid 'oohs' and 'aahs' from spectators. I waited but the crowd's disappointed chorus of 'oh no!' indicated that I had missed the target narrowly.'

During the 1948 tour of England, Miller belted 26 sixes, often at critical stages. In the second innings of the Lord's Test he came to the crease with Norman Yardley on a hat-trick. Miller was nearly dismissed first ball but hit a huge six soon after, the ball landing halfway up the grandstand.

Apart from towering sixes, Nugget also specialised in 'ponders', dispatching balls into ponds and rivers. At Eden Gardens, Calcutta (now Kolkata), in an unofficial test against India in 1945, he borrowed a bat from RS Whitington who warned Miller to be careful with it. Miller nodded and promptly drove India's spinner Vinoo Mankad over the sightscreen for four sixes, all landing in a pond outside the ground. To Whitington's relief, Miller was stumped soon after.

Top Test All-Rounders

Nugget gave two more balls a watery grave in South Africa in 1949-50, hammering six sixes in his breezy 131 against Eastern Province at Port Elizabeth. 'I remember reaching my ton with a six, one of the nicest and longest sixes I ever hit. It cleared the grandstand and landed in a pond in the park outside the ground. It was one of the shots that clicked.'

Although statistics did not mean much to him, his figures were impressive if not spectacular. He scored 2958 runs at 36.97 in 55 Tests, hitting seven centuries (with 147 runs as his highest) and 13 fifties and captured 170 wickets at 22.97 (7–60 being his best) and 38 catches. In 226 first-class matches he amassed 14,183 runs at 48.90 with 41 hundreds (top score 281 not out in 1956 when he was 36) and 63 fifties and took 497 scalps at 22.30 (best 7–12) and 136 catches.

He would have been ideally suited for one-day internationals with his furious hitting at no. 6 and with his express pace but unfortunately they came too late for him. Whether he would have enjoyed playing Twenty20 cricket is debatable as he played the game for the fun of it but at the same time hated the way current cricket was being cheapened.

Statistics, however, did not provide a yardstick for his greatness. It was his charisma, his glamour, his Errol Flynn-like persona that appealed to the spectators. As English author Gerald Brodribb wrote, 'Spectators saw in Miller the fine Tarzan-like physique they would all like to possess, the devil-may-care attitude to bowlers (and statistics) they would all like to adopt and the daring and powerful style of play they would all like to call their own.'

Mihir Bose added: 'Remove Miller from the scoreboard and he still lives. That can be said of few all-rounders.'

Born on 28 November 1919 in Sunshine, Victoria, Keith Ross Miller was named after the Smith brothers Keith and Ross who were about to complete their epic flight in a Vickers Vimy biplane from England to

Australia. He loved horse racing and wanted to be a jockey but he shot up to 6 feet in his teens and turned to cricket although he never lost his passion for punting.

His first-class debut for Victoria in 1938 was spectacular as the 18-year-old hit 181 against Tasmania at the Melbourne Cricket Ground.

> *He loved horse racing and wanted to be a jockey but he shot up to 6 feet in his teens and turned to cricket.*

'His outstanding potential was emphasised with a further century against Don Bradman's South Australia (with the cunning old spinner Clarrie Grimmett bowling) also at the MCG in the New Year 1940 Sheffield Shield match', recalled David Frith. So it was as a batsman that Miller took his bow to cricket. It was not until 1945 in the 'Victory Tests' that he showed his potential to rattle the stumps and scare batsmen.

In a way cricket saved his life. He served with 169 Squadron in England during the World War II, flying Beaufighter and Mosquito fighter-bombers. Given leave to play cricket in Dulwich, UK, he was devastated to learn on his return to Bournemouth that nine of his off-duty mates were killed when the local pub was bombed.

Miller made his Test debut against New Zealand at Wellington in March 1946, the first post-WWII Test after a break of seven years. Australia won by an innings in two days, the debutant scoring 30 runs (as 30 wickets tumbled for 295 runs) and took 2–6 in six overs. In his Ashes debut in Brisbane eight months later, he hit 79 and captured 7 for 60 as Australia won by an innings and 332 runs. But he was reluctant to bowl bouncers at his army friends (and now opponents), the English batsmen Bill Edrich, Wally Hammond and Cyril Washbrook.

Miller scored the first of his seven Test centuries (141 not out) in the Adelaide Test of the series. He was devastating in the rain-interrupted Trent Bridge Test in 1948 as he took 3–38 and 4–125. He frightened batsmen with his bouncers and was booed for the only time in his career.

The two Aussie legends Bradman and Miller often did not see eye-to-eye and Miller was dropped from the team to South Africa in 1949–50. He was later flown in as a replacement.

Miller remembered the Ashes Test on the MCG starting on the last day of 1954 with satisfaction. He had a dazzling spell of 3 for 5 in nine 8-ball overs, eight being maidens. His victims were skipper Len Hutton, Bill Edrich and Denis Compton and his final figures were 11–8–14–3. He was even more devastating in the Adelaide Test a month later. When England needed a token 94 to win the Test and retain the Ashes, Miller dismissed Hutton in his first over, Edrich in his second, Colin Cowdrey in his third and dived to catch Peter May as England struggled to 4 for 49. But the tumble damaged Miller's shoulder and England won by five wickets.

His most sensational bowling spell came during a Sheffield Shield match in 1955 between NSW and South Australia on the Sydney Cricket Ground. He had forgotten to pick up a team-mate and drove like a maniac to reach the ground just in time. He had hardly slept the previous night to celebrate the birth of his son. Not perturbed, he shot out South Australia before lunch for a record low of 27, 'Nugget' Miller capturing 7 for 12.

Neville Cardus called him 'The Australian in excelsis'.

On Australia's maiden tour of the West Indies in 1955, the 35-year-old Nugget hit three centuries and captured 20 wickets in the series. No wonder Neville Cardus called him 'The Australian in excelsis'.

Keith loved women and women loved him. But the one that meant the most to him was his wife Margaret 'Peggy' Wagner from Boston, Massachusetts who he had met during WWII. Their marriage lasted for over 50 years before Peggy died in 2003. He enjoyed classical music, especially

Beethoven. His last days were tragic as he endured hip replacement, cancer and stroke.

When he passed away, his team-mate Bill Brown said. 'He was the finest all-rounder I came in contact with; he could bat, bowl, field and he could fly an aeroplane.' Added ABC commentator Glenn Mitchell: 'It was said of him [Miller] that every woman wanted to be with him, while every man wanted to be him.'

I could imagine the Almighty standing in a queue to get his autograph when he returned to the eternal Dressing Room.

VINOO MANKAD
India

Mulvantrai Himmatlal 'Vinoo' Mankad was India's first genuine all-rounder and until Kapil Dev arrived on the scene three decades later he was the most versatile for his country, and certainly among all time greats.

In 44 Tests he scored 2109 runs at 31.47 with five centuries (top score 231) and took 162 wickets at 32.32 (best spell being 8–52) and 33 catches.

Ambidextrous, he batted right-handed and bowled left-arm leg spinners. In Tests he batted at all positions from no. 1 to no. 11 (only England's Wilfred Rhodes had done this before him). But it was as an opener that he excelled, scoring both his Test double centuries in the 1955–56 series against New Zealand, 223 in Bombay (now Mumbai) and 231 in Madras (now Chennai). Before him only Wally Hammond and Don Bradman had made two double centuries in the same series.

But it was as a bowler that Mankad was behind India's first ever Test victory in their 25th Test spanning 20 years. In this historic Test against England in Madras in February 1952 he captured 8 for 55 and 4 for 53. Eight months later in the inaugural Test against Pakistan in Delhi, he had a match haul of 13 wickets (8 for 52 and 5 for 79) as India triumphed by an innings and 70 runs. In between he played a memorable Test at Lord's where he scored 72 and 184 as an opener and bowled 97 overs, taking 5 for 196 in the first innings. This match is remembered as Mankad's Test and will be described later.

Born on 12 April 1917, his Test entry was delayed because of World War II. His debut at the age of 29 was against England at Lord's in June1946

It was Vinoo Mankad against England in the Lord's Test of 1952 when he scored 72 and 184 runs and captured 5 wickets.

when he top scored with 63 in the second innings. In the second Test in Manchester he bagged 5 for 101 in the first innings. This was just a warm up for Vinoo.

India's inaugural tour of Australia in 1947-48 started poorly for him. In the first two Tests he was dismissed by the great Ray Lindwall for 0, 7, 5 and 5. At a cocktail party at the end of the first day's play in the third Test in Melbourne, Mankad approached Lindwall and asked if he was doing anything wrong. In a happy mood, Lindwall told the keen Indian that he had been coming down too late on the yorker and suggested that he could do with a less pronounced back lift.

Thanking Lindwall and following his advice, Mankad made 116 the next day. His century came in only 135 minutes and he became the first Indian to hit a ton off an Aussie attack. Several times during the innings he asked Lindwall whether he had cut down his back swing sufficiently! He scored another century—once again off Lindwall and Keith Miller at their fastest—in the final Test in Melbourne.

During this tour Mankad was involved in an incident which gave him some unjustified notoriety. When bowling against Australian XI he noticed Bill Brown at the bowler's end leaving the crease before he delivered the ball. He warned Brown once but next time ran him out by whipping off the bails in the act of delivering the ball. Mankad did the same in the Sydney Test and a new cricket phrase was coined: *to be Mankaded*. Bradman defended Mankad in his autobiography *Farewell to Cricket*: 'In some quarters Mankad's sportsmanship was questioned. For the life of me I cannot understand why... By backing up too far or too early, the non-striker is very obviously gaining an unfair advantage.'

When the team departed for India, the Don presented him with an autographed photograph with the words 'Well played, Mankad' inscribed on it. Mankad treasured this till he died.

There were few things the plumpish gutsy Vinoo Mankad could not achieve. Although playing for a weak side known for its slack fielding and atrocious catching, and having an unsettled batting order, he reached the Test double of 1000 runs and 100 wickets in 23 Tests, which was then the quickest in Test history. He went on to top 2000 runs and 150 wickets in his 40th Test, also the quickest in Test annals at that time.

His batting symbolised cricket's glorious uncertainties and followed no set pattern. One day he would be sound and reliable, the next day a spectator's joy with thrilling shots everywhere and in the following match drab and stroke-less. But in his left-arm spin bowling he was always a delight to watch, a master on all wickets. His subtle variation of flight and spin kept the batsman guessing. As a fielder he was safe, especially to his own bowling.

> *His subtle variation of flight and spin kept the batsman guessing.*

Mankad reached his peak as an all-rounder in 1952. After taking 12 for 108 in the final Test in Madras in February which was instrumental in India's maiden Test triumph, only three things appeared certain—taxation, death and inclusion of Mankad in the Indian squad to England three months later. But his name was missing when the team was announced.

Being a professional cricketer who played in the Lancashire League, he wanted an assurance from the selectors that he would be picked for the tour of England. As he did not get a nod from them in advance, he went to play League cricket. Without him India was routed in the first Test in Leeds, losing four wickets for no runs in the second innings. The raw speed of debutant Fred Trueman and the clever seaming of Alec Bedser were too much for the tourists.

This forced the selectors to borrow Mankad from the Haslingden Club and he walked in from Lancashire League to Test immortality. With little practice at first-class level, he opened India's batting and top scored with 72 and bowled 73 overs to capture five wickets in England's first innings. His accuracy made skipper Len Hutton (150) ultra defensive for hours on an easy wicket, at one stage the Indian bowled 11 consecutive maidens.

When India started her second innings 302 runs behind, the iron-man Mankad opened the innings and captivated an appreciative Lord's crowd with a scintillating 184 with one 6 and 19 fours. 'His innings will take its place among the classics', wrote E.W. Swanton. But Mankad was not done yet. He opened the attack and bowled 24 more economical overs. In all he had bowled 97 overs and scored 256 runs. Although India lost, the Test is remembered as Mankad's Test.

'It is now Mankad against England', screamed the streamer headlines in London.

His 13 scalps in the inaugural Test against Pakistan four months later led to an innings victory for India. Yes, 1952 was a very good year for Mankad when he scored 540 runs at 41.54 and took 53 wickets at 22.08 in 10 Tests, a rare double at that time

When he turned 39 there were hints that he should retire. But he silenced his critics by recording two double centuries against New Zealand.

> *A Test record for the first wicket which stood till 2007.*

At Madras in the final Test of the series, he made 231, then the highest score by an Indian. During that innings he added 413 runs with Pankaj Roy, a Test record for the first wicket which stood till 2007.

When we remember Vinoo Mankad, we remember an unruffled robust character with the top two shirt buttons undone, usually uncapped (although at times he bowled wearing a cap) with a rhythmic bowling action, a beast of burden, an Atlas in flannels.

His son, Ashok, played 22 Tests for India in 1970s. Vinoo died in August 1978 aged 61 and is among few cricketers to have become a legend in their lifetime.

This is how John Arlott described him in 1950s: 'A great bowler, clearly the best of his type in post-war cricket and possibly as good as any in any period. Certainly he is entitled to stand with Rhodes, Verity and Parker in the line of classic slow left-arm bowlers.'

TREVOR BAILEY
England

A cricketer of strong character, Trevor 'Barnacle' Bailey had a mind of his own. Perceptive and intelligent, he was a tough 'cookie' who called an axe an axe. He was a useful rather than an outstanding all-rounder; an effective fast-medium bowler, a dour 'get-me-out-if-you-can' batsman and a brilliant fielder. His bat appeared a foot wide to his frustrated opponents as he lunged forward to play another defensive prod to save yet another match for Essex and England.

His innings of 50 in 357 minutes in the second innings of the Brisbane Test of 1958–59 was the slowest in first-class cricket. He made 68 to top score in a low-scoring match and his crawl lasted 458 minutes at an average of nine runs per hour. For sure, no selector would pick him in today's one-day internationals, let alone the Twenty20 slogathons.

Trevor Bailey was a crisis specialist and a strategist and his advice was sought by captains Len Hutton and Peter May. Bailey went on four overseas tours, sharing the new ball with Alec Bedser before the advent of super quickies 'Fiery' Fred Trueman, Frank 'Typhoon' Tyson and the pacey but metronome-like accurate Brian Statham. But the performances of 'Barnacle' Bailey were not eclipsed by the above bowling giants nor by the superb batting line-up of Hutton, May, Denis Compton, Colin Cowdrey and Tom Graveney. He was a quiet achiever and saviour, always there, playing a patient (frustrating?) innings here, bowling a swinging yorker there, pocketing a catch from apparently nowhere. He was as much responsible as any of the above legends for England emerging from post-WWII depression to world domination in 1950s.

Twice in 1953, England owed their survival to the back-seat driver Bailey. 'At Leeds he bowled leg-theory to slow down the Australian gallop to victory and at Lord's he batted for four and half hours for 71 on the final day in a famous stand with Willie Watson', according to *World Cricketers* (1996) edited by Christopher Martin-Jenkins.

Needing 343 runs to win the second Test at Lord's, England lost 4 for 73 with top-liners Hutton, Don Kenyon, Graveney and Compton dismissed. With defeat staring in the face, Bailey joined Watson and figured in one of the classic rearguard actions of Test cricket on the chilling final day. They added 163 precious runs which lasted from 12.42 p.m. to 5.50 p.m. as Bailey battled for 257 minutes for his 71. This saved England from what appeared a certain defeat.

With the first four Tests ending in draws, England won the final Test at The Oval to regain the Ashes after 19 years. Bailey's contribution in this Test was dismissing Keith Miller for one and making 64, the second highest score in the match.

In Kingston, Jamaica, the following year, he produced one of the most lethal spells in Test history, capturing 7 for 34 in 16 overs on a batsman's paradise. It was then England's best spell against the West Indians and his victims included Jack Holt and Everton Weekes for ducks and Jeff Stollmeyer for nine. In reply to the West Indies' paltry total of 139, England showed that there was no devil in the pitch by making 414, Hutton (205) outscoring the Windies' total and recording the first double century by an England captain in an overseas Test. Garry Sobers made his Test debut in this Test and had Bailey, his future biographer, as his first victim.

Born on 3 December 1923, Trevor Edward Bailey showed promise as a schoolboy cricketer at Dulwich and was a Cambridge Blue in both cricket and soccer in 1947–48. World War II delayed his cricket development. On leaving Dulwich he enlisted in the Royal marines and rose to the rank of Lieutenant before demobilisation in 1946. He represented Essex in County

Top Test All-Rounders

Allsport Hulton/Getty Images

cricket from 1946 to 1967, captaining them from 1961. He became the backbone of the England Test team for a decade from 1949 to 1959.

In 61 Tests he scored 2290 runs at 29.74 with one century and took 132 wickets at 29.21 and 32 catches. His first-class figures were more impressive: 28,641 runs at 33.42 with 28 centuries (top score 205), 2082 wickets at 23.13 (taking five wickets in an innings 110 times, best bowling 10 for 90 for Essex vs Lancashire at Clacton in 1949) and 426 catches. He passed 1000 runs in a season 18 times and 100 wickets in a season on nine occasions. Besides, he achieved the first-class double of 1000 runs and 100 wickets in a season eight times, the most for any post-WWII player along with Fred Titmus for Middlesex.

After retiring from cricket he wrote books and became a popular member of the Test Match Special team on the BBC. I enjoyed his analytical biography of Sobers titled *Sir Gary*. 'From the age of three, when I just began to play cricket I have always wanted both to bat and to bowl, a desire which remained with me throughout my career.'

'From the age of three, when I just began to play cricket I have always wanted both to bat and to bowl.'

Trevor Bailey square-cutting in the 1953 Oval Test against Australia.

RICHIE BENAUD

Australia

The name Richie Benaud means many things to many people. He was an all-rounder in every sense of the word, a crafty leg-spinner and googly expert who captured 248 wickets in 63 Tests, an attacking lower-order batsman who hit one of the fastest Test centuries, a brilliant gully fielder with amazing anticipation and reflexes and a crowd puller wherever he played. He was also a courageous and victorious leader of men who lost neither a series nor his cool. Now as a media personality he is the voice of cricket.

The Benaud saga begins with his father Lou who was of French origin. Selected for second grade for Penrith, teenager Lou tasted everlasting fame. For Penrith Waratah Club against St Mary's, he took all 20 wickets in the match, 10 for 30 in the first innings and 10 for 35 in the second.

But his bigger contribution was his encouragement to sons Richie and John to play single-handed cricket by bowling a tennis ball against a wall and hitting it on the rebound. More than the coaching, it was the atmosphere that captured the imagination of young Richie. In the words of A.G. 'Johnnie' Moyes, 'From the time he could toddle along, Richie lived in and breathed the cricket atmosphere'.

Born on 6 October 1930, Richie played his first competition match for Jugiong School when six and scored 11 runs. At eight, he played in the First XI of Burnside School near Parramatta and later led the team to a competition win. With his own cricket clothes packed ready, in case a player should fail to turn up, Richie travelled around to see his father play for

Richie Benaud weaving his magic spell against England in the 1958 Brisbane Test.

his district and club. Watching the great spinner Clarrie Grimmett was an inspiration to Richie and he recalls in his book *Willow Patterns*, 'I think it was the avid watching of Grimmett more than any one thing that made me want to be a leg-spinner'.

Thinking Richie's hands were not large enough, Lou did not allow him to bowl leg-spinners until he was 17. Instead, emphasis was kept on line and length. Till then he was considered more of a batsman. He was promoted to first-grade for Central Cumberland when 16 and made a brilliant 98 in his second match. However, the way to the top was not easy. There was a cracked skull, a broken thumb, a crushed finger and a ball in the mouth. But nothing could dent his determination to succeed. According to A.A.Thomson, 'He had courage in excelsis'.

The skull-cracking episode occurred when, as a teenager, he was batting for NSW Second XI. He tried to hook the ball, missed it and was struck a shattering blow on the forehead above the right eye. Oh for a helmet! He was out of cricket for a year but the blow left no psychological scar. Years later he hooked tearaway terrors Wes Hall, Fred Trueman and Frank 'Typhoon' Tyson with tremendous power.

His Test debut against the West Indies in January 1952 in Sydney was not impressive. Nor did he shine out in the Tests against South Africa in 1952–53 and when touring England in 1953. But in first-class matches on the 1953 tour to England he had magical moments as a batsman.

After reaching his first century in England, Richie drove Roy Tattersall for four successive sixes. Even the economical Alec Bedser and the crafty Johnny Wardle were belted over the fence as Richie plundered 135 in 110 minutes and the Australians won in the final over. Against Yorkshire he smashed 97 in two hours with four sixes and 11 fours and also took 7 for 46. At Scarborough against Pearce's XI—a virtual England side—Australia were set 320 runs to win in 220 minutes. Benaud opened with Arthur Morris and started steadily. When Len Hutton teasingly remarked, 'What's the matter laad, playing for average?' Richie's response was 11 sixes, a world record at the time. 'This was hardly liberty, it was licence', commented A.A. Thomson.

During this tour fellow spinner Doug Ring passed on valuable tips to the rookie Richie, especially how to bowl a top-spinner. Also on this tour the legendary Bill O'Reilly suggested a few changes in his bowling action.

Earlier, Richie had improved his batting stance by seeking Keith Miller's advice and practised in front of a mirror. The young Benaud was acquiring all-round excellence in first-class cricket, scoring three successive centuries against Queensland in the Sheffield Shield seasons of 1953–54 and 1954–55. Against Western Australia, he scored 112 and 59 as an opener and captured seven wickets as well.

As if saying, Test cricket, here I come, Richie hit a dazzling 121 in 85 minutes with two sixes and 15 fours in the Kingston Test against the West Indies in 1955. His century came in 78 minutes, then the third fastest Test century. This onslaught prompted a Jamaican barracker to shout, 'Do it to England, maan, not to us'. But there is a human angle story behind this belting of fours and sixes.

He had just heard that a close family member was seriously ill in Sydney. At one stage he walked down the pitch and told skipper Ian Johnson that because of this news he could not concentrate. Johnson replied, 'Well, just let your head go and hit'. And hit he did. Hooking and driving his way to 50 runs in 38 minutes of mayhem and 100 in 78 mad minutes.

Earlier in the series he had captured three wickets in four balls and ended up heading the bowling averages, taking 18 wickets at 27 apiece. After years of promise the 25-year-old was on his way to becoming a world class Test all-rounder.

Richie's second tour of England in 1956 started with a spectacular 160

Richie bowls with concentration and accuracy-—batsmen beware!

(three sixes, 22 fours) against Worcestershire in the opening match. Then in the Lord's Test, he put on a memorable performance, hitting a magnificent 97 off 113 balls in 144 minutes. Later he took what is described as the catch of the century when he caught Colin Cowdrey in the gully. Thus Richie had contributed sensationally to Australia's only win in the series.

Richie rates this Lord's Test as one of his most enjoyable games and, as for the Cowdrey catch, he modestly explains that instead of his catching the ball, the ball caught him, 'for good as it looked, I never saw the ball other than as a blur from the moment it left Cowdrey's bat'.

The same year Australia toured Pakistan and India. Shortening his run-up to save energy, he captured 7 for 72 in the Madras Test—his best Test figures— as Australia won by an innings. Then followed his most successful tour to South Africa in 1957–58. 'This experience', wrote A.A. Thomson, 'formed the springboard from which he leaped to three successive victories over England. It could be said that on the veldt, he eventually found his feet.'

On his South African performances, *Wisden* 1959 noted: 'The outstanding personality was R. Benaud who, in bowling and batting, enjoyed a tour of outstanding success'. He became the only player of the 20th century to take 100 wickets in a season outside England. His performances in the five Tests included: 122; 4 for 95 and 5 for 49; 5 for 114; 100, 4 for 70 and 5 for 84; 43 and 5 for 82. Seldom had an all-rounder performed so consistently in one series.

What is probably not known to many is that his career was resurrected by a pharmacist from a small New Zealand community. Leg-spinner Benaud was plagued by torn muscles in his fingers and as the tour of South Africa approached, with Australia the underdogs, he pinned his hopes on a trans-Tasman apothecary. At Timaru in February 1957, nine months prior to the South African safari, a Kiwi pharmacist had given him a potion he said would fix Richie's problem. 'And he was right', Benaud recalls. 'It was the single most beneficial thing that happened to me in cricket and I never had any trouble again.'

He started the tour sensationally, taking 9 for 16 in the country game in Kitwe, seven of his scalps with his new weapon, the flipper. His overall first-class figures of 817 runs at 50 (with four centuries) and 106 wickets at 19 apiece came about because he had the confidence of skipper Craig, vice-captain Neil Harvey and the entire team.

In the fourth Test in Johannesburg he scored 100 and grabbed 4 for 70 and 5 for 84 and totalled 329 runs (including two centuries) in five Tests at

54.83 and captured 30 wickets at 21.93, contributing largely to Australia's 3–0 win.

Benaud had worked hard for his phenomenal success. As Bob Simpson recalls: 'His practice sessions on that tour had to be seen to be believed. He laboured long after other players had left practice; a lonely figure bowling with a youngster to retrieve the balls aimed at a handkerchief placed on a good length spot. His legendary accuracy developed here.'

Benaud was appointed captain against England in 1959–60. He lost the toss four times out of five yet regained the Ashes 4–0. He contributed to this facile win by taking 31 wickets in the series and by his dynamic leadership. He had the whole team behind him. A born PR man, he had pre-Test match meetings where every player's viewpoint was considered and grievances settled.

The excellent team spirit that existed was very clear to the spectators. The fall of a wicket was greeted by ecstatic scenes in the middle, with the players swarming in to hug the bowler or fielder concerned. Thus Benaud could be called the father of modern cricket with all its extrovert expressions. These emotional get-togethers tended to nauseate the old-timers, but the players felt 10 feet tall and gave their all. He retained the series in England in 1961 winning 2–1 and in Australia in 1962–63, drawing 1–all.

Throughout the 1961 tour of England, Richie's right shoulder troubled him. At times it was so painful that he could not shave himself, let alone bowl googlies. Yet in the fourth Test in Manchester he converted a certain loss into a stirring victory. England were set 256 runs to win in 230 minutes and were galloping towards the target, with the score at 1 for 150 and Ted Dexter going great guns. It was then that Benaud produced his *piece de resistance*.

Because of his painful shoulder, he did not attempt excessive spin, but by going round the wicket and pitching in the rough of Trueman's footholds, he imparted an awkward lift. In an incredible spell, he took four crucial wickets for 13 runs: Dexter caught behind; Peter May, to his chagrin, bowled first ball; Brian Close caught after attempting a desperate shot and the sedate opener Subba Row bowled after batting for almost three hours. England lost 9 for 51 after being 1 for 150 and Benaud finished with 6 for 70. It was his biggest triumph—a victory against all odds. Following this tour he was awarded an OBE by the Queen.

But even more than in this series, Richie had gained immortality the previous season against the West Indies—the series that revived an interest in cricket. The rubber included the famous tie, a cliffhanging draw made possible by the last pair batting for two hours and a win by two wickets in the series-deciding final Test. Historian 'Johnnie' Moyes considered Benaud to be a more brilliant leader than Worrell. 'In applauding the West Indians for lighting the fires of cricket's rehabilitation, I give full marks to Benaud for providing all the fuel he could to keep it burning brightly, both then and in after years', he wrote.

'The fame of the series is Benaud's monument to cricket', added Bob Simpson, who played in that epic series.

In the first Test in Brisbane, resulting in the first of two Test ties in Test cricket and considered one of the greatest Tests of all time, Australia were set 233 runs to win at 45 runs an hour. They were in desperate trouble at 6 for 92 when Benaud joined Alan Davidson. Their 134 run stand tilted the match Australia's way. Then within one run, both were dismissed, Davidson for 80 and Benaud for 52. In the final chilling over, and with the scores level, the last two batsmen were run out.

Shoulder trouble forced Richie to retire at 33 during the series against South Africa in 1963–64. By then he had become the first cricketer to do the Test double of 2000 runs and 200 wickets. Because of mushrooming of Test cricket, 13 more have reached this milestone.

Top Test All-Rounders

As an all-rounder Benaud ranks with the truly great ones Garry Sobers, Ian Botham, Keith Miller, Imran Khan, Richard Hadlee and Kapil Dev. Moyes rated Benaud 'the finest captain I have seen since Bradman'. Concurred Ray Robinson, Australia's finest cricket writer, in *On Top Down Under*: 'His [Benaud's] achievements, put on the scale with his skippership successes, lead me to rank him first among captains I have known.'

Benaud's contribution to cricket went further than scoring runs and grabbing wickets. Pakistan cricket benefited from his advice when he suggested to the then President, Ayub Khan, that they do away with matting wickets. This was done and it led to an improvement in their cricket standard overseas. And in 1976, as manager of the International Wanderers, he toured South Africa and fought for multiracial cricket in that country. The news that South Africa would end segregation in sport in the late 1980s so pleased him that he referred to it as 'the best news I have heard in years'.

A professional journalist and a respected television commentator, Richie has written many books on cricket. He was one of the key figures in the formation of World Series Cricket in 1977. Today he is the most enduring face and voice in cricket world. He is recognised as the game's shrewdest analyst, delivering his insights with the dry humour and incisiveness which are his hallmark. Imitation is the best for of flattery and there are probably as many Richie Benaud impersonators as there are for Elvis Presley.

To quote fellow commentator Bill Lawry from the foreword in Mark Browning's *Richie Benaud: Cricketer, Captain, Guru*: 'There is no doubt that Richie Benaud has one of the most brilliant cricket brains in the world and on reflection, cricket has suffered from the fact that he has never taken an administration position in world cricket, apart from the fact that he had a part to play in the success of World Series Cricket, a dramatic period in the history of Australian cricket, a period which changed world cricket forever and fortunately, lifted the game into the modern era, both for players and spectators.'

ALAN DAVIDSON

Australia

A superb performer with both bat and ball, many of Davidson's exploits are legendary even 45 years after his retirement. For 'Davo' was a super dynamo as a teenager and remained so till his farewell appearance in Sydney in February 1963 when he took a wicket off his last ball in Test cricket.

It is always a pleasure to know a Test star personally. Except that Alan Davidson, known as 'Davo' and 'The Claw', never considered himself a star. He has time to talk with anyone who loves cricket. He is both a soldier and a gentleman and thinks of cricket as a game to enjoy.

Not that he ever took the game lightly. Although on figures (1328 runs, 186 wickets and 42 catches in 44 Tests) he cannot compete with some other all-rounders in this Chapter, he dominated the game with both bat and ball. As a fielder he was outstanding and always an inspiration to all around him.

So let's redefine the term 'all-rounder'. Selecting Davidson as one of the Five Cricketers of the Year, *Wisden* 1962 wrote, 'When a cricketer can make fifty runs in a Test match he immediately becomes a valuable commodity to his side. When he has the ability to add to that five wickets in an innings and a brace of catches he is beyond price to his associates and skipper. Such a cricketer is Alan Keith Davidson, born on 14 June 1929, of cricket loving parents at Lisarow on the Central North Coast of New South Wales, and latterly, one of the great all-rounders in the history of the game.'

The New Zealanders remember the match against Wairarapa in Masterton, New Zealand where he took all 10 wickets for 29 runs off 81

*Alan Davidson hits and misses and the ball is collected
by Godfrey Evans in the 1955 Adelaide Test.*

deliveries and then hit an incandescent 157 not out. 'It was a double without
a parallel in international cricket', Davidson recalls in his autobiography
Fifteen Paces. Statisticians delved through the record books and produced
the only similar achievement—by E.M. Grace who, according to *Wisden*,
carried his bat for 192 runs and took 10 wickets in the second innings of a
15-man a side match in 1862. So it was not *all* 10 wickets, as in the case of
'Davo'. In the next match young Alan ran out a batsman from the boundary
line with only one stump to aim at. This was just the beginning of a glorious
journey to all-round excellence.

Sir Donald Bradman wrote in the foreword of *Fifteen Paces*: 'I cannot
think of any all-round player at any time whose absence from the Australian
XI was of more importance.' Stressing on his fielding, the Don added,

'He wasn't nicknamed 'The Claw' for nothing. Some of his run-outs were phenomenal.'

Alan played most of his early cricket in the Gosford district of New South Wales and participated in a formidable family team of Davidsons and Cliftons. His greatest influence in early life was granddad 'Paddy' Clifton. A natural cricketer, Alan represented for three consecutive years the Northern High Schools. And their strong opponents were City High Schools which included his future Test captain Richie Benaud. Alan was then a left-arm spin bowler and turned to fast-medium bowling only after leaving the school.

In 1947 the teenager had taken 37 wickets at 4.30 apiece for Gosford in the John Bull Shield and topped the batting and bowling averages. But it was as a fastish bowler that he was selected for NSW in 1949–50. He soon became a feared personality among batsmen in State cricket. 'When you see that big right foot coming down the wicket, brother, you duck', was how he was spoken of by opponents, in hushed tones. 'The beauty of an almost perfect fast medium action with a disconcerting late swing has caused untold worry to opening batsmen the world over', wrote *Wisden* 1962.

As a batsman he was equally slam bang. His sixes in the famous Manchester Test of 1961 remain memorable. One flew over the cover fielder's head, the next crashed against brickwork alongside the railway line. And these sixes were clouted when Australians were on their knees and 'Davo' took them to a sublime victory. 'Every bit of six feet and fourteen stone went into those shots in the same way it has gone into all that Davidson has done over the years for Australia', added *Wisden*.

Bradman also remembered Alan's marvellous batting in the Manchester 1961 Test with awe and affection. 'I mention it to emphasise how great a batsman Alan might have been had not bowling taken so much of his energy.'

Top Test All-Rounders

That was a memorable Test series for both Benaud and 'Davo'. Before the second Test at Lord's both the all-rounders were unfit, skipper Benaud with a painful shoulder and 'Davo' with a sore back. But Benaud insisted that Alan should play to support the substitute captain Neil Harvey. 'I bowled that day as hard as I have ever bowled in my life', recalls Alan. His reward was 5 for 42 and 2 for 50 and Australia won, ending England's then longest unbeaten run of 18 Test victories since 1958–59.

With England winning the next Test at Leeds, the series was locked one–all when the fourth Test started at Old Trafford, Manchester. Trailing England by 177 runs, Australia were precariously poised at 9 for 334, only 157 runs ahead when Davidson added 98 runs for the last wicket with Graham 'Garth' McKenzie. This gave Australia a slim hope, which disappeared when England, chasing 256 for a win were 1 for 150. Then in an inspired spell, Benaud captured 6 for 70 and Australia won the Test by 54 runs and regained the Ashes. Those 98 runs added by 'Davo' and Graham were crucial.

To quote Davidson, 'There were moments when my heart pounded with anxiety as young Graham stood manfully erect to face the English bowling … At last I determined to take my life in my hands and try to hit him [spinner David Allen] out of the attack. When Allen began his next over I braced myself for the planned assault. I lashed at his first delivery and a rich, mellow sound from my bat indicated clean contact with the ball. I watched the ball fly higher and higher until it soared over the boundary at extra cover.'

Another huge six off Allen and 20 runs came in this over to remember for Alan and the over to forget for Allen.

Although Davidson had made his Test debut in England at Trent Bridge, Nottingham eight years earlier in 1953, it was in South Africa that he became an established Test cricketer. 'That was to be my greatest summer

'When you see the big right foot coming down the wicket, brother, you duck,' said batsmen when facing Alan Davidson.

abroad', he recalls. 'My bat felt as though it contained the magic of a wand and I averaged 54 runs each time I stepped out to the crease.' Injury-free for once, he hit four centuries and collected a rich haul of 72 wickets in all first-class matches at an economical average of 15.13. Also with the retirement of fast bowlers Ray Lindwall and Keith Miller he was used more as a lethal weapon rather than a spare part commodity.

The firm of 'Beno & Davo' was firmly established on that tour where the also-rans struck gold medals. Against Natal at Pietermaritzburg, the dynamic duo added 244 runs for the sixth wicket. And in the first Test at Johannesburg they shared a stand of 67 that eclipsed the previous seventh wicket record of 65 by the immortals Vic Trumper and Warwick Armstrong against South Africa in the Adelaide Test of 1910–11.

Another glorious season for 'Davo' was the exhilarating series against Frank Worrell-led West Indians in 1960–61. In the famous first Test in Brisbane, Australia were set 233 runs to win at 45 runs an hour. As described earlier, Benaud joined Davidson when Australia was on her knees at 6 for 92. The 134 runs added by the dashing duo tilted the match Australia's way. Then within one run, both were dismissed, Davidson for 80 and Benaud for 52. In the final chilling over, and with the scores level, the last two batsmen were run out. And the Test ended in a tie, the first of two in the game's history.

There were many heroes in this epic Test, Garry Sobers and Norm O'Neill who hit blazing centuries and Wes Hall who took nine wickets in the match at furious pace but Davidson's all-round excellence stood out. Despite a broken finger, he became the first cricketer to score more than 100 runs in a Test (44 and 80) and take more than 10 wickets (5 for 135 and 6 for 87) in the same match. Since then only two players have achieved this double of 100 runs and 10 wickets in a Test; Ian Botham against India in Bombay (now Mumbai) in 1979–80 and Imran Khan also against India in Faisalabad in 1982–83.

Although Davidson's batting was disappointing in subsequent Tests against the West Indies in that epic 1960–61 series, he captured five wickets per innings in the other three Tests he played, claiming 33 scalps at 18.55. The second most successful bowler from Australia, Benaud, had an average of 33.86. As *Wisden* 1962 summed up, '… it was Davidson, with his accurate left-arm pace, who gained most honours among the fast bowlers. He took 33 wickets, more than any other bowler on either side, despite the fact that he missed the fourth Test because of injury.'

According to team-mate Bob Simpson, ' 'Davo' was one of the greatest bowlers of my time because he took wickets when most needed by his team. His bowling average of 20 [20.53] was phenomenal.'

Alan Davidson recalls his final ball in Test cricket. It was in Sydney on 20 February 1963. 'I looked across inquiringly at Queensland umpire Lou Rowan. He smiled encouragingly and said: "Yes, Al, this is it.".… Now I was about to bowl my last ball for Australia. Was it possible that I could capture a wicket with my last delivery?'

He did, having England's wicketkeeper Alan Smith caught by the sticky fingers of Bob Simpson. 'It was a moment of pure exultation for me. A wicket with my last ball in my last Test match … The umpire walked up, handed me my cap and said: "Well done, Davo."'

'Apart from Test matches, I also took a wicket off my last ball in first-class cricket', he recently told me. 'It was for New South Wales against South Australia in Sydney in January 1963. And do you know who the victim was? Garry Sobers! I clean bowled him.'

'I respected every player I played with or against. They were my inspiration and I learned something from everyone. I was fortunate to have played in the tied Test against the West Indies in 1960 whereas the 1961 Manchester Test gave me the greatest satisfaction.'

From Lisarow to Lord's, from Johannesburg and Kanpur to Manchester and Sydney, it was a triumphant journey for the affable Alan Davidson.

JOHN REID
New Zealand

Was there anything John Reid, the stocky Kiwi, could not do on the cricket field? Born on 3 June 1928, he was a strong and sturdily built, attacking batsman and a medium fast outswing bowler. As a batsman he cut and hooked as if there was no tomorrow. And when his country was in trouble (which New Zealand often was) he hit his way out of crises rather than use a dead bat. When the ball was old, he turned to off-cutters, pitching an immaculate length. Reid was also a magnificent fielder and at times served as a deputy wicketkeeper.

Of the 58 consecutive Tests he played (which was a record then) he captained in 34 and led New Zealand to their first three victories. A genuine all-rounder, his efforts with both bat and ball were invaluable to his team. In 58 Tests he scored 3428 runs at 33.28, hit six centuries and took 85 wickets at 33.35 apiece, caught 43 and stumped one.

He is recognised as the best all-rounder produced by New Zealand before Sir Richard Hadlee. At one stage Reid held the New Zealand Test records for scoring most runs, hitting most centuries, capturing most wickets, holding most catches, leading his country in most matches and making most runs in first-class cricket as well.

He made a pleasing Test debut against England at Manchester in 1949 when he scored a fifty and followed it with 93 in the next Test at The Oval. On this tour he aggregated 1488 runs at 41.33 and hit four centuries.

The all-rounder in John Reid stood up on the tour of South Africa in

An aggressive shot by John Reid during a match between New Zealand and Surrey in 1949.

Top Test All-Rounders

1953–54 when he became the first player to score 1000 runs (1012 at 37.48) and take 50 wickets (51 at 19.33) in a South African first-class season. It was on this tour that he scored the first of his six Test centuries. This was in the Cape Town Test of January 1954 when he batted for 198 minutes for his 135 and added 174 runs in 150 minutes with 19 year-old John Beck who was unfortunately run out for 99. This partnership was then a record for New Zealand against South Africa. In the final Test in Port Elizabeth next month he took 4 for 51 in the first innings and was run out for 73 in the second.

He had a successful tour of India and Pakistan in 1955–56 when he topped the batting with 1032 runs at 54.31 and took more wickets than anyone else (39 at 23.87) in all first-class matches. In the third Test against India in Delhi he scored 119 not out and added 222 for an unbroken partnership with the elegant left-hander Bert Sutcliffe (230 not out).

Reid's performances with bat and ball fluctuated till he reached his peak in South Africa in 1961–62. On this epic tour he amassed 1915 runs at 68.39 including seven centuries 'leaving Denis Compton, Jack Hobbs, Len Hutton and Arthur Morris in his wake', to quote New Zealand author Don Cameron. He also took 27 wickets on the tour including 11 at 19.72 in the Tests.

According to Geoffrey Chettle in *Wisden* 1963, 'The tour of 24 matches must go down in history as belonging almost exclusively to Reid. This quiet, unassuming master of bat and ball smashed all records open to him. In the five Tests he scored more runs than any two of his colleagues. His tour aggregate of 1915 eclipsed Compton's 13-year-old record. He topped the century seven times, including a glorious 203 on his favourite Newlands and easily headed the fielding statistics with 22 catches.'

More important was his leadership, captaining his country to victories in the third Test in Cape Town when he scored 92 in the first innings, and in the final Test in Port Elizabeth he made 26 and 69 and took 2 for 26 and 4 for 44. South Africa led the series 2–1 and needed only a draw to win the rubber. Set 314 runs to win the Test, the home team played for a draw but were dismissed for 273 off 144 overs (at a pathetic run-rate of 1.89) to lose by 40 runs. Spinner John Alabaster bowled 52 overs and Reid had marathon figures of 45–27–44–4. This victory enabled New Zealand to square the rubber for the first time. There were no Man of the Match and Man of the Series awards then but we know who would have scooped the lot.

Thus John Reid's pre-tour prediction that he was leading the best team ever to represent New Zealand abroad was justified. To share the series against a strong South African side was a magnificent achievement. In fact never before had New Zealand won a Test match overseas. It was

In fact never before had New Zealand won a Test match overseas.

a personal triumph for Reid as he topped both the batting (546 runs at 60.64) and bowling (11 wickets at 19.72) averages in the Test series. He was also way above his colleagues in batting aggregate and averages in 17 first-class matches. After his monumental 1915 runs at 68.39, the next best in run aggregate was Graham Dowling (714 runs) and next best in batting averages was Murray Chapple (31.94).

He continued to jinx the South Africans, capturing 6 for 60 in the Dunedin Test of February–March 1964.

In 246 first-class matches he scored 16,128 runs at 41.35, hitting 39 centuries with 296 for Wellington against Northern Districts at Wellington in 1962–63 as his highest. It was the second highest number of runs scored in a day's play in New Zealand and included 15 sixes. This stood as a record for 32 years till eclipsed by Andrew Symonds (19 sixes in an innings for Gloucestershire against Glamorgan in 1995). Reid also snared 466 wickets at an impressive average of 22.60, picking up 5 wickets in an innings 15 times and 10 wickets in a match once. His best bowling was 7 for 20 for Otago against Central Districts in 1956–57. He also accepted 240 catches and stumped seven batsmen.

He was awarded an OBE for his splendid achievements, settled in South Africa where he did some coaching but returned home to spend some of his retirement fishing in the South Island. From 1993 to 2002 he became a front rank and respected International Cricket Council referee, establishing a reputation for his toughness and fairness.

Perhaps John Richard Reid was born a generation too soon. He retired in 1965 before one-day internationals had started. According to Don Cameron, 'Reid would have been a one-day team on his own—a batsman with thunderous strokes, a rapacious fielder especially at gully or cover, a bowler of what became known as right-arm busters which ranged from modest off-cutters to snarling bouncers.'

He could have become the ultimate all-rounder—a dual all-rounder—as his prowess in rugby overshadowed his cricket in early years. But a bout of rheumatic fever in his late teens forced him to give up rugby. Rugby's loss was cricket's gain.

TREVOR GODDARD

South Africa

Goddard's figures at both Test and first-class levels (11,279 runs at 40.57 and 534 wickets at 21.65) put him in a useful rather than an outstanding category. He was known for analysing opponents' strengths and weaknesses with uncanny accuracy. He would have made an ideal coach in these days of laptop 'autopsy'.

A left-hander, South Africa's Trevor Goddard is seldom acknowledged as a Test all-rounder. Figures of 2516 runs at 34.46, 123 wickets at 26.22 and 48 catches in 41 Tests does not make him an automatic choice in this Chapter. However, he was a perfectionist and a 'walking coaching manual, a left-hander of classically correct technique with bat and ball', according to Neil Manthorp in *Cricinfo*.

Tall, with short hair, his batting was firmly based on the back foot and his medium-paced new ball or stock bowling was naggingly accurate. He was one of few who opened both his country's batting and bowling.

A heavy scorer and wicket-taker in the national Currie Cup competition, Goddard's best season at home was in 1966–67 when he scored 830 runs and took 45 wickets in 10 matches. He was the first South African to reach 10,000 runs and 500 wickets in first-class matches and the first among South Africans to achieve the Test double of 2000 runs and 100 wickets.

Born on 1 August 1931, he made his Test debut against England in the Nottingham Test of June 1955. In the second innings he added 73 runs for the opening wicket with skipper Jackie McGlew. But after Goddard was dismissed, his team was 'typhooned' losing 8 for 65 as Frank 'Typhoon' Tyson grabbed 5 for 5 in a devastating spell.

Trevor Goddard bowls against England in the Trent Bridge Test of 1955.

In this his maiden Test series, Goddard captured 25 wickets at 21.12 apiece with two hauls of 5 for 69 in the fourth Test at Leeds and 5 for 31 in the final Test at The Oval. He also made two fifties in the series and was associated in a 176 run stand for the first wicket with McGlew in the Leeds Test. He was behind South Africa's victories in two Tests and an all-rounder was knocking at the door.

In the next two home series, against England in 1956–57 and against Australia the following summer, he proved himself a capable opening batsman. He scored 67 and 49 in the Johannesburg Test against England as South Africa recorded her first home win over England since 1930–31. Then against Australia in Johannesburg, the reliable opening pair of Goddard (90) and McGlew (108) put on 176 runs, then a record for the first wicket for South Africa.

Back to England in 1960 and he donned his all-rounder's cap, taking 5 for 80 in the Nottingham Test and scoring 99 in the final Test at The Oval. Appointed captain for the 1963–64 tour of Australia and New Zealand he shone out in both the Sydney Tests. In the third Test in January 1964 he scored 80 and 84 and in the final Test, also in Sydney the following month, he scored 93 and an unbeaten 44. In between in the Adelaide Test he had a haul of 5 for 60 as he led his team to a swashbuckling victory as the bespectacled Eddie Barlow and the elegant Graeme Pollock added 341 runs.

Then to New Zealand, the contrasting openers, the dour Goddard and the belligerent Barlow had century partnerships in each of the three Tests in Wellington, Dunedin and Auckland. He also took 4 for 18 in the final Test.

The faithful opening pair of Barlow and Goddard continued in the same vein in the home series against England. They added 134 runs in the fourth Test in Johannesburg Test and 114 in the final Test in Port Elizabeth. In the Johannesburg Test he followed his 60 in the first innings with a century (112) in the second.

Top Test All-Rounders

The indefatigable one had waited long for his maiden Test hundred. He had been dismissed in his nervous nineties (90, 99 and 93) in previous Tests and his first and only century came in his 62nd Test innings. He showed sportsmanship of the highest order in this Test against England. From leg slip, Peter van der Merwe threw down the wicket after the ball had been tossed to him by the wicketkeeper. The batsman, Michael J.K. Smith, who had gone down the pitch 'gardening', was declared out by umpire H.C. Kidson. But Goddard asked for the appeal to be revoked and Smith was recalled. This remains the most memorable Test for Goddard.

By the time Australia under Bob Simpson toured South Africa in 1966–67, Goddard had lost the captaincy to van der Merwe but not the sharpness of his away and inswingers. In the second innings of the first Test in Johannesburg, he captured 6 for 53, his best Test figures, and South Africa won by a huge margin of 233 runs. This was South Africa's first ever home victory against Australia at the 22nd attempt and 64 years after the series had commenced. It was a topsy-turvey Test when fortunes fluctuated. Trailing by 126 runs, the home team amassed 620 in their second innings. With Goddard claiming six victims, Australia collapsed for 261.

This was South Africa's first ever home victory against Australia.

South Africa went on to win the series 3–1, Goddard taking 3 for 36 and 3 for 27 in the fourth Test in Johannesburg and scoring 74 and 59 in the final Test in Port Elizabeth. In this series he scored 294 runs at 32.67 and collected 26 scalps at 16.23.

In *Sir Gary*, his namesake all-rounder Trevor Bailey describes Goddard as a 'highly competent workman rather than a genius'. Recognised as a reliable opening batsman and accurate medium-pacer, Trevor Goddard became an evangelist preacher after his retirement from cricket.

GARRY SOBERS

West Indies

Just as Sir Donald Bradman is considered the greatest batsman of all time, Sir Garfield Sobers has strong claims to be acknowledged as the iconic all-rounder. Having scored 8032 runs at 57.78 with 26 centuries (highest score 365 not out) and taken 235 wickets at 34.03 and 109 catches in 93 Tests, he was the first all-rounder to achieve the Test triple of 8000 runs, 200 wickets and 100 catches. South Africa's Jacques Kallis joined him in this exclusive club in January 2007.

Sobers' Test record puts him in the all-time great category. Add to it his first-class statistics; 28,315 runs at 54.87 with 86 centuries, 1043 wickets at 27.74 and 407 catches in 383 matches. He was also the first batsman to hit six sixes off a 6-ball over.

Bradman called Sobers a five-in-one cricketer; batsman extraordinaire, versatile fielder and three-in-one bowler (fast-medium, finger spin and wrist spin). Sobers later added one more dimension to his repertoire, captaincy.

Statistically, he was the *supremo*, yet number-crunching does not reveal the whole story. He was a remarkable man, unique, almost freaky. He was born on 28 July 1936 with 12 fingers, six on each hand. And after September 1959 he batted for two. 'For most of my international career I was playing for two—myself and my great friend Collie Smith who died one Saturday night in England in a car I was driving', he wrote in his autobiography *Garry Sobers*. Smith was only 26 then and at the height of his prowess.

Great all-rounder Garry Sobers bowling.

I have two indelible memories of the great Garry. In early 1980s, I attended a charity match at Dooralong, NSW, organised by The Primary Club of Australia. Sobers was there and he came over to my three-year-old son Zubin and patted him affectionately on his head, giving him his toothy smile. It was a spontaneous gesture I shall never forget.

Another incident I recall was when India played Australia in the Sydney Test in January 1981. Living in Sydney then, Sobers was in the Indian players' Dressing Room. So was I. India's opening batsman and skipper Sunil Gavaskar was out for a duck, caught Marsh bowled Lillee. When Gavaskar returned to the pavilion, head bowed, Sobers ticked him off, 'Is this the way you play an outswinger, hanging your bat out?' And Gavaskar listened dutifully as if he was an errant pupil in the headmaster's office!

Gavaskar has the highest opinion of Sobers and wrote in his book *Idols*, 'The greatest cricketer I've ever seen is Sir Garfield Sobers. He was the complete cricketer.'

Also he was superstitious. When India toured the West Indies in 1970–71, Sobers always touched the 21-year-old Gavaskar for luck. The Indian remembered the advice Sobers had given him before he toured England in 1971, 'In England, try and avoid cutting [the ball] in June but do so in July and August'. Gavaskar followed this advice and was the success of the tour.

My early memory of Sobers was in the first Test in Bombay (now Mumbai) in 1958 when he hit a classical unbeaten 142. He added 134 runs with Basil Butcher for the unbroken fifth wicket. Both of them used runners as they had sustained leg injuries, a rare instance at Test level.

This was Sobers' fourth century in four Tests. At his prolific best, he hit hundreds in the next two Tests against India in Kanpur and Calcutta (now Kolkata) to record six centuries in six Tests in 10 consecutive innings. And to think that he had failed to reach a ton in his first 16 Tests! He made up for this in his 17th Test, against Pakistan in Kingston in February 1958 when he amassed 365 not out, breaking Len Hutton's record score of 364. This record stood for 36 years till eclipsed by fellow West Indian Brian Lara.

It was the start of his amazing run spree: 365 not out, 125 and 109 not out, 14 and 27 against Pakistan in the West Indies; and then 25 and 142 not out, 4, 198 and 106 not out against India in India. In these six consecutive Tests, he amassed 1115 runs at an incredible average of 185.83. He never looked back after this Indian summer.

He hit three more centuries at home against England in 1959–60, totalling 709 runs at 101.29 in five Tests. In the first Test in Bridgetown he scored 226, adding a record 399 runs for the 4th wicket with Frank Worrell.

Top Test All-Rounders

This was followed by one of the greatest series ever, against Richie Benaud's Australians in 1960–61. In the famous tied Test in Brisbane, he scored 132 on the first day which set the tone for the rest of the series. It remains Sobers' favourite innings. He recalls in his autobiography *Garry Sobers*: 'Many people who saw it describe it as one of the better innings of my career. Frank [Worrell] went one better and thought it was the best he had ever seen, as did Sir Donald Bradman. He [Bradman] came straight up to me and said, "I told you, you would get them at the right time and you didn't disappoint me".'

Wrote Australian writer 'Johnnie' Moyes on Sobers on that tour: 'So often he touched greatness shared by few of his generation. His finest innings bore comparison with anything we have seen for many years and yet somehow he did not inspire the same confidence as [Rohan] Kanhai.'

Benaud added that Sobers was 'delightfully orthodox in his batting and yet, at the same time, a wonderful improviser against the ball that, for a fraction of a second, looks as though it will beat him'.

His debut as captain was impressive. In the first Test at Kingston in March 1965, the Windies recorded their first home win against Australia and it was the first time that they had led Australia in any series. Although he scored moderately, 352 runs at 39.11, his team won the Frank Worrell Trophy 2–1

He kept up the good work when he captained the West Indies to England in 1966. It was one of his happiest series, scoring 722 runs at 103.14 with three tons and 94 and 81, took 20 wickets at 27.05 and 11 catches, won all five tosses and retained the *Wisden Trophy* 3–1.

Sobers considers his unbeaten 163 in the second innings of the second Test at Lord's to be among his best Test innings. Trailing by 86 runs, the Windies were 5 for 95 when joined by his cousin David Holford. Both hit unbeaten hundreds as they added 274 and saved the match.

Garry Sobers nicks one and Colin Cowdrey dives to field it in the slip in The Oval Test of 1957.

One can go on and on about Sobers' magnificence at Test level. However, some of his greatest moments came outside Test arena. He played a magical innings of 254 in the Melbourne international as captain of Rest of the World XI against Australia. Bradman described it as 'the greatest exhibition of batting ever seen in Australia'.

In a county match for Nottinghamshire in 1968, he hit Glamorgan's Malcolm Nash for six sixes in a 6-ball over. This was the first such instance in first-class cricket and has been emulated only once since at that level.

Then in a Sheffield Shield match for South Australia against NSW in Adelaide in 1961–62, Sobers hit an amazing six. At first he went back then changed his mind and went forward to an Alan Davidson delivery and smashed it high and hard over mid-on. It flew about 150 metres. To quote Sobers, 'I was batting really well and had topped 150 when Alan Davidson bowled me a good bouncer just outside the off stump. I stood up and slapped it right over mid-on… It went so far that they still talk about it.'

What about Sobers the man? His personal life is also interesting. When touring India in 1966–67, the 30-year-old Garry fell in love with a beautiful Indian actress Anju Mahindu, 17, and got engaged to her. But it did not last long.

Two years later he met Prue Kirby, an Australian girl doing a public relations job in England for a canned fruit industry and fell in love with her. He married her on 11 September 1969 after asking Anju's permission to release him. The marriage lasted 15 years and it produced two sons Matthew and Daniel. They later adopted a daughter, Genevieve. Although divorced, Garry and Prue are still good friends. Their sons took up the Australian way of life and played Australian rules, cricket, football, tennis, judo and golf.

Garry Sobers retired from cricket in 1974 and was knighted in his beloved Barbados the next year where he was officially named one of Ten National Heroes.

TONY GREIG

England

Tony Greig will be remembered for his tall frame, tall hits and tall (but true) tales. Tall, fair, handsome and articulate, Tony Greig has gone through the gauntlet and has emerged unscathed. Born in South Africa, he shone out as an all-rounder for England, later captaining his adopted country to success, was one of the key figures in the formation of Kerry Packer's World Series Cricket in 1977 and currently his voice is recognised internationally as the cricket commentator on Channel 9 in Australia with that typical 'Greigy' style.

Larger than life size, he has that certain dash, a charisma that mostly attracts but he has his critics too. He is a leader of men, charming and multi-talented He knows what he wants and gets it. According to Christopher Martin-Jenkins in *World Cricketers* (1996), '[Greig] was a brave, determined and skilful all-round cricketer who seldom failed in Tests and many times seemed to be holding England's fortunes on his shoulders'. At times ruthless, he relished challenges, imposing his personality on matches and on events.

He usually batted at number six and showed to the bowlers who the boss was. And who would argue with his 6 foot 7 inch frame? He came out swinging his bat round his shoulders as he took the 'middle' from the umpire. Mostly a front-foot batsman, he specialised on the off-drive and lofted straight drives which went over the ropes and within the Stands. Like Keith Miller before him he had 'six appeal' and he was a crowd favourite, especially in India. Many of his best innings were played on his two tours to India.

Tall Tony Greig in aggressive form against
Australia in the 1972 Old Trafford Test.

In 1972–73 he shone out as a batsman playing unbeaten innings of 68 and 40 (and accepting five catches) in the Delhi Test which England won by 6 wickets. In the final Test in Mumbai, he hit 148. During this innings he added 254 runs with Keith Fletcher. In the series he scored 382 runs at 63.67.

Greig achieved all-round success when England toured the Caribbean the next season. He scored 430 runs (including two centuries) at 47.77 and captured 24 wickets at 22.62 runs apiece. In the third Test in Bridgetown, he made 148, his joint top score, and bagged 6 for 164, becoming the first to record a hundred and take five wickets in an innings of the same Test for

England. Inspired, Greig scored another century in the Georgetown Test and captured 8 for 86 and 5 for 70 in the final Test in Port-of-Spain. Both his 8 for 86 in the innings and 13 for 156 in the match were records for England against the West Indies at that time. On this tour he had switched from swing to quickish off-spin, which may explain his success. This bowling bonanza enabled England to win the Test and draw the series.

However, his copybook was blotted somewhat by a controversy in the first Test in Port-of-Spain. When West Indian batsman Bernard Julien played the last ball of the second day down the pitch, Greig picked it up. Then observing that Alvin Kallicharran was out of the crease, he threw down the stumps and appealed. Kallicharran was given run out by umpire Sang Hue and the crowd was furious. After long consultations between captains, umpires and administrators, the appeal was withdrawn. Greig apologised and peace was restored.

He carried on his fine batting form in Australia in 1974–75, playing a buccaneering innings of 110 against Dennis Lillee and Jeff Thomson at their peak. This was the first century in a Brisbane Test by an England player since 1936–37. He put in an impressive all-round performance in the third Test in Melbourne, scoring 60 in the second innings, lofting off-spinner Ashley Mallett for a monstrous hit in the outer and taking valuable wickets.

Appointed captain, Greig led England to a successful tour of India in 1976–77. England won the Test series 3–1 as he totalled 342 runs at 42.75. His 103 in the Kolkata Test, his 49th, was memorable as he became the first one to achieve the double of 3000 runs and 100 wickets for England.

He led England in the historic Centenary Test in Melbourne in March 1977, which attracted the largest collection of international cricketers in history. Although England lost, Greig remained a very popular player on and off the field. At that time he was 'earning upwards of £50,000 a year from various cricket contracts and allied business activities', according to Christopher Martin-Jenkins in *World Cricketers* (1996). He was also certain of leading England for many years.

Then was born Kerry Packer's rebel World Series Cricket (WSC) with Greig as one of the key figures and he lost credibility with the establishment. Although he was the captain of England, he travelled the world between March and May 1977 to sign up many of the world's best cricketers on Packer's behalf including some of his own team-mates. The WSC was born soon after and Greig was dismissed as captain of England for

> *Then was born Kerry Packer's rebel World Series Cricket (WSC) with Greig as one of the key figures and he lost credibility.*

what was regarded as 'his betrayal of trust' but he continued to play for them successfully under Mike Brearley in 1977.

In 58 Tests he scored 3599 runs at a healthy average of 40.43 with eight centuries and took 141 wickets at 32.20, claiming 5 wickets in an innings six times and pouched 87 catches. And in 350 first-class matches, he amassed 16,660 runs at 31.19, took 856 wickets at 28.85 and held 345 catches. As a slip fielder he was superlative, the safest and the most brilliant of his era. Well, his height helped too.

Greig migrated to Australia in 1978 and started as a chairman of an insurance company and a successful television commentator on Channel 9. Along with WSC pioneers Richie Benaud and Ian Chappell, Greig has been broadcasting the game and presenting his views on the box for 30 years. He speaks his mind without fear or favour and is popular with TV viewers from the time the coin is tossed (with his key in the pitch as his trademark) to interviewing the man of the match at the end.

One cannot speak for hours on end without a gaffe here and there and Greig is known for putting his foot in the mouth on occasions. He was once 'caught out' when commentating on Channel 9 during a one-day international between Australia 'A' and West Indies on the Sydney Cricket Ground on 10 January 1996. When a batsman hit a sizzling six, he yelled in excitement 'It's a HUGE shit' instead of 'It's a HUGE six'.

A lively after-dinner speaker, he told a humorous story at a cricket function. He had just started playing county cricket for Sussex after leaving South Africa. The bowler steamed in and had Greig out plumb lbw. That was the first ball he had faced and to his relief the appeal was turned down. He took a single off the next ball, which brought him near the umpire who whispered to him: 'Do you know Sandy Greig from Queenstown?' 'He's my father,' Tony replied. 'Damn good decision, then!' was the retort from the umpire who was Sandy's mate. Greig went on to make 150-plus, captured newspaper headlines and never looked back.

Greig is one of four Test cricketers who has averaged more than 40 with the bat and less than 35 with the ball in Test arena; the others being Aubrey Faulkner, Garry Sobers and Jacques Kallis.

IAN BOTHAM

England

The recently knighted Ian Botham did not care about statistics but they have been breathtaking. In 102 Tests, he scored 5200 runs at 33.54 with 14 centuries (highest 208) and 22 fifties, took 383 wickets at 28.40 (capturing 5 wickets in an innings 27 times, 10 wickets in a Test four times, best bowling spell being 8 for 34) and took 120 catches. He is the only cricketer to do the triple of 5000 runs, 300 wickets and 100 catches.

Cricket has produced many characters; W.G. Grace, Merv Hughes, Derek Randall, Javed Miandad, Greg Matthews, Shane Warne amongst others. And then there was Ian Botham, who, according to Sunil Gavaskar was 'the craziest cricketer I have known'. Gavaskar should know. Not only were they worthy opponents (arguably the best opening batsman of all time against probably the best all-rounder) but they also played together for Somerset.

A character yes, but crazy? Gavaskar who idolised Botham, explains in his book *Idols*: 'In the [Somerset] dressing room, he [Botham] was an absolute terror because he could never sit still . . . If he did not find anything to do, he would punch you on the arms, dip his teaspoon in a pot of hot, boiling water and while you were sitting unawares, he would try to cause burns on your hands with the spoon or just a lighted match stick.' Dressing room or dungeon?

Botham may have been a prankster off the field but a mighty warrior on it, irrepressible and cheerfully insubordinate. With another Test immortal Vivian Richards, he formed a flamboyant and in later stages an ungovernable

Ian 'Biffy' Botham bowling an unplayable delivery.

partnership for Somerset. Richards had traces of arrogance and ego, Botham had no artifice. With Botham you got what you saw, a man without malice. Underneath the tough exterior, he cared for humanity. His marathon walks to raise funds for leukaemia sufferers have been exemplary. He was a great all-rounder and remains a good humanitarian.

Top Test All-Rounders

Botham was the quickest to accomplish the Test double of 1000 runs and 100 wickets (in only 21 Tests and within 25 months). He did the double of a century and 5 wickets in a Test innings an incredible five times. Garry Sobers, Mushtaq Mohammad and Jacques Kallis are the next best with twice each. Once Botham scored a century and took 13 wickets in the same Test which is unique. More important, he converted apparently lost Test matches into glorious victories.

Ian Terrence Botham was born in Heswall in Cheshire on 24 November 1955. He made an instant impact, his debuts in both one-day internationals and in the Test arena were impressive. At 18, he played his first important match for Somerset against Hampshire in a one-dayer in 1974. Shortly after arriving at the crease, when Somerset was 8 for 113 and needing 183 to win, he was hit full in the mouth by a bouncer from West Indies fast bowler Andy Roberts. Botham bled profusely, eventually lost four teeth but declined to leave the field. He hit two soaring sixes while making an unbeaten 45, guiding Somerset to a victory.

He took 5 for 74 on the first day of his Test debut against Australia at Nottinghamshire in July 1977. In his second Test at Leeds, he again shone out, capturing 5 for 21 off 11 economical overs in the first innings as England won to lead the series 3–0. Cricketers reach truly great status when a match is named after them. At least two Tests are called 'Botham's Tests'. One was against India in Mumbai in 1980 and the drama-packed topsy-turvy 1981 Leeds Test against Australia the following year was the second.

Botham ('Both' and 'Beefy' to his friends and fans and 'Gorilla' to his victims) played perhaps his finest Test match in the Golden Jubilee Test in Mumbai in February, 1980. His feat of scoring a century and taking 13 wickets has remained unparalleled in over 130-year history of Test cricket. On the opening day, he captured 6 for 58 to dismiss India for 242 (helped by wicketkeeper Bob Taylor who accepted seven

The ebullient English all-rounder Ian Botham drives for a four against India in The Oval Test of 1982 as Syed Kirmani keeps.

catches). Botham came in to bat with England in trouble, 5 down for 58. Unconcerned, he added 171 runs with Taylor (43), scoring 114 runs in 206 resolute minutes which included 17 fours. He got better each day as he captured 7 for 48 (for amazing match figures of 13 for 106) to rout India for 149 and England won by 10 wickets with a day to spare. His versatility was in full bloom.

He touched rock bottom next season, only to rise to everlasting fame. Despite his all-round excellence, his captaincy record was poor. He was too much of an individual to lead a team, too undisciplined to impose authority. It was darkest before the dawn for the beleaguered captain in the Ashes series against Australia in 1981. Under him, Australia lost the first Test, he made a pair in the second Test and lost captaincy to Mike Brearley. This was, to use a cliché, a blessing in disguise for Botham. It was as if iron chains had been removed from his body and the 'Gorilla' was his old exuberant self.

The third Test at Headingley, Leeds, was the stuff miracles are made of. It was one of the most fascinating and bewilderingly fluctuating Tests. One up in the series, Australia declared at 9 for 401, John Dyson scored 102, skipper Kim Hughes 89 and Botham took 6 for 95, indicating his return to form as a bowler. Despite his 50, England was dismissed for 174 and forced to follow-on. They appeared sunk at 7 for 135, still 92 runs behind when Graham Dilley joined Botham. Amid rising tension, the two fast-medium bowlers started the rescue act, adding 117 runs in 80 minutes, Dilley contributing 56 precious runs. Botham refused to budge as he added 67 more runs with tail-ender Chris Old and remained unbeaten with 149 out of England's respectable total of 356. Still the win target for Australia was only 130 runs. It appeared easily achievable when the visitors reached 1 for 56. Just then tall Bob Willis, inspired by Botham's heroic deeds, struck crippling blows by grabbing 8 for 43 and England incredibly won by 18 runs. Botham had made it all happen scoring 199 runs and capturing seven scalps in this epic thriller.

Still not satisfied, Botham took 5 for 11 off 14 overs (nine being maidens) in the second innings of the next Test in Birmingham which England won to lead 2–1 in the series. Botham was adjudged Man of the Match for the second Test in a row. He wasn't quite finished with the Aussies yet though. In the following Test in Manchester, England was tottering at 5 for 104 but then came Botham with his pocket full of miracles. He smashed 118 in 123 minutes off 102 balls, with six sixes (three off Dennis Lillee) and 13 fours. He completed his century with a six as England totalled 404 and won her third Test in succession to retain the Ashes. In the final Test at The Oval, a draw, he took 6 for 125 and 4 for 128. What a series for him—especially the last four Tests when he amassed 365 runs at 52.14 (with two hundreds) and took 28 wickets at 19.68 (with three 5 wickets per innings hauls and 10 for 253 in the final Test).

After this superhuman effort, everything he did appeared as an anti-climax. His love for fast food made him put on pounds and his hunger for runs and wickets diminished somewhat as he approached his 100th Test. This was against New Zealand in the third and final Test in Wellington in February 1992. He was not in the original XII but was brought back in the side, due to injuries to opening bowlers Derek Pringle and Chris Lewis. Botham, now approaching 37 was no more the charging rhino he was in his heyday. As a colt he was aggressive and brash—steaming in and blasting out batsmen with a splendid outswinger. At his peak he was a hell-raiser in the middle with his sixes and bouncers and in the dressing room with his 'weapons of mass destruction', superheated spoons and lighted matches! However, wear and tear took their toll and the old devil lost his horns. Describing his last seasons, John Woodcock wrote in *Wisden 1994*: 'But his batteries were pretty nearly run down by then [1993], and once the England selectors were not interested in him they went flat.'

In 116 one-day internationals he made 2113 runs at 23.21 and captured 145 wickets at 28.54. At any level and in any situation, he made the game buzz with excitement. His tirades with Ian Chappell in 1970s continue to make headlines.

In June 2007, Botham was knighted by the Queen for his cricketing prowess and his commendable efforts in raising funds for leukaemia research. Arise, Sir Ian.

IMRAN KHAN

Pakistan

Imran Khan is rated one of the greatest all-rounders; colourful, charismatic and dynamic. He is fair, handsome and a ticking dynamo. His 12 wickets in the Sydney Test of January 1977 represented one of the finest pieces of sustained swing-bowling I have seen. And, unlike lightning, he struck twice on the same spot. That was Imran's finest hour—as, indeed, it was Pakistan's before their World Cup win in Melbourne in 1992.

Born on 25 November 1952, he made his first-class debut in 1969–70 and toured England in 1971, playing his first Test when only 19. He stayed on in England, playing for Oxford University from 1973 to 1975—as captain in 1974. When captaining a Combined Oxford-Cambridge side against the touring Indians in 1974, he hit 160 and 49. He was awarded his County cap for Worcestershire in 1976.

He scored 1000 runs in the English seasons of 1975 and 1976, hitting 10 centuries. His highest score was 170 for Oxford against Northamptonshire in 1974. The same year he hit two centuries in one match, against Nottinghamshire—117 not out and 106. In 1976 he totalled 1092 runs at 40.44, with four centuries and a highest score of 160.

However, in Australia, it was as a bowler that he gained renown and respect. In the Sydney Test, assisted by Sarfraz Nawaz, keen fielding and ideal swing conditions, he worried the best of Australian batsmen. Imran was soon among the Aussie bats—like a wolf among pigeons—scattering them and shattering their morale. On 14 and 16 January 1977, Imran, to some, appeared as the David who had cut the 'Go-Lillee-aths' to size. To

Adrian Murrell/Getty Images

*Charismatic all-rounder Imran Khan in action
during the Lord's Test against England in 1982.*

others, he seemed as direct descendant of the dreaded Genghis Khan!

Imran is an interesting talker. 'When I was young, I just wasn't interested in bowling fast, which was nothing unusual because no one in Pakistan was particularly interested in bowling fast. The wickets over there don't encourage fast men and the climate isn't particularly friendly. I did not start bowling seriously until I was 16 or 17. However, as there was such a shortage of quick bowlers in Pakistan, I used to get put on by my club. It was when I got into the Pakistan team that I began to realise that my team-mates relied on my bowling more and more.'

For Oxford University and Worcestershire he was considered a batsman who could bowl medium pace. 'Whenever I bowled a bit faster, the experienced players in my teams in Oxford and Worcestershire would tell me to cut down on pace and concentrate on line and length. Thus I arrived in Australia in 1976 a batting all-rounder. All that changed in the second innings of the second Test at Melbourne. My team-mates encouraged me to try and bowl faster, to become a bit more aggressive and I said, 'Why not?' We were all looking forward to the Sydney Test which followed the next week. That was the game of my life when I actually went into it thinking of myself as a genuine fast bowler. I can't tell you how satisfying my figures were. I will never forget that match.'

When Alan Davidson presented Imran with the Man of the Match award, he complimented the Pakistan icon that it was one of the most outstanding feats he had seen on the SCG. 'To my intense embarrassment, favourable comparisons were being made between the pace of Lillee and myself ', he wrote in his autobiography *Imran*.

Both Imran and his cousin Majid played stellar roles when Pakistan toured the West Indies in 1977. Majid scored 530 runs and Imran captured 25 wickets in the series. In the following Test at Port-of-Spain, Imran took 4 for 64 and Pakistan recorded a series-levelling win. At Kingston, Jamaica, in the final Test, he bowled at his fastest to pick up 6 for 90 in the first innings.

Then came the World Series Cricket (WSC) revolution and the Khan cousins were among the first to be signed up. Imran did not suffer in comparison with the fastest bowlers in the world. In fact, he was timed third quickest in the world, after Jeff Thomson and Michael Holding.

After Pakistan's miserable performances in England in 1978, its Cricket Board decided to include WSC players in the series against India which Pakistan won 2–0. Sixteen months later, with Majid out of form and Imran unfit, Pakistan surrendered the series 0–2.

During the 1980s, Imran emerged as a world-class all-rounder, charismatic and glamorous, a sex symbol with a playboy image. He considers the time spent with World Series Cricket in the late 1970s as decisive in making him a complete cricketer. During this series he learnt from masters of the craft; Mike Procter improving his run-up and John Snow assisting him in turning the left shoulder more towards square-leg to help achieve the outswinger.

He was at his best technically in Australia in 1981–82 when adjudged Player of the Series. Earlier he had scored his first Test hundred (against the West Indies at Lahore in 1980–81) after coming in during crisis when Pakistan was five down for 95. During this series he became the second Pakistani after Intikhab Alam to achieve the Test double of 1000 runs and 100 wickets. This was followed by his capturing 14 for 116 against Sri Lanka at Lahore the same season—his best Test figures.

Pakistan cricket is replete with controversies and internal dissension. Javed Miandad, a magnificent batsman, did things his way as captain which did not endear him to senior players—Imran included. There was a strong protest against Miandad's leadership and he was replaced by Imran as Pakistan's captain in 1982.

Captaincy brought out the maturity in him without affecting his all-round performances. He was a natural leader of men, perhaps autocratic at times—especially in selecting players he wanted. A talented but undisciplined Pakistan team needed a strong man at the helm and Imran was just that. Players were at times in awe of him but he insisted on discipline and got it.

His happiest moment was in Melbourne on 25 March 1992, when he lifted the 1992 World Cup in front of nearly 90,000 wildly cheering spectators. After the presentations he said it was 'the most fulfilling and satisfying cricket moment of my life'. He described the victory as a triumph for his young team's talent over finalist England's experience.

Imran's role in the World Cup triumph went deeper. He had virtually hand-picked the squad and after losing the key fast bowler Waqar Younis to

'Howzzat' appeals Imran as batsman Rod Marsh applauds sarcastically.

a stress fracture before leaving Pakistan. They had a disastrous start when they lost four of the first five matches. But he urged his players to imitate the action of a cornered tiger and they went on to five consecutive wins.

Apart from his inspiring leadership, Imran had enjoyed an all-round triumph himself, top scoring with 72 in the final, adding 139 with Miandad for the third wicket and capturing the final English wicket.

He was then 40 and soon hung up his cricket shoes after scoring 3807 runs at 37.69 in 88 Tests (with six centuries, 136 being his highest score) and taking 362 wickets at 22.81 (capturing 5 wickets in an innings 23 times and 10 wickets in a Test six times, his best effort being 8 for 58) and 28 catches.

He was among four all-rounders (Ian Botham, Kapil Dev and Richard Hadlee being others) to achieve the Test double of 3000 runs and 300 wickets when he retired. Since then Shaun Pollock of South Africa and Australia's Shane Warne have joined this exclusive club. Imran Khan's figures were equally impressive in one-day internationals, 3709 runs at 33.41 and 182 scalps at 26.61, best being 6 for 14, in 175 matches. He was an adornment of cricket.

He remained in news even after retiring from cricket. His marriage and subsequent divorce to socialite Jemima Goldsmith made headlines. These days Imran is in the news again as a politician who wants to introduce democracy in Pakistan. An opponent of President Pervez Musharraf, Imran Khan was arrested in November 2007 after making his first public appearance since emergency rule was declared in Pakistan.

But it is as an outstanding cricket all-rounder that Imran will be remembered by posterity. In a poll conducted by *Cricinfo* in 2007, he finished on top, getting 37 % votes from about 10,000 readers. Garry Sobers came second with 14% votes, followed by Wasim Akram (13%), Kapil Dev (11%), Ian Botham (7%), Jacques Kallis (6%), Learie Constantine (5%), Richard Hadlee (3%), Adam Gilchrist (2%) and Shaun Pollock (1%).

Polished, learned and supremely talented, Imran gave cricket sex appeal in the 1970s and 1980s, just as Keith Miller had done so in the 1940s and 1950s.

KAPIL DEV

India

Kapil Dev is unique. The only Indian fast bowler to dominate the international scene for over a decade, he is the only all-rounder to achieve the Test double of 5000 runs and 400 wickets, the youngest to do the 1000 runs and 100 wickets Test double and the first all-rounder to play 100 Test matches.

In July 2002 he was chosen by a panel of 32 international judges (cricketers, writers and broadcasters) as the *Wisden Indian Cricketer of the Century* ahead of legends Vinoo Mankad, Vijay Hazare, Sunil Gavaskar, Sachin Tendulkar and the spin trio of Prasanna, Bedi and Chandrasekhar.

The 1980s have been recognised as a decade of all-rounders with New Zealander Richard Hadlee, Pakistan's Imran Khan, England's Ian Botham and Kapil vying for top honours. All four were outstanding cricketers with Hadlee and Imran better bowlers and Kapil and Botham entertaining crowds with their lofty hitting.

Kapil held the record of being the most prolific wicket-taker (434 wickets in 131 Tests) till West Indian quickie Courtney Walsh (519 wickets) overtook him in March 2000. To be a fast bowler and an Indian sounds like an oxymoron but Kapil succeeded on lifeless Indian pitches with dedication and natural talent. Not as fast as Tyson, Hall, Marshall, Ambrose, Thomson, Shoaib or Lee, Kapil swung the ball like a boomerang and his snake-like break-back struck with the speed of a cobra.

Gavaskar remembers Kapil's debut in the Faisalabad Test in October 1978. Sadiq Mohammad was a seasoned opener for Pakistan and came out to bat in the national green cap. 'No need for helmets, we're playing

A small bat but a huge all-rounder. Kapil Dev was an energiser; when batting, bowling or coaching.

Top Test All-Rounders

India', he must have said to himself. Wrong! 'He had a scare as a Kapil bouncer whistled past his head with the kind of hiss only those who have faced deliveries of that speed can hear', Gavaskar recalled. Sadiq asked for a helmet pronto! Just as well. In the next over another bouncer from Kapil hit Sadiq flush on his helmet and went for four byes. Imagination boggles had Sadiq not worn the helmet. Kapil had arrived and stayed on the Test scene for 16 years. India at long last had found a bowler who could deliver knockout punches. He also scored 59 as a nightwatchman in that match and a quality all-rounder had emerged.

Kapil Dev Nikhanj was born in Chandigarh, Hariyana, on 6 January 1959 (give or take a few years, as Kapil himself is not sure). Gavaskar was among the first to spot his talent. Kapil is a rare jewel. As he was a world record-holder in taking most Test wickets in the last millennium, he is considered more of a bowler than a batsman. In future, however, he may be remembered equally for his carefree and exhilarating batting and his six appeal for he was a mighty tonker of sixes.

To him bowling was a serious job, he was often a one-man demolition squad whose job it was to dismiss batsmen—day in and day out—from 1978 to 1994. Batting, however, was a relaxation. He stood tall and hit tall; he loved his 'sixomania' and shared his exuberance with spectators. 'Test cricket is for batsmen, not bowlers', he once said. 'Bowlers are like slaves.' His bowling restricted and troubled batsmen but his batting enchanted and often won matches for India, especially the 1983 World Cup.

Oddly, his careless batting led to his being dropped in a Test after playing 66 Tests in a row from October 1978 to December 1984. Subsequently he played 65 consecutive Tests from January 1985 to March 1994. The Kolkata Test of December-January 1984–85 was the only gap in his 131 Test career. He was blamed for India's eight wicket defeat to England in the previous Test in Delhi when he played a risky shot when prudence was needed. Selectors, when will they learn? To expect Kapil to bat defensively is equivalent to asking a Formula One driver to keep to a speed limit of 80 kmh. The Indian selectors are known for their short memories. It was Kapil's daredevil hitting which led to his country's finest hour—India winning and lifting the World Cup at Lord's on 25 June 1983 under Kapil's captaincy.

Prior to 1982, he was a bowler who could bat. His Test batting average overseas was a pathetic 13. He announced himself as a batsman on the tour of England where he played sizzling innings of 41, 89, 66 and 97. Every time he appeared set to score the fastest century in Test history, he got out. In the Lord's Test India was tottering at 5 for 45 when in walked Kapil with his characteristic swagger and made 41. India was forced to follow-on and Kapil defended for a while with Dilip Vengsarkar. Soon Kapil broke loose and smashed 89 runs out of 117 added in mere 15 overs. His 89 adventurous runs included three sixes and 13 fours. The quickest century was his for the taking when Botham had him caught at short mid-wicket. Kapil also bagged eight wickets (5 for 125 and 3 for 43), which was a marvellous all-round performance.

Not quite satisfied, he reached 50 in 33 minutes in the second Test at Manchester—cover-drives predominating. In the third and final Test at The Oval, India faced the follow-on but Kapil did the rescue act—again—by savaging 97 runs off just 92 balls in 102 minutes, slashing two sixes and 14 fours. India had lost her 'dull dog' image thanks to Kapil Dev.

Between this Test series and the 1983 World Cup, Kapil played county cricket for Northamptonshire. His clear and tall hitting reminded the home spectators of Colin Milburn, a big hitter alas no more with us. Kapil was named as one of the Five Cricketers of the Year in *Wisden 1983*, 'his all-round displays of rubbery exuberance' emphasised.

Kapil's best was to come a year later. Appointed as captain of India, he went on to win for India her only World Cup. No one had given India a chance to make it to the semi-final but the match against lowly Zimbabwe lifted their spirit. 'Today Zimbabwe, tomorrow the world', was how Kapil's men felt. India's World Cup record was woeful, having won only one match in 1975 and none in 1979. However, they started the 1983 campaign well by defeating the mighty West Indies in the opening round.

They had to beat the L-plated Zimbabweans to enter the semi-final. Batting first, India was in all sorts of trouble at 4 for 9, their acclaimed openers Gavaskar and Srikkanth out for ducks. Kapil entered, his usual toothy smile missing. India lost her fifth wicket for 17 in the 13th over. Put Kapil in a corner and he fights like a tiger. 'Leave it to me,' he told his batting partners as he added valuable runs with Roger Binny and Madan Lal and then an incredible 126 with Syed Kirmani (who made only 24) for the unbroken ninth wicket—not only a World Cup record but a record in all one-day internationals.

From a disastrous 5 for 17, India had recovered to a healthy 8 for 266, Kapil striking an unbeaten 175 with six sixes and 16 fours. It was then the highest score in a one-day international and still regarded as one of the most spectacular innings in any form of cricket. The Zimbabweans batted courageously but fell 31 runs short.

Inspired by this narrow win, India went on to beat Australia in a qualifier, England in the semi-final and met West Indies, the winners of the previous two World Cups, in the final. Sent in to bat, India was dismissed for 183. An easy win for the Windies was on the cards but Kapil Dev and his medium-pacers had different ideas. 'Master Blaster' Viv Richard and Desmond Haynes took the score to 1 for 50. Haynes was dismissed but Richards kept attacking. He lifted Madan Lal for what appeared to be a six but Kapil ran like an Olympian and caught it. This was the turning point, the crucial catch had tilted the game India's way. Incredibly, India won by 43 runs and nearly 10,000 Indian supporters gathered around Lord's pavilion to cheer their heroes. Back in India there were all night celebrations and a holiday was declared the next day.

Kapil was the national hero, an international superstar. The following year, West Indies extracted revenge by routing India in the one-dayers and the Test series and Kapil lost his captaincy. Fortunately, Kapil the rustic with a simple smile, had his feet on the ground in moments whether grand and ignoble, and carried on playing with the same spontaneous verve.

In November 1989, against Pakistan at Karachi, Kapil became the first non-specialist batsman to play 100 Tests. R. Mohan wrote in *Sportstar* (India), 'There was an air of celebration to the Karachi Test besides the regular competitive spirit. Kapil Dev was being feted left and right for his hundredth Test appearance. There was a genuine feeling of warmth for a person accomplishing such a feat... The charming thing about his 100th appearance was that the Pakistani organisations connected with the cricket that came up with many commemorative plaques.' The Pakistan International Airlines was the first to present him a silver salver on the eve of the Test. The Board of Control for Cricket in Pakistan followed and so did Habib Bank of Pakistan. The Indian Board also presented a silver plaque to Kapil at the team meeting before the Test. He bowled with his customary fire on his special day to capture 4 for 69 in 24 overs.

India started badly and was in strife at 6 for 85 but was rescued by Kapil (55) and Ravi Shastri (45) who added 78 runs for the seventh wicket and India totalled 262, still 147 runs in arrears. Pakistan went for quick runs but Kapil restricted their run-rate, his analysis being 36–15–82–3 as he swung the ball appreciably. Thus he took seven out of 15 wickets to fall. When capturing his third wicket in the first innings, he became the fourth bowler to take 350 Test scalps. And he had dismissed quality batsmen Aamer Malik, Shoaib Mohammad and Javed Miandad (twice each) and Shahid Saeed once. India was challenged to make 453 runs to win and was

3 for 303 at stumps. Kapil did not get a chance to bat in this drawn Test. It was a Test to remember for him, 55 runs, seven wickets and four shining plaques.

He went on to play 31 more Tests and set records as mentioned earlier. A year after his 100th Test, he played a cameo role in the Lord's Test against England. Now remembered as the Graham Gooch Test (who made 333 and 123), India needed 24 runs to avoid the follow-on with only tail-ender Naren Hirwani at the other end. Kapil got those 24 runs in four balls, four successive sixes off spinner Eddie Hemmings.

Kapil was an energiser; when batting, bowling or fielding for 16 years. In 131 Tests he scored 5248 runs at 31.05, hitting eight centuries (163 being his highest) and 27 fifties. He also snared 434 wickets at 29.64 taking 5 wickets in an innings 23 times and 10 wickets in a Test twice, and held 64 catches. His best bowling was 9 for 83 against West Indies at Ahmedabad in 1983–84.

His performances in one-day internationals were equally spectacular. He hammered 3783 runs (with an unbeaten 175 as his top score) at 23.79 and took 253 wickets at 27.45 (best being 5 for 43) in 225 matches.

Bowling was his wife, his life, his 10 to 6 job, his bread and butter. Batting was his mistress, his indulgence. He seldom strayed when bowling and hardly ever batted with a straight bat; his cross-bat flings giving spectators almost orgasmic delight.

RICHARD HADLEE
New Zealand

The real Richard Hadlee—as we know and admire him—stood up in the 1980s. The promising performer of the 1970s became a supremo; not the fastest bowler on the globe but among the brainiest. He plotted the dismissals of his opponents strategically. Not only did he watch the videotapes of Dennis Lillee, the bowler he admired most, but also those of contemporary batsmen. He studied weaknesses in their technique 'in the manner of a surgeon studying x-rays before probing for the source of the problem', to quote Don Mosey from Wisden *(1991).*

In one of the most explosive series in Test history when hardly a day passed without an umpiring controversy, the home team New Zealand defeated the star-studded West Indians 1–0 in early 1980. The margin of victory was a leg-bye in the first Test at Dunedin which New Zealand won by one wicket.

The Kiwi win staggered the critics since only a month previously, the Windies had won the Benson and Hedges World Series Cup in Australia and then thrashed a full-strength Australian side. The man behind New Zealand's surprise victory was the tall, razor-sharp all-rounder, Richard Hadlee. In the Dunedin Test which New Zealand won with a solitary wicket to spare, he took 5 for 34 and 6 for 68 and scored 51 and 17, the second highest score in either innings. In the visitor's second innings he became the highest wicket-taker among New Zealanders at Test level.

In the second Test at Christchurch, he scored his maiden Test century and in the process became the first New Zealander to achieve the Test

Richard Hadlee appeals for a wicket in his last Test; against England, Birmingham, 1990.

double of 1000 runs and 100 wickets. He bowled splendidly throughout the series, his 5 for 34, 3 for 58 and 4 for 75 in the first innings of all three Tests contributing to the world champion West Indians failing to reach 230 in the first innings of any of the Tests.

Another memorable moment in New Zealand's 50 years of international cricket came on March 13, 1974. In the second Test at Christchurch the New Zealand 'mouse' roared at the mighty Australians under Ian Chappell, defeating them by five wickets. With centuries in both innings, Glenn Turner was the architect of this shock win. However, the Hadlee brothers, Dayle and Richard, contributed just as handsomely. Between them, the fast-medium pacers took 12 wickets—eight of them in the second innings.

In a way, elder brother Dayle was responsible for Richard's rise to the top. Just before a Plunket Shield match, Dayle's toe was caught in the motor while mowing the lawn. This gave Richard the opportunity to represent Canterbury. He took a hat-trick in that match and subsequently was chosen to tour Australia with the New Zealand B team in 1972.

Richard and his namesake, Richard Collinge, were the fastest bowlers in New Zealand in the 1970s. Richard Hadlee had a series of injuries, including a painful shoulder, which put him out of the game for most of the 1975 season. However, acupuncture helped him. He performed brilliantly in the Wellington Test against India in 1976, with a match haul of 11 for 58, including 7 for 23 in the second innings.

When New Zealand toured Pakistan and India in 1976–77, Richard was their most effective bowler. He topped the batting averages as well against Pakistan in the Test series. In the final Test at Karachi, Richard made 87, then his highest Test score, and was associated in a 186-run partnership with Warren Lees. This show of defiance helped the Kiwis to save the Test.

Richard became the spectators' favourite during the second Test against Greg Chappell's Australians at Eden Park, Auckland in 1977. He stood up to the blistering pace of Dennis Lillee, scoring 44 and a well-hit 81 out of the team total of 175 which prompted writer Don Cameron to comment: 'New Zealand has never known crowd fever quite like this'. Later that year, Richard was named New Zealand's Cricket Personality of the Year and received the Nugget Cup. The cricket-mad Hadlee family (father Walter, brothers Barry and Dayle, wife Karen who had all represented New Zealand internationally) was there in full force during the presentation.

The last time Dayle and Richard played together in a Test was at Wellington in February 1978. In this historic Test, New Zealand defeated England for the first time. Richard took 10 wickets in the match, his second innings spell of 6 for 26 causing England's sensational collapse: 64 all out. It was England's lowest score since 1948 and her lowest against all countries except Australia.

In this historic Test, New Zealand defeated England for the first time.

After much deliberation, the New Zealand Cricket Council gave Richard Hadlee permission to play World Series Cricket (WSC). He was probably the first cricketer to play WSC without losing his Test status.

He took his 100th wicket in the second Test against Pakistan at Napier in 1979 in his 25th Test. The following season, in the first Test against the strong West Indies, his 27th, he became the highest wicket-taker in New Zealand's Test history, surpassing Richard Collinge's record of 116 wickets in 35 Tests. In the second Test of the series, his 28th, he reached his Test double. Only four all-rounders had achieved this in fewer Tests; Ian Botham in 21 Tests, India's Vinoo Mankad and Kapil Dev in 23 and 25, respectively and Australia's 'Monty' Noble in 27.

Respected by opponents for his controlled seaming and pace variations, Richard Hadlee worked hard for his success. He told Richie Benaud in *World Series Cricket 1978–79*: 'Cricket is now very much my life. I'm totally involved and committed to it. If you want to get to the top, it means getting off your backside and working hard.'

The real Richard Hadlee—as we know and admire him—stood up in the 1980s. The promising performer of the 1970s became a supremo; not the fastest bowler on the globe but among the brainiest. He plotted the dismissals of his opponents strategically. Not only did he watch the videotapes of Dennis Lillee, the bowler he admired most, but also those of contemporary batsmen. He studied weaknesses in their technique 'in the manner of a surgeon studying x-rays before probing for the source of the problem', to quote Don Mosey from *Wisden* (1991).

He moved the ball late either going away or coming in. He specialised in 'leg cutters' and called his slower ball 'dangly' (which swung in to a bewildered batsman). He rarely used the bouncer, keeping it only as a surprise weapon. Subtlety was the name of his game. He often played cat and mouse and without warning, turned into a cat among the pigeons. He had a ball for every occasion.

He was neither a batsman-hater nor a spectacular appealer a la Lillee or Brett Lee. He did not supply 'killer' quotes to journalists like Jeff Thomson did. He just pocketed his 5-fers efficiently and ruthlessly, felt 'very happy and proud' and won for New Zealand quite a few Test matches.

That is why his unpopularity in certain sections of the crowd in Australia in the mid-1980s was difficult to understand. Some offensive chants upset him but he carried on regardless, reaching new milestones. He became the first cricketer to capture 400 Test wickets and his 431 scalps in 86 Tests was a record when he retired in July 1990. Since then it has been eclipsed by many bowlers. Richard's taking 5 wickets in a Test innings 36 times and 10 wickets in a Test nine times were both records when he called it a day.

Son of Walter Hadlee who had captained New Zealand in 1940s, Sir Richard Hadlee had many outstanding bowling achievements in his Test career from 1972 to 1990. His favourite Test was in Brisbane in November 1985. Australia was cruising at 1 for 70 when he struck crippling blows. He took the first nine wickets to fall and accepted a catch of the last man, Geoff Lawson, off Vaughan Brown. Richard scored 54 out of New Zealand's total of 7 declared for 553 and captured 6 for 71 in the second innings as the Kiwis won by an innings and 41 runs. He had match figures of 15 for 123 which stunned Australia.

Was Richard disappointed in missing out on the *ultimate* achievement of taking all 10 wickets in a Test innings? 'No. That was, I suppose, as near-perfect a performance one hopes to achieve and one in which the whole team shared', he replied.

He was also a useful lower-order batsman who scored 3124 runs at 27.16 in 86 Tests, hitting two centuries, his highest being 151 not out against Sri Lanka at Colombo in 1986–87.

Richard played County cricket for Nottinghamshire and Sheffield Shield for Tasmania. For Notts in County Championship of 1984, he became the first to achieve the double of 1000 runs and 100 wickets since 1967, scoring 1179 runs at 51.26 and 117 wickets at 14.05.

In first-class cricket he scored 12,052 runs at 31.71 in 342 matches, hitting 14 hundreds (highest score 210 not out for Nottinghamshire against Middlesex at Lord's in 1984). He also captured 1490 wickets at 18.11, taking 5 wickets in an innings 102 times (best being 9 for 52 against Australia in the Brisbane Test of 1985–86).

His record in one-day internationals is also impressive. In 115 matches he scored 1751 runs at 21.61 and took 158 wickets at 21.56, best being 5 for 25.

Just before the Lord's Test against England in June 1990, the 39 year-old Kiwi received a knighthood in the Queen's Birthday honours' list. To fit the occasion, Sir Richard gave a Man of the Match performance, taking

3 for 113 and 1 for 32 and scoring 86 runs embellished with 12 fours and two sixes. Then followed his final Test at Birmingham a month later. He captured 3 for 97 and 5 for 53, dismissing Devon Malcolm for a duck with his *last* ball in Test cricket. He was made New Zealand's Man of the Series. 'That was no sentimental gesture: the world's leading Test wicket-taker had called it a day at the peak of his powers', summed up *Wisden* (1991).

WASIM AKRAM

Pakistan

Taking into account both forms of international cricket—Test and the one-dayers, Wasim Akram was arguably the best all-rounder. His record in the two versions of the game—especially in bowling—has been awe-inspiring. He has many onlys, firsts and mosts to his credit; the only one to take more than 500 wickets in limited-overs internationals, the first one to capture more than 50 wickets in World Cup, the only one to perform two hat-tricks in successive Tests, the first bowler to perform two hat-tricks in limited-overs internationals and the hitter of most sixes (12) in a Test innings.

Statistics aside, Wasim and his partner in pace, Waqar Younis, formed a lethal opening bowling partnership. They can be placed in the same class as Larwood and Voce, Lindwall and Miller, Trueman, Tyson and Statham, Hall, Gilchrist and Griffith, Lillee and Thomson, Roberts and Holding, Marshall and Garner, Ambrose and Walsh. Peter Roebuck was moved to write in the *Sydney Morning Herald* of 11 February 2003, '[Wasim] Akram is the most remarkable cricketer his country has produced and among the best the game has known… In Akram's hands a ball does not so much talk as sing. With a flick of the wrist and an arm that flashes past his ears like a thought through a child's brain he pushes the ball across the batsman and makes it dip back wickedly late, or bends it early where upon it changes direction after landing.'

Born on 3 June 1966, into a moderately affluent middle-class family in Lahore, Wasim Akram was educated in a private school which encouraged

Pakistan's left-hander Wasim Akram was arguably the best all-rounder at both forms of international cricket. Here he is bowling to West Indies in Canada in 1999.

sports. At 12, he was opening the bowling and batting for the school, at 15 he was appointed captain. His life was consumed with cricket—at school, home, in the garage with his brother and on the streets with a tennis ball. At 18, his big inswing and powerful hitting attracted attention. Pakistan's former fast bowler Khan Mohammad taught him to lift his arm in the delivery stride which added to his speed.

He was lucky to be at the right place at the right time. He was practising in the Under-19 nets when who should pass by but Javed Miandad. The great Pakistan batsman was so impressed by Wasim's ability to move the ball at speed, while retaining control that he insisted that the youngster be included in a squad of 14 for a three day Patron's XI match against New Zealand at Rawalpindi in 1984–85. At Miandad's insistence, Wasim displaced the better known Tahir Naqqash in the final selection.

Fewer first-class debuts have been more sensational than Wasim's.

Fewer first-class debuts have been more sensational than Wasim's; 7 for 50 and 2 for 54 as all around people asked 'who's this Wasim boy'? His victims included Test players John Wright (both innings), Bruce Edgar and John F. Reid (both innings). This is not the end of a fairy story, just the beginning.

Wasim went on to make his limited-overs international debut against the Kiwis at Faisalabad that season and was selected to tour New Zealand two months later. In his second Test in Dunedin in early 1985, the 18-year-old took 5 for 56 and 5 for 72. In 1987, he signed a lucrative six-year contract with Lancashire. His best match that summer was against Surrey when he captured 5 for 15 including a hat-trick and scored 98 runs off 78 balls.

He established himself as a Test all-rounder on the tour of Australia in 1989–90. In three Tests, he scored 197 runs at 39.40 with one match-saving century and took 17 wickets at 18.70 with three 5 wickets per innings hauls. He was made Man of the Match in the first two Tests and was undoubtedly the player of the tour with his brisk and varied left-arm bowling and belligerent left-hand batting. In the first Test in Melbourne in January 1990, he captured 11 wickets; 6 for 62 in the first innings and 5 for 98 in the second but still could not stop Australia winning by 92 runs.

In a seesawing second Test in Adelaide, Pakistan almost lost the match, then almost won it thanks to a memorable 191 run partnership between Imran Khan (136) and Wasim Akram (123) for the sixth wicket. Trailing Australia by 84 runs, Pakistan lost 4 for 22 and was 5 for 90 when Wasim joined Imran. Wasim, not noted for his batting in a crisis, played splendidly for 244 minutes and hit 18 fours and a six with tremendous power all round the Adelaide Oval. The fluctuating Test was drawn when Australia needing 304 to win were 6 for 233 at close. It was Wasim's match as he had scored 52 runs off 89 balls in the first innings and captured 5 for 100 and 1 for 29. He won over the Australian spectators with a match aggregate of 175 runs and six wickets and becoming only the third Pakistani after Mushtaq Mohammad and Imran Khan to score a century and take 5 wickets in an innings in the same Test.

After this tour, Wasim established himself as a top-class bowler but his batting was disappointing, although he did hit a century and a double century in a Test career embracing three decades. Wasim and Waqar Younis were enormously successful when Pakistan toured England in 1992. Wasim captured 82 wickets at 16.21 on the tour, the most by a visiting bowler since 1964. In four Tests he took 21 wickets at 22.00. 'It would be surprising if there has been a better left-arm bowler of pace; and he was the coolest of match winners with the bat at Lord's', wrote Scyld Berry in *Wisden 1993*.

Wasim was adjudged Man of the Lord's Test after bagging 2 for 49 and 4 for 66 and playing a match-winning innings. Set 138 to win, Pakistan lost 8 for 95 when Wasim (45 not out) and tail-ender Waqar (20 not out) carried them to victory. Amid mounting tension, Wasim drove spinner Ian Salisbury through covers in the last over of the fourth day to win the thriller by 2 wickets.

He continued with his deadly spells in the drawn Manchester Test when he took 5 for 128 in the second innings, and 6 for 67 and 3 for 36 in the final Test at The Oval which Pakistan won by 10 wickets to win the series 2–1. Wasim and Waqar were adjudged joint Men of the Series for Pakistan. There were some speculations about ball tampering after the series. England's manager and former Test cricketer, Micky Stewart, hinted that he knew how the Pakistani speedsters managed to swing the old ball more than the new one but was not prepared to say how.

Earlier, in 1990–91, Wasim became the third player after England's Maurice J.C. Allom (vs New Zealand in Christchurch in1929–30) and Chris Old (vs Pakistan, Birmingham, 1978) to take four wickets in five balls at Test level. This was against the West Indies at Lahore. He was on a hat-trick after dismissing Jeff Dujon and Curtly Ambrose off successive balls in the second inning. He almost got a hat-trick when Ian Bishop edged the ball past Imran Khan who could not hang on to it. Off his next two deliveries he dismissed Malcolm Marshall and Courtney Walsh. One near miss and he had missed the hat-trick twice in one over! He had to wait for eight years for his first hat-trick and then got his second in the next Test.

In the Asian Test Championship held in 1998–99, Wasim performed hat-tricks in successive Test matches against Sri Lanka in March 1999, at Lahore and then at Dhaka. He became only the third bowler after Australia's Hugh Trumble and Jimmy Matthews to achieve two Test hat-tricks and the only one to do so in consecutive Tests.

Wasim was also the first player to take two hat-tricks in one-day Internationals (ODIs) against West Indies and then against Australia, both at Sharjah in 1989–90. So far, fellow Pakistani Saqlain Mushtaq and Sri Lanka's Chaminda Vaas are the only other cricketers to perform two ODI hat-tricks.

Wasim also holds the record of hitting most number of sixes in a Test innings. Against Zimbabwe at Shekhapura in 1996–97, he hit his highest Test score of 257 not out which included 12 sixes and 22 fours. He got past English great Wally Hammond's record of 10 sixes in his unbeaten 336 against New Zealand in the 1932–33 Auckland Test. Wasim's 257 off 363 balls in 490 minutes is the highest score by a no. 8 batsman in Test arena. He came in to bat at 6 for 183 and took the score to 553, adding 313 exhilarating runs with Saqlain Mushtaq (79); a record for the eighth wicket.

In 104 Tests he scored 2898 runs at 22.64 with three centuries (highest 257 not out). He also captured 414 wickets at 23.62, capturing 5 wickets in an innings 25 times and 10 wickets in a Test five times. His best bowling spell was 7 for 119 against New Zealand in 1993–94. Two more runs and Wasim would have joined the elite group of all-rounders who have achieved the 3000 runs and 400 wickets Test double.

He will be remembered for his feat of scoring a fifty (52), a century (123) and taking five wickets in an innings (5 for 100) in the Adelaide Test against Australia in January 1990. Only six cricketers before him and only Jacques Kallis after him have achieved this rare triple in Test annals.

In ODIs, his record is just as impressive. In 356 matches he scored 3717 runs at 16.52 (highest score 86) and took a record 502 wickets at 23.52, bagging 5 wickets in an innings six times, the best being 5 for 15. He is the only one to grab more than 500 wickets. Wasim also led in World Cup; being the first one to take more than 50 wickets. In 38 World Cup matches, he took 55 wickets at 23.83; a record broken by Australia's Glenn McGrath in the 2007 World Cup.

*Oh, what a feeling, he's out! A compelling figure, Wasim Akram
has the grin of a playboy and the powers of a cricketing genius.*

'The Adelaide Test of January 1990 has been my cherished memory in Test cricket,' he recently told me. 'But my most memorable moment in cricket is when Pakistan won the World Cup in Melbourne in 1992.' No wonder, he scored 33 runs, adding 52 valuable runs with skipper Imran Khan, captured three scalps (Ian Botham for a duck and then clean bowling Allan Lamb for 31 and Chris Lewis for nought off successive balls), was adjudged Man of the FInal as Pakistan beat England by 22 runs in front of a crowd of almost 90,000.

A complex character requires a perceptive writer to sum him up. So over to Peter Roebuck: '[Wasim] Akram's cricket has been not so much a career as a merry-go-round. Along the way he has dazzled many batsmen, taken hundreds of wickets, helped his team win a World Cup [in 1992], captained his country a few times, refused to talk to his successor and been implicated in several scandals, always protesting his innocence with the air of a cat appalled at claims he was responsible for devouring a nearby fish... A compelling figure, he has the grin of a playboy, the face of a gangster and the powers of a cricketing genius.'

CHRIS CAIRNS
New Zealand

On his performances at Test and limited-overs levels, Chris Cairns could be considered as a genuine all-rounder. He was made Man of the Series against England in 1999 and the readers of Wisden Cricket Monthly *voted him as the Best All-rounder of the 1999 English season, winning 186 votes, 139 votes more than South Africa's Lance Klusener (who finished at number 3). The same poll ranked him as the fourth best Player of 1999 after Andy Caddick, Steve Waugh and Klusener. As a climax,* Wisden *honoured him as one of the Five Cricketers of the Year 2000.*

Chris Cairns reserved his best for his 43rd Test. He was 29 then and had played Test cricket for 10 years with only few outstanding feats with bat or ball. He then had more lows than highs, suffering from injuries, a kidney operation and mood swings, which retarded his progress.

This changed in a hurry in the Hamilton Test against the West Indies in December 1999. And what a pulsating, topsy-turvy Test it turned out! On the first day, Chris was hammered by the West Indies opening pair of Sherwin Campbell (170) and Adrian Griffith (114) who piled on 276 runs. Medium-pacer Chris had laboured on to 0 for 62 before he took his first wicket on the second day. Inexplicably, the visitors collapsed and were shot out for 365, losing their last 10 wickets for 89 runs as Chris claimed 3 for 73. New Zealand were 6 for 258 when Chris went in to bat and was almost run out before he had scored.

The third (TV) umpire, David Quested, scanned several unsatisfactory replays and gave Chris the benefit of doubt. Fortunately for Chris, the

Chris Cairns had 'six appeal' and here he is striking a tall six against England in the 2004 Lord's Test.

special side-on cameras were not filming at that time and he admitted later that he was lucky to survive. He went on to top score with 72 which included two sixes and nine fours. When 48, he reached his 2000th run.

The Kiwis led by 28 runs. Demoralised, the Windies fell to pieces and were bowled out for a paltry 97. Man of the Match, Chris Cairns was their nemesis, capturing 7 for 27 to finish with a rather symmetrical match figure of 10 for 100. By taking 10 wickets, he joined his dynamic Dad, Lance Cairns, who had grabbed 10 for 144 (7 for 74 and 3 for 70) against England in the Leeds Test of 1983. The two form the *only* father–son combination to capture 10 wickets in a Test. Two months earlier, in the Kanpur Test against India, Chris had claimed his 131st Test wicket, to get past his father's Test tally of 130 scalps.

Chris was not finished with the Windies yet. In the Boxing Day Test at Wellington, he captured 5 for 44 and 2 for 25 and scored 31 runs as New Zealand won the Test and the series 2–0. The New Zealanders completed the whitewash by slaughtering the Windies 5–0 in the one-day internationals (ODIs). Chris had contributed to two victories by hitting a whirlwind 75 (six sixes, two fours) and adding 136 runs with Nathan Astle in the first ODI at Auckland and by capturing 3 for 25 in the third ODI in Napier.

His next series was against Steve Waugh's all-conquering Australians in March–April 2000. Although Australia extended their Test win sequence to ten by beating the Kiwis 3–0, they could not curb Chris Cairns, the cavalier batsman. He belted 13 sixes in the series while making 341 runs at 56.83. He sparkled in the Wellington Test where he played two spectacular innings, 109 with two sixes and 14 fours and 69 (six sixes and four fours) besides taking four wickets.

In the first innings, he came in to bat when his country was on her knees at 5 for 66. Boldly he plundered 72 runs in 54 minutes with Astle and 109 in 113 minutes with Adam Parore. Reported Phil Wilkins in the *Sydney*

Morning Herald, 'For almost 3½ hours, Australia felt the bludgeoning bat of the beefcake no. 7 batsman [Cairns]. Shane Warne's Test record was forgotten in twin puffs of smoke as Cairns sent two deliveries hurtling back overhead in four balls, the first disappearing high into the top tier of the Bob Vance Stand on the straight hit, the second over the mid-wicket fence.'

He was even more of a daredevil in the second innings when 75 per cent of his score came in sixes and fours. In the next Test in Hamilton, the swashbuckling Kiwi hit 37 and 71 (including two sixes) in a bid to rescue his country. Although he disappointed as a bowler in the series, often delivering loosely and taking 10 wickets at 37.90, he was a colossus as a batsman.

This was sweet revenge for him as a leaked document from the Australians prior to the series had stated that Chris Cairns was fragile. 'A good frontrunner but lacks confidence if you get on top of him', said the secret dossier on him. Perhaps this inspired him to a Man of the Series performance in the three Tests. He not only topped the batting average among the New Zealanders, but outscored the Australians as well. 'Fragile, me? Forsooth!', he could have been forgiven for saying, which he did not. He let his bat do the talking.

He let his bat do the talking.

Prior to the Wellington fireworks in 1999 and 2000, his happiest Test was at Eden Park, Auckland against Zimbabwe in January 1996. He scored his maiden Test hundred, belting nine sixes in his 120 off 86 balls. One of the sixes was lifted over the covers on the roof of the Stand. His first 50 had come in 58 minutes off 49 balls, and his next 50 in 48 minutes off 37 deliveries.

He had missed by only one six to equal the then Test record of 10 sixes, hit by English great Wally Hammond (also at Auckland against New Zealand in 1932–33). Subsequently, Pakistan's Wasim Akram lifted 12 sixes against

Top Test All-Rounders

Zimbabwe at Sheikhupura in 1996–97. The tall hitting by Chris delighted his father Lance who was a six symbol of his time.

Exit Lance Cairns in 1985 and enter Chris Cairns in 1989. A similar type of cricketer, Chris had a sounder batting technique. To quote Sir Richard Hadlee from *Wisden Cricket Monthly* (January 1997): 'A match winner, probably more with the bat than the ball… Hits hard and straight… I think he should bat higher up than he does in one-day games where he could tear an attack apart—he's wasted coming in with only a few overs to go… shows the potential to become a very good opening bowler or first change. A different type of player than his father [Lance], he's technically a better batsman, although he hits the ball nearly as hard! Seems to be enjoying his cricket more these days.'

Despite being close to Lance, Chris proclaims himself a self-made bowler. 'Dad never pushed me. In fact, he taught *me* nothing at all until I was about 14.' Chris made his Test debut against Australia in the Perth Test of November 1989. He was flown in as a replacement for an injured Brendon Bracewell but developed back strain himself and could not bowl from second day onwards.

He appeared a threatening bowler in the Auckland Test against England in 1991–92 when he took 6 for 52 and 2 for 86. In the earlier Test at Christchurch he scored 61 with 11 fours and added 117 for the 7th wicket. His other notable Test performances were:

- *4 for 136 and 5 for 75 vs Sri Lanka at Auckland in 1990–91*
- *6 for 52 and 2 for 86 vs England at Auckland in 1991–92*
- *4 for 113 and 78 runs vs Australia at Perth in 1993–94*
- *4 for 90, 3 for 54 and 64 runs vs Australia at Brisbane in 1997–98*
- *4 for 95 and 52 runs vs Australia at Perth in 1997–98*
- *6 for 77 vs England at Lord's in 1999 and 5 for 31 and 81 runs vs England at The Oval in 1999*

His 72 and 10 for 100 against the West Indies at Hamilton in December 1999, his 109 against Australia in March 2000 and his swashbuckling 120 off 86 balls against Zimbabwe in 1995–96 have already been detailed. When in the mood, he can devastate any attack but often he went into a shell and appeared non-communicative.

According to Dave Crowe in *ABC Cricket Book 1999–2000*, Chris 'is only a touch away from greatness. Injury, illness and personal tragedy have dogged his career, but he keeps coming back with sensational performances—although, not always consistently. Hits like a mule with straight sixes a specialty and can make a ball sit up on a shirt front. A world-beater on his day but enigmatic and unpredictable.'

His tour to Australia in 1993–94 became controversial when he withdrew unexpectedly from the team on the morning of the Hobart Test, citing a bruised heel. He then faced a play-or-go-home ultimatum from the management before the next Test in Brisbane. He played but under-performed.

The personal tragedy mentioned above happened in 1994 when his 19-year-old sister Louise was killed in a freak train accident near Christchurch. It took Chris a long time to get over this loss.

His statistics in both Tests and ODIs are eye-catching. In 62 Tests he scored 3320 runs at 33.53 hitting five centuries and took 218 wickets at 29.40, capturing five wickets in an innings 13 times. His 87 sixes in Test matches remained a record until surpassed by Australia's six-king Adam Gilchrist and West Indies legend Brian Lara in 2006 and 2007. In 215 ODIs he amassed 4950 runs at 29.46 and took 201 wickets at 32.80.

Chris also played county cricket for Nottinghamshire and is remembered for his blistering 114 against Gloucestershire at Trent Bridge in June 1996. He broke the dressing-room window with one of his three straight sixes and Notts won by an innings in three days. This was their first victory in their

Top Test All-Rounders

13th championship match in 11 months. There was wide-spread jubilation in the Notts camp with Chris (who also had taken four wickets) as the hero.

He brushed aside the praises saying that he had not achieved enough for his county. Instead he got inspired by photographs of well-known cricketers on the wall. 'These are my biggest source of motivation, those photographs on the pavilion walls, because I've achieved very little compared with many of them', he said modestly.

One does not normally associate modesty with bulky opening bowlers and six hitters but with Chris Cairns they do co-exist.

SHAUN POLLOCK
South Africa

Along with England's Andrew Flintoff and team-mate Jacques Kallis, Shaun Pollock is the leading all-rounder of the 2000s. In 108 Tests he scored 3781 runs at 32.31 with two centuries and took 421 wickets at 23.11. Kapil Dev, Richard Hadlee and Shane Warne are the only others to achieve the Test double of 3000 runs and 400 wickets. He is also one of the few to reach the ODI double of 3000 runs (3519 runs at 26.45) and 300 wickets (393 at 24.50) in 303 matches.

Like Chris Cairns, Shaun Pollock was also born into a family with a strong cricketing heritage. Both his father Peter and uncle Graeme were outstanding Test cricketers for South Africa. The apartheid policy led to South Africa's exclusion from international cricket for two decades from 1970 which interfered with the two older Pollocks reaching their pinnacles.

With the dismantling of apartheid, South Africa made a welcome return to international sports in early 1990. It was too late for Graeme and Peter to stage a comeback, but it seemed that the Pollock cousins, Anthony (Graeme's son) and Shaun (Peter's son) would start from where their illustrious fathers had left off. Anthony had more pressure to perform because Graeme was still an active player and a legend. Still, he represented Transvaal when a teenager, struggled and played with their B team until the late 1990s.

Shaun had to face less unfavourable comparisons because Peter had retired from the scene in 1975. Shaun's progress was steady and without consciously trying, fitted well into his Dad's shoes. In fact, he took more

Shaun Pollock dives to take a catch against Zimbabwe in the 2005 Cape Town Test.

wickets than his father did and at a better average, 421 wickets at 23.11 in 108 Tests against Peter's 116 at 24.18 in 28. But for his country's boycott for 20 years, Peter could have achieved much more.

Was the name Pollock a big cross to bear? 'As a kid I realised that people took an interest in me because of my name', he told Jonathan Agnew in *Wisden Cricket Monthly.* 'But I didn't feel there was any pressure on me. Dad had finished by 1975 so he was out of the limelight.' Also, Peter was very easy with him when at school and if he did not want to play cricket, he never forced him to don the pads. He did not often come to watch him play, and if he did, he would stand far away behind a tree.

Shaun was keen on the game and competitive. He made his Test debut at 22 against England at Centurion in November 1995. It was an impressive series for him as he topped his country's bowling averages, claiming 16 wickets at 23.56 (best being 5 for 32) and scoring 133 runs at 26.60.

Wisden 1997 opined that he was the find of the series and added, 'He immediately looked the part and his cricket combined some of the best features of both his famous relatives, uncle Graeme and father Peter.'

Shaun was even more successful in the limited-overs internationals that season against England and was adjudged Man of the Match in the first and third matches. In the Cape Town Test, he top scored with a run-a-ball 66 not out and grabbed 4 for 34. He went on to form a frightening opening bowling partnership with Allan Donald, just as his father had with Mike Procter. Unlike Peter and Mike who could compete only against England, Australia and New Zealand, Shaun demonstrated his swing, cut and pace all over the cricket world.

After scoring 92 against Sri Lanka at Cape Town in 1997–98, he played his most memorable, yet paradoxically, his most frustrating Test. This was against Australia in Adelaide in early 1998. He captured 7 for 87 (his best spell to date) and 2 for 61, scored 40 runs and was adjudged Man of the Test. So why was it frustrating? In the second innings, with the South Africans scenting victory, Shaun bowled a lifter to a well-set Mark Waugh. It hit the Australian on the arm and as he walked away in pain, his bat brushed the stumps and dislodged a bail. After repeated replays lasting about five minutes, Waugh was declared not out by the TV umpire.

To add to Shaun's agony, Waugh was dropped the next ball by Adam Bacher. Australia saved the Test and won the series. It was Shaun's most disappointing match despite his heroic performance. It was sweet revenge for him and his team-mates when under his captaincy, South Africa beat Australia in the final of the Commonwealth Games held in Kuala Lumpur, Malaysia, in September 1998. Shaun took 4 for 19.

He was also behind South Africa's whitewash of the once mighty West Indies who they humbled 5–0 in the 1998-99 Test series. He captured 29 scalps at 16.65, with match-winning performances at Johannesburg (5 for 54 and 4 for 49), Port Elizabeth (5 for 43 and 2 for 46) and Durban (1 for 45 and 5 for 83).

He was at his all-round best against New Zealand in 1999 when he bagged 13 wickets at 14.85 in the 3-Test series and scored 112 runs without getting out. Such consistency against all countries made South Africa's English coach Bob Woolmer describe Shaun as 'one of the finest all-rounders since Garry Sobers'. This appeared going over the top as he had at that time not scored a Test hundred (against Sobers's 26). Quite embarrassed at Woolmer's hyperbole, he told *Wisden*'s Agnew, 'Ach, the coach is always blurting his mouth off! . . . I really won't know how I can be measured up until my career is over and until then I really can't be bothered with it at all.'

The shock revelation of skipper Hansie Cronje's involvement with an Indian 'bookmaker' thrust Shaun into captaining his country in three one-dayers against Australia in April 2000. He passed this fiery assignment in flying colours by beating Steve Waugh's rampaging Aussies 2–1.

Shaun is a shining role model for aspiring young cricketers. He neither smokes nor drinks and very rarely swears—surprising for a fast bowler. Also, he is playing a vital role in his country's development program—which aims to unearth the likes of Vivian Richards, Curtly Ambrose and Brian Lara by introducing cricket to black African children in the under-privileged townships.

His progress as the world's leading fast bowler is a matter of immense pride to his family. Now his Dad watched him play from the stands and not from behind a tree!

In his final ODI in February 2008 Shaun hit the winning run as South Africa defeated the West Indies in Johannesburg and tributes poured in for his career spanning two decades.

Shaun Pollock is delighted after claiming India's
Rahul Dravid in the Johannesburg Test of 2006.

JACQUES KALLIS
South Africa

On figures and usefulness for his country, Kallis could be termed the leading all-rounder of the day with his away swingers at about 135 km per hour and sharp slip fielding supplementing his dour batting at number 3.

In the Cape Town Test of January 2007, stocky South African Jacques Kallis became the second all-rounder after West Indies icon Garry Sobers to achieve the Test triple of 8000 runs, 200 wickets and 100 catches. Statistically, their achievements appear almost identical, as shown below:

Player	Tests	Runs	Average	100s	Wickets	Average	5w/i	Catches
Garry Sobers	93	8032	57.78	26	235	34.03	6	109
Jacques Kallis	116	9477	57.78	29	229	30.91	5	121

5w/i = 5 wickets per innings

Also both have achieved the double of scoring a century and taking five wickets in an innings in the same Test twice each. As Kallis is under 33, there are quite a few years of cricket left in him and he may become the first player to perform the Test triple of 10,000 runs, 200 wickets and 100 catches.

Also Kallis is close to the one-day international (ODI) triple of 10,000 runs, 200 wickets and 100 catches, having amassed 9541 runs at 45.21, 239 wickets at 31.53 and 101 catches in 274 ODIs. As Sobers did not play one-day internationals, we cannot compare the two at the shortened

*Jacques Kallis drives powerfully against
Pakistan in the 2007 Lahore Test.*

Kallis celebrates his century against Pakistan in the 2007 Karachi Test.

version of the game but at Test level they have run neck to neck. However, on personality and flamboyance they are poles apart. Also the standard of bowling has fallen considerably in recent times.

Sobers was an extrovert left-hander who oozed crowd appeal and put entertainment above statistics. Without trying to be unkind to Kallis, the right-hander thrives on facts and figures and craves for averages rather than accolades. He guards his wicket as a fortress á la Trevor Bailey and Geoff Boycott; reaching milestones being his main goal. Not that he is selfish, his long tenures at the pitch have saved many matches for his team. He prefers ruthless efficiency to adventurous hitting. And no one can even approach Sobers's three-in-one bowling style which has put him in a class of his own as an all-rounder. Although not as different as chalk and cheese, Sobers and Kallis represented vastly different varieties of cheese.

After a tentative start in Test cricket as a 20-year-old in 1995, he made his mark in the Rawalpindi Test against Pakistan in October 1997 when he scored 61. This Test was watched by Queen Elizabeth and the Duke of Edinburgh celebrating Pakistan's 50th Independence Anniversary.

Then in the first Test against Australia in Melbourne two months later, he scored a match-saving 101 in the second innings. Needing 381 runs to win in 122 overs, South Africa managed to survive, thanks to Kallis's maiden Test century. His patient innings contained many stylish drives as he ignored a volley of sledging by the frustrated opponents. His stolid defence earned him the Man of the Match award. In Sydney in the next match he became Shane Warne's 300th Test victim.

Although he has hit 29 Test centuries, he remembers his 87 against Sri Lanka in Kandy in 2000 with pride as it resulted in a surprise win for his country. Earlier South Africa had lost the first Test in Galle by an innings (ace spinner Muttiah Muralitharan claiming 13 Proteas wickets) and crowd came for the second Test in Kandy in droves to see their country clinch the rubber. Instead, South Africa delivered a knockout blow on the fourth day to square the series. It was a cliffhanger as the tourists won by seven runs. Trailing by 55 runs in the first innings, South Africa was in trouble at 3 for 50. But a typically fighting innings from Kallis in four hours on a difficult pitch with a quirky bounce gave them a whiff of success. Sri Lanka needed only 177 to win the Test and the series but lost both the openers Marvan Atapattu and skipper Sanath Jayasuriya for ducks. They never recovered from this horror start and lost.

After scoring back-to-back centuries in ODIs in two days in June 2003 he said that he was happy because it would boost his father's morale as he fought cancer. Normally Kallis shows little emotion after scoring a century, not even after recording his first double century against England in The Oval Test of August 2003. He had batted for seven hours for his 200 and was probably too exhausted to lift and twirl his bat around!

But 2003–04 proved to be a very good season for Kallis when he became only the second player in Test history after Sir Donald Bradman to score centuries in each of his five successive Tests. This was his amazing run sequence against the West Indies: 158 and 44; 177; 73 and 130 not out; 130 not out. Then in his next series against New Zealand he made 92 and 150 not out in Hamilton to complete five centuries in five Tests. He was going for his sixth consecutive ton in Auckland but could make only 40 and 71. Just 29 more runs in the second innings and he would have equalled Bradman's record of 6 hundreds in six Tests. However, in five consecutive Tests in 2003–04, he had amassed 954 runs at 190.80.

Although labelled a slow coach, he hit the fastest Test fifty by number of balls faced. Against Zimbabwe in Cape Town in March 2005 he reached his 50 off 24 balls. Pakistan's master-tonker Shahid Afridi comes next with a 26-minute fifty.

Kallis's best bowling feat was against the West Indies in the Bridgetown Test of March–April 2002 when he took 6 for 67 and 2 for 34. It was a controversial match which South Africa should have won but for some blatant time-wasting tactics by the home team.

Kallis is one of four cricketers to have scored a century and taken five wickets in an innings in the same Test twice. The Cape Town Test of January 1999 is remembered as Kallis's Test. He confirmed himself as an all-rounder when he became only the eighth player in Test history to score both a century and a fifty and take five wickets in an innings in the same match.

> *The Cape Town Test of January 1999 is remembered as Kallis's Test.*

South Africa won the toss and batted but opener Gary Kirsten was out to the first ball off Curtly Ambrose and in walked Kallis to face some chin music. He scored 110 and added 235 runs for the third wicket with Daryll Cullinan. Kallis took 2 for 34 as his team led by 194 runs. He remained not out with 88 in the second knock as skipper 'Hansie' Cronje declared, thus narrowly missing the distinction of hitting two tons in a match. Kallis captured 5 for 90 to enable South Africa to win the Test and lead 3–0 in the series. Man of the Match Kallis was on the field for all but four hours of the match, having batted for 12 hours and bowled 42.4 overs.

Jacques Kallis repeated the century and '5-fer' double in the Potchefstroom Test against the L-plated Bangladeshis in October 2002. He took 2 for 26 and 5 for 21 and stroked an unbeaten 139 as his team won by an innings. However, the Cape Town Test gave Kallis greater satisfaction as it was achieved against Ambrose and other quickies.

As narrated before, 2004 was the year he shone out as a pure batsman as injuries forced him to bowl less. But advice from team-mate Mark Boucher and a passionate plea from skipper Graeme Smith helped Kallis to regain his zing as a bowler. Boucher compared Kallis's bowling to Pakistani Wasim Akram's. He wrote in *The Wisden Cricketer*—South Africa edition: 'To me, the key to Jacques's performance as a bowler is his change of pace. Wasim Akram was brilliant at that. He was very difficult to line up by batsmen. The same is true of Kallis, he can suddenly turn on the heat and bowl at 145 km per hour.'

> *The same is true of Kallis, he can suddenly turn on the heat and bowl at 145 km per hour.*

In 2005 he was honoured as the ICC's Test and overall Player of the Year after all-round performances against the West Indies and England. 'Until the emergence of Andrew Flintoff, he was by some distance the leading all-rounder in the world game, capable of swinging the ball sharply at surprising pace off a relaxed run-up', wrote *Cricinfo*.

On the Autralian tour in 2005–06, he had problems facing Brett Lee's pace-like-fire in the Melbourne Test. But he made a patient 111 in the first innings of the Sydney Test in January 2006. His slow unbeaten fifty in the second innings perhaps cost South Africa the match which is remembered for Australian captain Ricky Ponting scoring centuries in both innings in his 100th Test.

Against Pakistan at home in early 2007, Kallis continued to perform well as an all-rounder, being the leading run-scorer and an effective bowler.

In the 2007 World Cup in the West Indies he scored 485 runs (highest for South Africa and fifth highest in the tournament) at 80.83. His run sequence was 128 not out, 48, 86, 66 not out, 32, 81, 22, 17 not out and 5. But he failed against champion Australia in both the Super-8 and in the semi final and his sluggish approach at the crease drew criticism. In bowling he had an economy rate of 4.44. On the whole it was a disappointing World Cup for South Africa because so much was expected from them.

However, the words of Brian Lara must have comforted Kallis. The West Indian legend said during the 2007 World Cup, 'If you want someone to bat for your life, you get Jacques Kallis to bat for your life'.

Encouraged, he was at his supreme best against Pakistan in October 2007, hitting three centuries in two Tests. In Karachi he stroked 155 and an unbeaten 100 as his country won by 160 runs and followed with 59 and 107 not out in Lahore the following week and was adjudged Man of the Match for both the Tests and Player of the Series. But wait, there is more! In his next two Tests, against New Zealand he continued his prolific rungetting, 29 and 186 in Johannesburg and 131 in Centurion. Thus he totalled 767 runs in four consecutive Tests at an astounding average of 153.40. Raved Osman Samiuddin in *The Wisden Cricketer* (UK), 'The first [century in Karachi] was the best, a Kallis displaced from his bubble, Kallis as entertainer… Key wickets and a stunning slips catch or two added another layer.'

Neither pace nor spin bothers Jacques Kallis. Nor do top quality batsmen or critics who doubt his all-round ability.

DANIEL VETTORI
New Zealand

Vettori does not have the charisma of Miller, Botham, Imran, Warne, Flintoff or Tendulkar but his figures are impressive if not spectacular. Vettori has been on international scene for only 10 years and more is expected of him. Youngest to play Test cricket for New Zealand—he was only 18 years and 10 days when he made his Test debut—and Sir Richard Hadlee's record of 431 Test scalps for a New Zealander is not beyond him.

As you watch Daniel Vettori getting ready to bowl his subtle variety of spin or walking in to bat at number seven for a rescue act, he resembles an academic trying to explain his latest scientific discovery. Perhaps it is those spectacles which give him a scholarly look. But the quiet achiever does his job as a bowler and, in crises, as a batsman. So little is written on this left-hander that it comes as a shock that he is one of select 14 cricketers to achieve the Test double of 2000 runs and 200 wickets, scoring 2627 runs at 27.36, has hit two centuries (he is one of only 15 in Test history to score a century batting at number nine) and 16 fifties, taken 241 wickets at 34.51 including five wickets in an innings 13 times and 10 wickets in a match in three Tests. And he is under 30.

Born on 27 January 1979, the teenager had his Test initiation against England at Wellington in February 1997 after playing only two first-class matches. Sent in to bat at no. 11, he remained unbeaten in both innings and impressed with his left-arm spin taking 2 for 98 off 34.3 steady overs.

His best came against Australia in the Auckland Test of March 2000 when he captured 5 for 62 and 7 for 87. His victims included Steve

"Oh no!" Vettori laments as a West Indian batsman is dropped off his bowling in the 2006 Auckland Test.

Daniel Vettori is ecstatic after taking Shane
Warne's wicket in the 2004 Brisbane Test.

Waugh, Damien Martyn (twice), Greg Blewett, Justin Langer, Mark Waugh and Adam Gilchrist. When Vettori clean bowled Martyn, he had his 100th wicket in 29 Tests at the age of 21 and became the youngest spinner to reach this milestone. His 12 wicket haul was second best for a New Zealander after Hadlee's epic 15 for 123 also against Australia in the Brisbane Test of November 1985. Like Hadlee, Vettori enjoys bowling against Australian batsmen.

He had his form slump in 2002–03 when he could take only 16 wickets in nine Tests but he came back with a bang in Bangladesh in October 2004. New Zealand trounced the home team by innings in both the Tests and the victorious Vettori took 2 for 26 and 6 for 28 in Dhaka and 6 for 70 and 6 for 100 in Chittagong. He captured 20 wickets in the series, more than twice as many as any other player, at an astounding average of 11.20 and was a unanimous choice for the Man of the Series award.

In the one-day series that followed he took over captaincy from Stephen Fleming and won 3–0, Vettori snaring seven wickets at 9.86. Admittedly, the opposition was weak but to capture 27 wickets at 10.85 in five Internationals was pleasing for him and his supporters.

A handy left-hand batsman, he has registered two Test hundreds. Against a strong Pakistani attack, he scored an unbeaten 137 in Hamilton in December 2003. He came in at number 9 and reached his maiden Test hundred from 131 balls and hit 20 fours dispatched to all parts of the field as he added 99 runs for the ninth wicket. 'He unfurled a range of strokes of the purest quality', wrote *Wisden* 2005.

His second century was against Zimbabwe in the first Test in Harare in August 2005. Batting at number 8, he top scored with 127 and added 76 runs with Brendon McCullum. He took 2 for 1 and 4 for 28 as Zimbabwe collapsed for 59 and 99 and the Kiwis triumphed by an innings. It was one of the shortest Tests ever, finishing in two days. He scored 48 and pocketed 2 for 56 and 3 for 66 in the next and final Test in Bulawayo. But these all-round successes gave Vettori little joy as the opposition was embarrassingly weak.

The youngest spinner to take 100 Test wickets, he was considered in 2005 as among three world's best spinners after Shane Warne and Muttiah Muralitharan. He was selected in the World team which toured Australia in October 2005. Although he did not set Melbourne's Telstra Dome on fire, along with Muralitharan, he twice restricted Australia to attainable totals. But the batsmen in the star-studded World XI flopped and they lost all three one-dayers in Melbourne and the Super Test on the Sydney Cricket Ground.

It is as a bowler rather than as an all-rounder that Daniel Vettori will be remembered. His subtle variations in flight and length, his mastery of drift and usual lower-order batting make him his country's most valuable player. It is his guile that sometimes converts what appears a harmless delivery into an unplayable hand grenade. Taking over from Stephen Fleming as the captain in 2007, Vettori promises to be New Zealand's best bowling all-rounder after Richard Hadlee and Chris Cairns.

ANDREW FLINTOFF
England

Andrew 'Freddie' Flintoff, the bulky English all-rounder described as the second Ian Botham, is a three-in-one cricketer. He was behind England regaining the Ashes in 2005. He has a magnetic persona, a joie de vivre that draws spectators in, that indefinable 'lure of the animal'. Those who put enjoyment above technique feel that he has made cricket exciting again. Like Keith Miller, Imran Khan and Ian Botham before him, he has that certain appeal. Brian Lara may not pick Flintoff to save his life but what would life be worth without the likes of Denis Compton, Frank Worrell, Neil Harvey, Miller, Botham, Adam Gilchrist and 'Freddie'?

A simple Lancastrian, Flintoff divides items in two categories, things that matter and things that shatter. In his relatively short career of 67 Tests, he has hit 77 sixes. (Australia's Gilchrist tops the list with 100 sixes in 96 Tests, followed by Lara 88 in 131, New Zealander Chris Cairns 87 in 62 and 'Master Blaster' Viv Richards 84 in 121.) One of Flintoff's sixes almost landed in his father Colin's palms on the upper tier of the Ryder Stand during the Birmingham Test against the West Indies in July 2004. But Dad dropped it for which Andrew roasted him during his end of play interview. He could afford to be facetious because this was after his effervescent 167 off 191 balls, inclusive of 17 fours and 7 sixes.

His nickname Freddie was coined by John Stanworth, the coach of Lancashire Second XI, when he was 15 as his surname rhymed with the lovable cartoon character Fred Flinstone.

'Freddie' Flintoff is in seventh heaven after dismissing
India's Rahul Dravid in the 2006 Mumbai Test.

To quote Stephen Moss from *The Guardian*, 'He [Flintoff] is funny, unaffected by and unchanged with stardom. He is still the big, brawny boy from Preston who likes a pint and a laugh, and most of all, loves the game of cricket.' *Wisden* 2004 named him as one of the Five Cricketers of the Year and described him as a farmhand delighting in the coconut shy and a blond Apollo.

Born on 6 December 1977 in Preston, a cricket town north of Manchester, he strikes sixes and shatters stumps with the delight of an uncomplicated schoolboy. 'He is so laid-back, he should be an Australian really', says Stuart Law who represented Australia in one Test in 1995 and played county cricket for Lancashire with Flintoff. In the 2003 County Championship, Law averaged 91.00 with the bat, second only to Flintoff's average of 103.80. Law added, 'Freddie would give [David] Boon's 52 cans [of beer] on a London to Melbourne trip a real nudge'.

Australians have a high esteem of 'Freddie'. Isn't esteem a second cousin of awe? Bob Simpson, as shrewd a judge of cricketers and characters as any, wrote in *Sportstar* (India) a few years ago, 'He is one hell of a cricketer and no matter what status he reaches, he will remain the same easygoing giant. I first met him when I coached Lancashire in 1990 and 1991. He was a respectful, gentle giant then and I doubt whether stardom will change him.'

Simpson was impressed with his ability to judge the length of the ball and his technique. Early in his career, the English selectors and management saw his bulk as fat, and the English press joyfully jumped on the bandwagon and harassed young Flintoff. According to Simpson, these criticisms were unfair: 'Like Merv Hughes, Flintoff is always the life of the party and kept the spirit of the dressing room high'. Also like Merv, Flintoff works hard at the nets.

The impression he sometimes gives that he is all brawn and no brains is false. He is bright and was his Lancashire school's chess champion. When batting he hits cleanly and runs fast, picking up ones and twos. As a bowler he is accurate and was earlier used as a stock bowler. Later, skipper Michael Vaughan tried him as a strike bowler with devastating effect. He fields well and has taken some spectacular catches.

He is a good listener and welcomes advice. He is courteous and says 'Thank you' for the smallest favour given. He is 193cm tall, currently weighs 101kg and resembles a Viking rather than Fred Flintstone. He is a softy really and a dog lover who owns three boxer dogs. A team man, a century does not mean much to him unless it brings victory. He made an unimpressive Test debut in July 1998 against South Africa in Nottingham, scoring 17 runs and taking one wicket. The next Test in Leeds was a disaster for him as he made a pair and failed to take a wicket. He was probably too overwhelmed or too overweight or both.

He was pulled up by his manager 'Chubby' Chandler, former Lancashire teammate Neil Fairbrother and England's team coach Duncan Fletcher. They bluntly told him that he was wasting his talent. He cut down on his beer and pies, visited gym regularly and lost 15kg as fat Freddie turned into fit Flintoff in 2004. Against New Zealand and the West Indies that summer, he scored 597 runs at 59.70, hitting a century and six fifties, and captured 24 wickets at 24.50. A star was born.

Among his memorable moments in 2004 were:

- *blasting a six-studded 167 off 191 balls against the Windies in the Birmingham Test*
- *dismissing Brian Lara on the verge of a century in the same Test*
- *scoring an unbeaten 57 which guided England to victory in the Manchester Test*
- *registering 50s in seven successive Tests*
- *hitting 104 off 91 balls against Sri Lanka in the ICC Championship Trophy at the Rose Bowl. He smashed 9 fours and 3 sixes, scoring his first 50 off 69 balls and then racing to his next 50 off only 20.*

Soon after, he was voted Player of the Year by Professional Cricketers' Association, ahead of Andrew Strauss, Steve Harmison and Vaughan. This was after scoring three centuries and a 99 in his last seven one-day internationals (ODIs). To top it all, he became a father in 2004, a Bam-Bam for Dad Fred Flintstone—sorry Flintoff!

He belts the ball all over the ground and bowls at around 145kph without sacrificing his accuracy. He is also the master of reverse-swing. Well, this was before his ankle injury which affected his progress in 2006 and 2007.

In the Ashes summer of 2005, Flintoff established himself as England's greatest all-rounder since Ian Botham, producing a succession of inspirational performances to score 402 runs and take 24 wickets in five exciting Tests and carry his team to glory in one of the greatest Ashes series of all time. It was a performance that delighted the nation starved of success, and propelled Flintoff to superstar status.

He single-handedly inspired England to a two-run victory over Australia at Edgbaston, in one of the greatest Tests of all time by scoring 68 and 73 (belting 9 sixes) and taking 3 for 52 and 4 for 79. He followed it with a maiden Ashes hundred at Trent Bridge, sealed the series with a marathon five-wicket haul at The Oval, and was presented the Compton-Miller Medal for Man of the Series. The celebrations for the Ashes triumph went on all night, culminating in an open-top bus parade through the streets of London. By now, he was a global superstar a la Shane Warne or Sachin Tendulkar.

> *Flintoff's finest hour was the manner in which he stepped into the breach as England's captain, on an injury-plagued tour of India.*

But arguably Flintoff's finest hour was the manner in which he stepped into the breach as England's captain, on an injury-plagued tour of India the following season. Leading from the front, he put up a grand all-round performance, grabbing 11 wickets and making five fifties in six innings, as England defied the odds to draw the series 1–1.

In July 2006 he underwent surgery on his left ankle, missing the Test and one-day series against Pakistan but recovered ahead of schedule. He was named England's captain for the Ashes in 2006–07 but both his batting and bowling were disappointing and England was routed 0–5 by the rampaging Australians. Led by Ricky Ponting, the Aussies were thirsting for revenge for the 2005 Ashes loss. Flintoff's batting deteriorated under pressure and the troublesome ankle required further injections throughout the series.

It was a sad fall from sublime to ridiculous for Freddie and at the end it was a sharp contrast to the beer-fuelled celebrations 16 months earlier. He atoned in part by leading England to a surprise victory in the subsequent one-day Commonwealth Bank Series, after being handed back the captaincy by the injured Michael Vaughan.

His form deserted him again in the Caribbean for the 2007 World Cup and he will be sadly remembered for one incident—capsizing a pedalo in the sea in St Lucia following England's defeat to New Zealand. As a consequence he was dropped from the next match against Canada and stripped of the vice-captaincy. He continued to pound away with the ball but his efforts with the bat became embarrassing. By the end of the World Cup he appeared broken and exhausted and missed the start of England's international summer against the West Indies because of an ankle injury. His 'escapade' in St Lucia was soundly criticised by skipper Vaughan.

Flintoff has scored 3381 runs at 32.50 with five centuries (highest score 167) in 67 Tests and taken 197 wickets at 32.02 (best 5–58) and 44 catches. Equally prolific in one-day internationals, he has amassed 3090 runs at 31.53 and captured 146 wickets at 25.10 and took 41 catches.

His all-round form is essential for England to regain its 2005 supremacy. Many factors contributed to England's rise and rise in 2004 and 2005, batsmen Strauss and Marcus Trescothick, fast bowler Steve Harmison and the steadying influence of skipper Vaughan. But Flintoff was the catalyst, the enzyme that digests the opponents, the syringe that injects the fear factor as he transfused red corpuscles into a once anaemic England.

Michael Brearley, the former England captain, wrote: 'Like Botham, Flintoff has become a hero who makes visible the link between village green and Test arena. Each embodies the small boy wish of us all, to have superhuman strength, power and flair. He is a charismatic all-rounder with a huge grin. He has given England self belief—he is the Australian among Englishmen. His presence lifts the morale.'

After Flintoff's slide in 2007, Simon Wilde wrote in the December 2007 issue of *The Wisden Cricketer* (UK), 'The spirit is willing but the foot is weak and future bleak … He has gone from national treasure to holy relic in a year of diminishing returns.'

But not everyone is that pessimistic. 'Flintoff brings everything to the party. On his day there are not many cricketers who can match up. He is the best all-rounder of the day.' And who said that? Brian Lara, arguably the best batsman of his day.

2 Wicketkeeping Test All-Rounders

A wicketkeeper is like a pianist in an orchestra, there is room for only one. The second best keeper can get in the side only if he is a capable batsman.

Having featured Test cricketers who stood out with both bat and ball, let us train our binoculars on wicketkeepers who won Test matches using their bats and gloves. To this author, expertise with bat and gloves also constitutes all-round excellence.

This could start a debate. Why not include outstanding fielders who batted prolifically as all-rounders? But then the ability to take catches has been a criterion in including bat/ball all-rounders, namely Wally Hammond, Alan Davidson and Jacques Kallis to give three examples. However, unlike fielders, wicketkeepers rarely bowl and can never be counted as all-rounders unless the dismissals they make (catching and stumping) are added to their batting prowess.

If Australia lacks a genuine batsman–bowler all-rounder at Test level since the retirements of Richie Benaud and Davidson in early 1960s, Rod Marsh, Ian Healy and Adam Gilchrist have helped in Australia reaching the top rung of cricket with their aggressive batting and acrobatic work behind the stumps. They were, to some extent, as much match-winners as Keith Miller, Garry Sobers, Ian Botham, Imran Khan, Richard Hadlee and Kapil Dev were for their respective countries.

All 15 cricketers featured in this chapter are all-rounders, good at keeping and batting.

So let us profile the gloved all-rounders from England's Les Ames and Godfrey Evans to the current terrific trio of Gilchrist, South African Mark Boucher and Kumar Sangakkara of Sri Lanka.

LES AMES
England

In many ways LEG (Leslie Ethelbert George) Ames epitomised a gloved Test all-rounder. His legs were always padded, whether batting or keeping. This whimsical opening does not do justice to Ames as he took cricket very seriously, spending most of his life as a professional cricketer—either in front or behind the stumps.

A cheerful and bubbly character, he was strongly built and equally at ease keeping to the thunderbolts of Harold Larwood, the fastish swing of Bill Voce or the spin wizardry of 'Tich' Freeman. Also he kept scoreboard operators busy with his entertaining batting as he was the first world-class wicketkeeper batsman.

He was good enough to play for England as a batsman. No other wicketkeeper has scored 100 first-class centuries (102, including nine double hundreds). In 593 first-class matches he amassed 37,248 runs at 43.51, including 2434 runs (with eight centuries) at 40.56 in 47 Tests. He also made 1121 dismissals (703 caught and 418 stumped) in first-class matches including 97 (74 caught and 23 stumped) in Tests. His total of 418 stumpings at first-class level remains a record after six decades.

Born on 3 December 1905 in Elham, Kent, he dominated both keeping and batting for Kent and England. He remains the only player to achieve the double of 1000 runs and 100 dismissals in a season three times, in 1928, 1929 and 1932. The only other cricketer to do this double subsequently was John T. Murray for Middlesex, in 1957. In 1932 Ames became the only one to score 2000 runs (2482 at 57.72 with nine centuries) and make 100 (104) dismissals

Les Ames drives with power and precision against the West Indies in 1939.

including a record 64 stumpings. The next season he amassed 3058 runs hitting three double centuries and six centuries. His highest score was 295 in only four hours against Gloucestershire in 1933. It included a six and 34 spanking fours.

His performances at Test level were no less impressive. His best moment as a batsman was in the Lord's Test against Australia in 1934. Australia was full of confidence after winning the first Test at Nottingham by 238 runs.

Wicketkeeping Test All-Rounders

England was struggling at 5 for 182 at Lord's when Ames joined Maurice Leyland. They added 129 precious runs for the sixth wicket and with left-arm spinner Hedley Verity capturing 15 wickets in the match, 14 for 20 in a single day, England won by an innings. Ames's 120 was the first century by a wicketkeeper in an Ashes series and he was more proud of this innings than anything else he achieved. As icing on the cake, he caught Don Bradman off Verity for 13 in the second innings.

Earlier, in the Lord's Test against New Zealand in June 1931, Ames (137) added 246 runs with 'Gubby' Allen for the eighth wicket. Then in the Christchurch Test, also against the Kiwis, in March 1933, Ames (103) added 242 runs in 145 minutes with the majestic Wally Hammond (227) for the fifth wicket. Ames (115) had another memorable partnership with Hammond against South Africa in the Cape Town Test of 1938–39 when adding 195 runs in 145 minutes for the fourth wicket.

Ames recorded his top Test score, 149, against the West Indies in 1929–30 and aggregated 417 runs at an excellent average of 59.57 in the series. The West Indians remained his favourite foes and he dismissed eight of them in The Oval Test of 1933, (caught two, stumped two in the first innings and caught four in the second) as England triumphed by an innings and clinched the rubber 2–0. He stumped the legendary George Headley for nine in the first innings and caught him for 12 in the second.

As a wicketkeeper Les Ames was unobtrusive and efficient. No flamboyant gestures for him. His glove work was neat and economical, he was more like Australia's Bert Oldfield rather than his successors in Kent and England, Godfrey Evans and Alan Knott. With fellow Kentish man 'Tich' Freeman, a spinner, Ames formed a celebrated bowler–keeper combination in the 1930s as Alan Davidson and Wally Grout did in the the 1950s and 1960s, and Dennis Lillee and Rod Marsh ('caught Marsh, bowled Lillee') in the 1970s and 1980s.

The Ames–Freeman partnership reached its zenith in 1928 when Freeman captured a record 304 wickets and Ames made 122 dismissals and scored 1919 runs as well.

After retirement, Ames became a national selector in 1950s when England was on top. He was the manager of England's touring teams on three occasions. 'He was without doubt the greatest wicketkeeper batsman the game has so far produced', wrote *Wisden* 1991.

There were discussions that there were better wicketkeepers in England than Ames and he was a permanent member of the team because of his batting. *Wisden* disagreed. 'If this was so, would [Douglas] Jardine, for example, have preferred him to [George] Duckworth in Australia in 1932–33? Surely not.' When fit, Ames was England's first choice wicketkeeper from 1931 to 1939 and an integral part of Kent cricket from 1927 to 1951.

I had the pleasure of seeing him score an unbeaten century during the Commonwealth team's tour of India in 1950–51 with Ames as the captain and Duckworth as the manager. In 18 tour matches, Ames scored 595 runs at 37.18 with two centuries, his highest being an unbeaten 116 against Prime Minister's XI in Bombay in March 1951.

Ames died on 26 February 1990 aged 84. Thousands turned up at his memorial service held in Canterbury Cathedral. This was a worthy tribute to a man of outstanding all-round talent.

GODFREY EVANS
England

Exuberant, ebullient and extrovert are the terms that describe this daredevilishly outstanding wicketkeeper batsman. He dived full length to collect balls on either side, making difficult catches look easy and at times easy catches look difficult.

He loved entertaining the crowd and was delighted to receive applause. He appealed with gusto and delighted in lifting the ball skywards. Evans scored over 2000 runs in Test cricket (2439 at 20.49 in 91 Tests). He hit two Test tons and narrowly missed out on scoring a century before lunch against India at Lord's in June 1952. Being theatrical, he made nonsense of the theory that wicketkeepers should not be showy.

In 1950s, Godfrey Evans dominated the play in front or behind the stumps. Until fellow Kentish man Alan Knott surpassed him, Evans held the record for most dismissals in Test arena. He was brilliant in everything he did. As a keeper he took catches few others could have reached and as a batsman he had a rich repertoire of strokes, some of his own invention. In 465 first-class matches he scored 14,882 runs at 21.22 with seven centuries and made 1066 dismissals (816 caught, 250 stumped).

Two of his seven first-class centuries were hit in Tests; 104 vs the West Indies in Manchester in 1950 and 104 vs India at Lord's in 1952. He also holds a most un-Evans-like batting record, experiencing the most agonising wait by a batsman on the verge of a 'pair'. In the Adelaide Test against Australia in February 1947 he remained scoreless for 97 minutes.

After being bowled first ball in the first innings, he came to the crease 45 minutes before stumps on the fourth day. It was crisis time and the normally

*A sight for the Gods. Don Bradman cuts and
Godfrey Evans keeps in the 1948 Trent Bridge Test.*

dashing Denis Compton controlled the strike. Evans faced 20 balls in 45
minutes that day and could have taken a single or two but Compton sent
him back to farm the strike. Still on a 'pair', he had a restless night. After a
further 52 run-less minutes on the final day, he scored his first run. He went
on to make an unbeaten 10 and the Test was drawn.

His favourite memory was the Lord's Test against India in 1952 when he
struck 98 runs before lunch on his way to a breezy 104 and, in the same match,
became the first wicketkeeper from England to make 100 Test dismissals. He

went on to make 219 dismissals (173 caught and 46 stumped) which was then a record. Trevor Bailey remembers one catch in the Melbourne Test of 1950–51 when Evans caught Neil Harvey off Alec Bedser 'one-handed, horizontal and airborne down the leg side off a genuine leg-glance'. After retirement, his huge and graying mutton-chop whiskers became his trademark as he lent boundless energy to charity matches and was employed by bookmaker Ladbrokes to organise odds at big matches.

A jovial character and fond of nightlife, he once joked that the CBE he received stood for Crumpet Before Evensong! He died on 3 May 1999 aged 78. In his obituary, *Wisden* 2000 wrote, 'Godfrey Evans was arguably the best wicketkeeper the game has ever seen… What is beyond question is that he was the game's most charismatic keeper: the man who made the game's least obtrusive specialism a spectator sport in itself. His energy and enthusiasm brought the best out of other fielders, whatever the state of the game. But he added to that a technical excellence that has probably never been surpassed.'

Colin Cowdrey eulogised at his memorial service, 'Behind the stumps, Godfrey Evans was a genius—no doubt about that. In a sense, he was something of a genius off the field too, for being such enormous fun and for his eternal optimism.'

FAROKH ENGINEER

India

Nicknamed 'Rooky', Farokh Engineer was the best wicketkeeper batsman produced by India. Handsome and athletic, he batted with gusto and kept wickets like an acrobat in a circus. He was a young man in hurry, took risks and mostly got away with it. His 94 before lunch against a fierce Windies attack in the Chennai Test of January 1967 was unforgettable.

Like Evans, Engineer scored over 2000 runs in Test cricket and just missed out on scoring a century before lunch; against the West Indies at Madras (now Chennai) in January 1967.

As a wicketkeeper he was brash and brilliant and often airborne. No wonder, his hero was Godfrey Evans! Like Evans he could reach the wildest leg-glances with a horizontal dive and flick off the bails in an instant, if the batsman's heel was raised a millimetre. In 46 Tests he scored 2611 runs at 31.08 with two centuries and 16 fifties and dismissed 82 batsmen, 66 caught and 16 stumped. In a first-class career spanning from 1958 to 1976 for Mumbai, India and Lancashire, he made 13,436 runs at 29.52 with 13 centuries and affected 824 dismissals (704 caught and 120 stumped).

Surprisingly, he was not an automatic choice for India, facing stiff challenge from the aggressive batsman keeper Budhi Kunderan. Only from 1965 onwards, he became a fixture in the Indian Test team.

Of all his innings, he remembers his 53 and 40 (top score against Wes Hall on the rampage) at Kingston in March 1962. However, his most audacious Test innings came against the West Indies in January 1967 in Chennai. Opening India's innings for the first time, he hammered 109 runs, 94 coming

*India's agile wicketkeeper Farokh Engineer runs out
England's John Jameson in The Oval Test of 1971.*

before lunch on the first day, against a formidable attack of Wes Hall, Charlie
Griffith, Garry Sobers and Lance Gibbs.

Engineer toured Australia in 1967–68 and then with Rest of the World XI
under Sobers in 1971–72. It was on the latter tour that he made his top score
in first-class cricket, 192 against a Combined XI in Hobart.

Against England in India in 1972–73, he topped the Test batting average
with 415 runs at 41.50. In the final Test of this series in Mumbai in February
1973, he opened India's innings and played an attacking innings of 121,

his highest at Test level, and 66 in the second. He had added 192 runs with skipper Ajit Wadekar in the first innings and 135 with Sunil Gavaskar in the second. India won the series 2–1 so it was a match to remember for 'Rooky' Engineer.

On the tour of England in 1974, he once again headed the Test batting average, 195 runs at 39.00 but India was whitewashed 0–3. His highest score in that series was 86 in the Lord's Test when he added 101 runs with Gavaskar for the first wicket. After retirement from Test cricket he settled in Lancashire playing county cricket with the same intensity and aggression. His popularity there was reflected by the lucrative amount he received in his Testimonial in 1976. Here are some of the plaudits he earned in the Testimonial Year Book *Farokh*:

Fellow stumper Alan Knott: 'Farokh is capable of really brilliant things behind the stumps. I'll never forget him catching John Edrich in an India against England Test match at Lord's off the bowling of left-arm spinner Bishan Bedi. John got a thick edge which saw the ball hit Farokh on the body and as it fell towards the ground he flicked it up into the air with his left foot to take a truly unbelievable catch.'

Former great English batsman Tom Graveney: 'He [Farokh] was acrobatic and had tremendously fast reflexes, getting to the ball and removing the bails in a flash if the batsman's foot was raised. Farokh was also a top-flight batsman and served both India and Lancashire with distinction.'

Colin Cowdrey wrote in Farokh's biography *From the Far Pavilion*: 'In all my cricket years I have not known anyone who has embodied the true spirit of cricket more completely than Farokh Engineer. He is the keenest and liveliest of cricketers.'

I had the pleasure of renewing our acquaintance in Sydney in February 2007. Currently the vice President of Lancashire Cricket Club, he has put on some weight but has remained the same charming self. As expected, Godfrey Evans featured in our conversation.

Farokh's heroes? Frank Worrell and Godfrey Evans. People who helped him reach the top? Polly Umrigar and Godfrey. Bowler he hated to face: No-one! This was typical of Farokh who would talk with anyone on the street but still look like a prince. No wonder he is referred to as King Farokh, and jokingly as the Persian Pirate—being a Parsee, he has a Persian ancestry. Mutton-chop Godfrey Evans and Persian Pirate King Farokh had cricket in their veins and spectators at their feet.

JAMES M. PARKS

England

James M. Parks was an outstanding batsman and part-time but efficient wicketkeeper. He was the famous son of England's Test cricketer James H. Parks. JM (Jim) Parks was at his best against spinners.

Jim Parks was born on 21 October 1931 in Sussex and made his mark as a batsman in his early twenties. However, he donned wicketkeeping gloves for the first time in 1958 when the regular Sussex keeper was injured. He was so successful standing back that he took over the job on a regular basis the next season. He had made his Test debut in July 1954 as a batsman in Manchester against Pakistan.

He was in and out of the team and was flown to the Caribbean as a replacement in 1959–60. Coming in the final Test in Port-of-Spain in March 1960 at the eleventh hour, Parks made 43 and a match-saving 101 not out (adding 197 runs with MJK Smith for the seventh wicket), stumped Clyde Walcott in the first innings and caught him in the second, and also stumped Conrad Hunte. What a fairy tale Test for the newly arrived!

When John T. Murray was injured in 1963, Parks established himself as England's gloveman, taking some brilliant catches standing back and scoring runs, his forte. He toured Australia, New Zealand, India, South Africa and the West Indies from 1963 to 1967. In 46 Tests he scored 1962 runs at 32.16 with two centuries and nine fifties and made 114 dismissals, 103 caught and 11 stumped. He did not keep wickets in three Tests when he took two catches and scored 86 runs at 28.66.

England's wicketkeeper batsman Jim Parks hooks—and no need to run. It's a four.

In 739 first-class matches from 1949 to 1976, he accumulated 36,673 runs at 34.76 with 51 centuries and 213 fifties and effected 1181 dismissals (1087 caught, 94 stumped). Not all of his catches were taken as a keeper.

ALEC STEWART
England

Alec Stewart was a paradox. When in full flow he could pulverise any attack. At his best against fast bowlers, he cover drove with flourish and pulled with panache. His two centuries as an opening batsman against the fiery pace of Curtly Ambrose and the nagging accuracy of Courtney Walsh in the Bridgetown Test of April 1994 were memorable. Alec Stewart was in his element against quickies but less secure against spin bowlers.

He scored 118 in the first innings off 221 balls, spanking 18 fours, on his 31st birthday. Three days later he stroked 143 off 319 balls with 20 fours to become the first England batsman to score a hundred in each innings of a Test against the Windies. He added 171 runs for the opening wicket with skipper Michael Atherton in the first innings and 150 with Graham Thorpe for the seventh wicket in the second. After losing the first three Tests, a victory in this Test by 208 runs was some consolation for England and a moment to cherish for Man of the Match Stewart.

What pleased him even more was that his twin hundreds had enabled England to inflict only the second defeat on their hosts in 30 Bridgetown Tests. England became only the second visiting team to win a Bridgetwon Test since Bob Wyatt's England team had done 60 years previously in 1934–35.

But he had weakness against the turning ball and was inconsistent as a batsman. To quote Lawrence Booth from *Cricinfo*, '… his instinctive style meant that he was a sequence of purple patches and less colourful troughs'.

In 1990s he swapped keeping gloves with R.C. 'Jack' Russell but eventually

England opening batsman Alec Stewart hits as Adam Gilchrist looks on behind the sticks in the match against Australia at The Oval in 2001.

became England's regular wicketkeeper. Taking over captaincy from Atherton in 1998, he led England to her first series win in 12 years. This was against South Africa. In the Leeds Test he took five vital catches as a keeper which contributed to England's thrilling victory.

Stewart also remembers the Melbourne Test of December 1998 which England narrowly and surprisingly won, thanks to his 107 and 52. But he lost captaincy after England's failure in the 1999 World Cup.

He was once again in the news when he scored a century in his 100th Test which was against the West Indies in Manchester in August 2000.

Coincidentally his 100th Test hundred was scored on Queen Mother's 100th birthday. Alec Stewart will always remember 4 August 2000 when he joined all-time greats Colin Cowdrey, Javed Miandad and Gordon Greenidge to record a century in his hundredth Test match. He recalls the standing ovation he had received after this landmark innings. 'It was a special feeling, in a way more important than my other centuries—especially as England was in trouble when I walked in to bat', he told me.

His final Test, against South Africa in September 2003 at The Oval, is also special to him. He scored only 38 but England won by nine wickets despite the opponents scoring 484 in the first innings and the popular Alec was chaired from the field. He had taken four catches as well to farewell Test cricket on a high note. To quote *Wisden* 2004: 'A deafening cheer greeted Stewart, collar up, as he strode through the South Africans' generous guard of honour'.

Alec Stewart had worn many hats in his 13 year Test career—as an opening batsman, middle order bat, wicketkeeper, captain, technician, tactician … But the parts had made an accomplished whole.

Here are the statistics of Alec Stewart when he kept wickets and when he did not:

Player	Tests	Runs	Average	HS	100s	50s	Caught	st
As a wicketkeeper	82	4540	34.92	173	6	23	227	14
Not as a wicketkeeper	51	3923	46.70	190	9	22	36	0
Total	133	8463	39.54	190	15	45	263	14

HS = Highest score; st = Stumped

JOHN WAITE
South Africa

Before Mark Boucher came on the scene, John HB Waite was the best wicketkeeper batsman to represent South Africa. He was a Springbok legend for over a decade in the 1950s and 1960s as he became the first cricketer to represent his country in 50 Tests and the only one to do so in the pre-isolation era.

On the tour to England in 1951, John Waite replaced Russell Endean as wicketkeeper and was selected in the first four Tests against England. His debut was in the Nottingham Test when he opened and scored 76 runs and took four catches. Mainly through a gritty double century by skipper Dudley Nourse, South Africa won their first Test in 16 years. In all matches on the tour, Waite scored 1011 runs at 33.70 and made 148 dismissals (124 caught and 24 stumped).

Johnny Waite was a self-effacing perfectionist, neat behind the stumps although tall for a keeper. He took slow bowlers unobtrusively and efficiently and accepted diving catches standing back to fast bowlers. As a batsman he had a sound defence and a wide range of strokes.

In the final Test against Australia in Melbourne in February 1953, he did not concede a single bye as Australia piled on 520 runs. It was the famous topsy-turvy Test which Australia lost by six wickets despite their huge first innings total. It was heart-breaking for Neil Harvey who had scored a glorious 205.

Waite's first Test century (113) was in the thrilling Manchester Test against England in July 1955 which the visitors won by three wickets. His best all-round series was against Australia in 1957–58 when he scored 362

South Africa's John Waite keeping against Nottinghamshire in 1955.

runs at 40.22, including 115 and 59 in the first Test in Johannesburg and 134 in the third Test in Durban when he added 231 runs for the third wicket with Jackie McGlew. Waite continued his good batting form in England in 1960 when he headed the batting average at 38.14.

He had a memorable home series against New Zealand in 1961–62 scoring his fourth and last century (101) at Johannesburg and making 26 dismissals (23 caught and three stumped) in the series, then a world record. He was prolific in Australia and New Zealand in 1963–64 when he amassed 552 runs at 42.46 in all first-class matches.

His final Test was against England in February 1965 when he caught MJK Smith and Jim Parks in the first innings and Geoff Boycott in the second.

Wicketkeeping Test All-Rounders

In 50 Tests he scored 2405 runs at 30.44 with four centuries (top score 134) and 16 fifties. He took 124 catches and stumped 17. Most of his records in Test cricket for South Africa have been surpassed by Dave Richardson and Boucher although he still holds, with Boucher, the record for most dismissals, 26, in a Test series for his country.

Born in Johannesburg on 19 January 1930, he collected 9812 runs at 35.04 with 23 centuries and 45 fifties and made 511 dismissals (427 caught and 84 stumped) in 199 first-class matches. His highest score was 219 for Eastern Province against Griqualand West at Kimberley in 1950–51.

He was a dynamic player and reacted when provoked. When the South Africans were slow handclapped in their match against Lancashire in 1951, he along with Eric Rowan sat down on the pitch as a protest and resumed batting only when the barracking stopped.

ALAN KNOTT

England

All eyes are on Alan Philip Eric Knott when he is on the field, whether wicketkeeping or batting. His fidgeting, twisting and calisthenics made compulsive, and at times irritating, viewing.

As a wicketkeeper, he surpassed all records for an Englishman during his 14 hectic years between 1967 and 1981. Small, nimble-footed and quick-witted, he was an impish genius, as suggested by his initials APE! Not surprisingly, his nickname was 'Flea'.

He was prone to stiff muscles and therefore exercised constantly to keep his limbs supple. His pads had to have four straps instead of three. Every clothing and protection had padding inside which absorbed sweat. He changed his clothes and showered at each interval and existed mostly on a diet of fruit and milk.

He was preferred to his wicketkeeping rivals—especially Bob Taylor—because of his superior batting. Knott batted in two gears; slow and defensive when England was in trouble but once the runs were on the board he switched to top gear, pressing down the accelerator pedal to the full. According to Christopher Martin-Jenkins 'His right-handed batting was shrewd, increasingly unorthodox (his top hand holding the bat with the palm facing the bowler) and often outrageous, as when he repulsed the dangerous swing bowling of Bob Massie by carting him to all parts of the leg-side field in 1972.' Also on two tours to India in 1972–73 and 1976–77, he hit his way out of trouble against the master Indian spinners by skipping out of the crease and hitting the ball over the top.

Whereas more accomplished England batsmen were on the back foot

Alan Knott hooks against India in the 1971 Oval Test.

against the pace and bounce of Dennis Lillee and Jeff Thomson in 1974–75, Knott preferred the front foot and was the second highest scorer for England in that series of broken limbs and shattered confidence. His unbeaten 106 in the Adelaide Test of January 1975 remains one of the finest by a keeper in Test history, and he was the second keeper after Les Ames to hit a century in an Ashes Test. His wicketkeeping was quick and dazzling as he became the second keeper after Godfrey Evans to make 200 dismissals in Test cricket when he caught Ian Chappell off Derek Underwood in the first innings of that

Test. He had also scored 51 in Perth, 52 in Melbourne and 81 in Sydney to aggregate 364 runs in the Test series at 36.40. And to make this a Test series to cherish for him, he made 23 dismissals (including a stumping), just one short of his 24 dismissals (including three stumpings) also against Australia in 1970–71.

He always put a high price on his wicket and in his fourth Test, at Georgetown in April 1968 against the West Indies, he scored an unbeaten 73 and helped Colin Cowdrey, also from Kent, save the Test by adding 127 invaluable runs for the sixth wicket. Needing 308 to win, England were 5 for 41 before the two Kentish men got together, and were 9 for 206 at the end of a tantalising drawn match.

He was 'robbed' of his first Test century in March 1969 against Pakistan in the Karachi Test. He was unbeaten on 96 when a mob stampeded on the field just before lunch on the third day. The play was abandoned with England 7 for 502. Not a nervous ninety, shall we call it a riotous 90?

His first Test hundred came in the Auckland Test of March 1971 when he scored 101 in the first innings and 96 in the second, narrowly missing becoming the first wicketkeeper to register a century in each innings of a Test. Perhaps this was a nervous ninety! He reached 1000 runs in Test cricket in this Test, his 25th.

Born on 9 April 1946 in Belvedere, Kent, he scored 4389 runs at 32.75 in 95 Tests, hitting five centuries (highest score 135) and 30 fifties and made 269 dismissals (250 caught and 19 stumped). He was the first player to achieve the Test double of 4000 runs and 200 dismissals. In 511 first-class matches from 1964 to 1985, he amassed 18,105 runs at 29.63 with 17 centuries (156 being his highest) and 97 fifties, caught 1211 and stumped 133.

'He hardly missed a catch that anyone remembers', wrote John Thicknesse in *Cricinfo*. Describing him as a genuine all-rounder, Thicknesse added, 'Yet

The fastidious Knott playing a firm stroke against Pakistan in the 1974 Lord's Test.

to see his wicketkeeping at its most spectacular, you had to catch him standing up to [spinner Derek] Underwood on a rain-affected pitch for Kent in county cricket … Most of the time, despite the obvious problems, Knott would take the ball so nimbly he might have been keeping in the indoor nets.'

His Test figures would have been even more awe-inspiring had he not joined Kerry Packer's World Series Cricket and the rebel tours to South Africa in late 1970s. But for two decades he had given pleasure to millions of cricket fans watching cricket live or on television. He was an entertainer and a perfectionist, a gyrating genius.

SYED KIRMANI

India

One does not expect a short bald man to be artistic and elegant. But India's most successful wicketkeeper, SMH Kirmani managed it very well. He wore a wig but you can't fool all the people all the time and once when the wig fell off, Kirmani's shining bald head became an occasion for giggles for the spectators during India's historic tour of Australia in 1977–78. Why historic? The tour coincided with the inauguration of Kerry Packer's World Series Cricket and Kirmani was promptly nicknamed 'Kirry Packer'. On this tour he scored valuable runs and kept wickets with brisk efficiency.

Kirmani took to wicketkeeping as a duck takes to water. 'I started playing when I was six and always liked to keep wickets', he told me. 'As gloves were not affordable, I used bricks to stop balls.' From bricks to Test cricket was not an easy passage as Farokh Engineer was established as India's wicketkeeper and Kirmani had to await his turn. He toured England three times without playing a Test. But he persevered and went on to make 198 dismissals—an Indian record—in 88 Tests.

Born on 29 December 1949 in Madras (now Chennai), he had to wait till he was 27 to make his Test debut. In his second Test against New Zealand in Christchurch in February 1976, he equalled the then record of six dismissals in an innings. Kirmani remembers that match vividly.

'I had taken four catches and stumped one in the Test after New Zealand's incomplete second innings when Geoff Soulez, the English statistician, told me that I needed one more victim to equal a Test record. I was so excited I

India's Syed Kirmani behind the stumps in the 1981 Bangalore Test against England.

could not sleep that night. Fortunately I caught the tall Richard Collinge the next morning and joined the greats, Wally Grout of Australia, Denis Lindsay of South Africa and John Murray of England.'

Following Engineer's flamboyant footsteps was not easy but Kirmani had a distinctive style; he was an efficient and hard-working ant and not a colourful butterfly. For most of Kirmani's career he had to keep to spin wizards Bhagwat Chandrasekhar, Bishan Bedi and Erapalli Prasanna, as also to the seam attack spearheaded by Kapil Dev.

Earlier, Kirmani was an aggressive batsman and was called 'a schoolboy Rohan Kanhai' by an English critic. But later he became more circumspect and scored two centuries in Tests and 13 in first-class matches. Both his Test tons were scored in Mumbai. His first century was against Australia in the sixth Test in November 1979 when he was sent in as a 'night-watchman'. Keeping a cool head, he made an unbeaten 101, adding 127 runs with Karsan Ghavri for the seventh wicket. India won this Test by an innings as also their first ever series against Australia 2–0.

He made his highest Test score of 102 against England, also in Mumbai in December 1985. He added 235 runs for a record seventh wicket stand with Ravi Shastri (142) and India won by eight wickets.

Kirmani's finest series as a wicketkeeper was against England in India in 1981–82 when he did not concede a single bye in three successive Tests when England aggregated 1964 runs. In the third Test in Delhi, Kirmani (67) added 128 runs for the eighth wicket with Shastri. Then against the West Indies in Madras in December 1983 he went in at number 10, scored an unbeaten 63 and put on 143 runs with Sunil Gavaskar (236 not out) for the unbroken ninth wicket. In 88 Tests, Kirmani scored 2759 runs at 27.04 with two centuries and 12 fifties and made 198 dismissals (160 caught and 38 stumped).

Wicketkeeping Test All-Rounders

He had also played a crucial role in India's triumph in the 1983 World Cup with some useful contributions with the bat and immaculate glove work. His 126 run stand with skipper Kapil Dev after India were at one stage teetering at 5 for 17 against Zimbabwe was vital in India reaching the final.

On retirement he became the national selector and rose to become the chairman. At his best Syed Mujtaba Hussain Kirmani was a scintillating wicketkeeper and a stylish bat who rescued India time and again. The Indian keeper with Chinese eyes, Kojak hairline and an Australian temperament remains an entertaining character.

JEFFREY DUJON
West Indies

As a wicketkeeper he was as good as any against super quicks, nimble on his feet and acrobatic in his movements. He was less impressive against spin but he hardly got the opportunity as the Windies attack had little room for spinners in his era. The cool-headed Dujon was a diving pigeon among soaring hawks.

If facing the West Indies pace like fire was like walking on burning coals for batsmen, keeping to the likes of Andy Roberts, Michael Holding, Joel Garner and Curtly Ambrose was like placing a burning coal on the tongue. Ask Jeffrey Dujon.

As Mike Selvey wrote, 'It was one of the most spectacular sights of cricket in 1980s. A great West Indian fast bowler—any of several suspects—roared on by a partisan Caribbean crowd, a short ball rearing, the batsman fending and edging, and behind the stumps, a lithe athlete leaping and plunging to take another one-handed blinder. Jeff Dujon was the gymnastic hub of these all conquering Windies sides.'

Dujon never played in a losing series and his 272 dismissals was a Test record which was later eclipsed by the Aussie trio of Rod Marsh, Ian Healy and Adam Gilchrist and the South African Mark Boucher. Dujon's sideways and horizontal leaps were spectacular. He made his international debut when touring Zimbabwe and Australia in 1981–82. He impressed with an unbeaten 104 against New South Wales in Sydney and played many dashing innings in one-day internationals, studded with strong drives and hooks.

Wicketkeeper Jeff Dujon and slip fielders Viv Richards and Gordon Greenidge rejoice at the fall of a wicket in the 1988 Lord's Test against England.

Born in Kingston, Jamaica on 28 May 1956, Peter Jeffrey Leroy Dujon made five Test centuries and his top score of 139 came during a critical juncture. In the first Test in Perth in November 1984 the Windies were struggling at 6 for 186 and his 149 runs stand with 'Larry' Gomes enabled them to total 416. During this innings he was struck a nasty blow off Terry Alderman's bouncer and retired with blurred vision. The pitch was so difficult with an uneven bounce that the Australians were shot out for 76 and 228 and the visitors won by an innings and plenty.

In 81 Tests he scored 3322 runs at 31.94 with five centuries and 16 fifties and made 272 dismissals (267 caught and five stumped). A genuine all-rounder he could have represented the Windies as a pure batsman as he scored a century against all countries except New Zealand. He was made one of the five cricketers of the year 1989 by *Wisden*. 'He always had the special touch which gave his batting the stamp of class', wrote Tony Cozier in *Wisden*. 'His build is slim and he lacks the sheer power of those, such as Vivian Richards, Gordon Greenidge and Clive Lloyd.' But Cozier added there was unmistakable evidence of Lawrence Rowe's influence in Dujon's classically stylish batting.

ROD MARSH

Australia

Although Marsh will be remembered as a tough and tumbling keeper of wicket and faith, his lower-order batting lay at the core of many stubborn performances by Australia as he rescued Australia from mid-innings crises. But he was more than a wicketkeeper-batsman.

Rodney William Marsh started his Test career under a cloud but ended it 14 years later among the stars. Selected in the Australian team in the Ashes series of 1970–71 to replace the popular Brian Taber, he dropped a few catches in his Test debut in Brisbane and was nicknamed 'Iron Gloves'. The following month in the Sydney Test he was booed by a section of the pro-Taber crowd.

But the tough, mustachioed Marsh did not let this negative crowd reaction upset him. If any, it only increased his determination to succeed. In his Test swan song against Pakistan in Sydney in January 1984, he was cheered lustily by the crowd as he took five catches in his final innings and became the first wicketkeeper to make 350 Test dismissals. It was the Test where the three icons of Australian cricket—Greg Chappell, Dennis Lillee and Marsh—said farewell to Test cricket simultaneously. With fellow West Australian Lillee, Marsh had formed a fabulous partnership; 95 of Lillee's 355 wickets were caught by Marsh. It remains a record more than two decades later and the term 'caught Marsh bowled Lillee' has become a folklore.

Caught Marsh Bowled Lillee is also the title of Ian Brayshaw's biography of the Aussie legends. In the foreword of this book, captain Ian Chappell emphasised the role the Lillee–Marsh combination played in Australia's

Rod Marsh going out to bat.

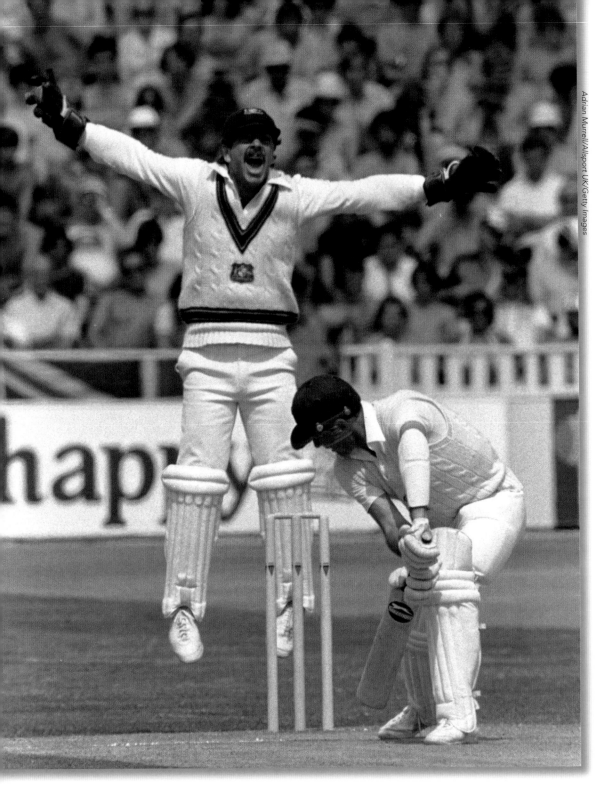

*Rod Marsh jumps with joy after catching
Geoff Boycott in the 1981 Birmingham Test.*

success in the 1970s and 1980s. 'As players they were a captain's dream. At one end a talented fast bowler who, with huge heart, was always ready to give just one last effort for his team … At the other end a man whose skill with the gloves could lift a team with a brilliant catch or who could offer some tactical advice that might turn a game in the team's favour.'

Marsh was the first of the three world-class wicketkeeper-batsmen from Australia. Ian Healy and Adam Gilchrist followed his padded footsteps and between them the trio took 1088 catches, made 78 stumpings (that is 1166 dismissals) and scored 13,559 runs at 32.83 in 311 Tests. Healy and Gilchrist will be featured later in this chapter.

Born in Aradale, Perth on 4 November 1947, Marsh scored 3633 runs at 26.51 with three centuries and 16 fifties and caught 343 and stumped 12. In 257 first-class matches he aggregated 11,067 runs at 31.17 with 12 centuries (236 being his highest score) and 55 fifties and took 803 catches and stumped 66. He was among the first to play one-day internationals on January 1971 in Melbourne and had a strike-rate of 82.26 as he made 1225 runs at 20.08 in 92 matches. He hit four fifties and made 124 dismissals in the shorter version of cricket, 120 caught and four stumped. He would have stumped more had champion leg-spinners Shane Warne and Stuart MacGill played in his time.

Thickset in build with hairy feet and hairier lips, Marsh was combative in approach. His combination of concentration, determination, diving athleticism and skilled glove work made him an object of admiration and inspiration. His tactical expertise and people skills provided a recipe to make him into an ideal captain but doors did not open for him. He had pleaded with skipper Greg Chappell not to instruct Trevor Chappell to bowl that notorious underarm delivery in a one-dayer against New Zealand in Melbourne on 1 February 1981. But Greg did not listen and it turned out to be one of the worst controversies of cricket.

Wicketkeeping Test All-Rounders

Marsh became the first Australian keeper to record a Test century when he scored 118 against Pakistan in Adelaide in December 1972. He hit two more, against New Zealand, also in Adelaide a year later and in the historic Centenary Test against England in Melbourne in March 1977. This was also the first century by an Australian keeper against England. Also, in this Test Marsh surpassed Wally Grout's Australian record of 187 Test dismissals.

Earlier, Rod 'Bacchus' Marsh had narrowly missed hitting a Test hundred in the Melbourne Test of January 1971 when captain Bill Lawry declared the innings closed with Rod not out on 92. Let Marsh narrate this tale of missed milestone from his autobiography *You'll Keep*. 'Even his [Lawry's] own partisan crowd could not remain faithful to him after he declared with my score only eight runs short of a century, which would have been the first by an Australian keeper in a Test match. I wasn't at all upset about it.'

Knowing Marsh, the last sentence is hard to believe!

After retirement he joined the Channel 9 commentary team. But his views on too many one-day matches angered Kerry Packer and Marsh was sacked on the spot. This turned out well for him and Australia as he enhanced his reputation as the head coach of Australian Cricket Academy in Adelaide in 1990s and early 2000. He was quick to spot the talents of Ricky Ponting, Glenn McGrath and Brett Lee among others. In 2002 he ventured overseas where he was appointed coach of England and an English selector. He stepped down in September 2005 after helping England regain the Ashes after 16 years. What a glove of irony!

In January 2005 he was inducted into Australian Cricket Hall of Fame. The Iron Glove had a silk lining after all.

IAN HEALY

Australia

For almost a decade, Ian Healy was the pulse of the Australian squad. His record of 395 dismissals was recently overtaken by South Africa's Mark Boucher but that cat-like finesse of Healy will be difficult to emulate. He prided himself on his professionalism, his total commitment in training and in team meetings.

Ian Healy is recognised as among the best wicketkeeper-batsmen in the game's history and the first keeper to play 100 Tests. A veteran of 119 Tests, he held the record of making most dismissals (395) in Test history till Mark Boucher of South Africa went past him in October 2007. Healy's 29 stumpings are exceeded by Australia's Bert Oldfield (an incredible 52 stumpings in 54 Tests), England's Godfrey Evans (46 in 91), India's Syed Kirmani (38 in 88) and Australia's current go-getter Adam Gilchrist (37 in 96).

Healy also scored 4356 runs at 27.39 at Test level hitting four centuries, his unbeaten 161 against the West Indies in the Brisbane Test of November 1996 being his highest. He considers this Test as the highlight of his career. He went in to bat at 5 for 196 on a moist, swinging Gabba pitch when Michael Bevan was dismissed by Courtney Walsh for a first ball duck. Calmly Healy added 142 runs with Steve Waugh and had valuable partnerships with tailenders enabling Australia to reach 479. He had batted for six hours and hit 20 fours. He also made an unbeaten 45 from just 50 balls in the second innings. Thus, he had scored 206 runs in the match without getting dismissed and was adjudged Man of the Match.

Wicketkeeping Test All-Rounders

'Apart from my strokes against the likes of Curtly [Ambrose] and Courtney [Walsh], my glove-work was satisfying, we won the Test to go one up in the series', Healy reminisced to me during the 2003 Sydney Test against England made memorable by Steve Waugh, his partner of many summers, scoring a stirring last-ball century to equal Don Bradman's Australian record of 29 tons.

Healy has a mischievous look and a satisfied grin. He almost purrs as he talks; his eyes sparkle through his glasses, encouraging you to ask him provocative questions. One wonders how he could have ever sledged on the field but he often indulged in mind games. Just ask Sri Lanka's captain Arjuna Ranatunga with whom he had an on-field altercation during a one-day final in Sydney.

As a batsman, Healy was in the same groove, if not the same class, as Ian Chappell. Both were compulsive hookers and were indefatigable in temperament. These days, the Ians go hand-in-glove in the Channel 9 TV box, intelligently analysing a game and dissecting a player's technique.

Ian Andrew Healy ('Heals' to friends) was born in Brisbane on 30 April 1964. His father, a bank manager, was a sports fanatic. As a boy, Healy was inspired by the wicketkeeping of Rod Marsh. In 1972, he moved to the town of Biloela, 600km north of Brisbane. Young Ian was stimulated by the town's passion for all sports. He rode his bicycle to practise and play cricket, soccer, basketball, squash and rugby league. He became cricket captain at 11 and at a clinic conducted by Queensland wicketkeeper John MacLean, he was allowed to examine his gloves. He still cherishes the memory.

Boy Healy played with adults, which perhaps explained his hardheaded approach to cricket. By the age of 17, he had developed that mental and physical toughness which typified his first-class and Test career. Despite solid performances with gloves and bat, he found it difficult to break into the Queensland Sheffield Shield team, as Peter Anderson was their regular

A compulsive hooker, Ian Healy is seen in action against Sri Lanka at Colombo in 1999.

keeper. Healy had played only six first-class matches when, out of the blue, he was selected for the tour of Pakistan in 1988. It was the most surprising selection since wrist-spinner John Watkins was picked in 1972–73 and off-spinner Peter Taylor in 1986–87. Many asked 'Healy, who?'

Healy was just as staggered at his selection. 'Was I being had?' he wondered. 'I phoned my parents and it was my father who actually confirmed the news.' Healy has national selector Greg Chappell to thank for this sudden promotion. Having played with Rod Marsh throughout his Test career, Greg was aware of the advantages offered by a wicketkeeper batsman. To him, Healy was ideally suited for the dual role. It turned out to be an inspired choice as 'Healy who' became a fixture of the Australian team for 12 summers, giving his unconditional support to captains Allan Border, Mark Taylor and Steve Waugh.

'Greg was impressed by Healy's tough temperament and efficient glove work', remembers John Benaud. 'What I like most about 'Heals' is the way he takes up a challenge with his opponents. A forceful personality, he was a revivalist and the best in the world in the 1990s. More importantly, he kept so well to Shane Warne who turns the ball square. Healy was up there with the best.' His nasal 'Bowwwling Warnie' was his signature tune and it echoed in all cricket grounds. Added Steve Rixon, former Test wicketkeeper and later the NSW coach: 'He [Healy] had his limitations earlier, but given the responsibility, he became a top-liner.'

Healy's most dramatic moment was as a batsman. It came in the thrilling Port Elizabeth Test against South Africa in March 1997. After more than three days of twists and turns, it peaked to a climax. Australia needed five runs to win, South Africa needed two wickets. Amid cliffhanging suspense, skipper Hansie Cronje came to bowl the final fateful over. Let Healy take over the narration: 'Mmm, well really, I didn't know what was going to come out. My legs were stiff, my adrenaline pumping and my nerves running everywhere. Well, the ball drifted down the leg and I thought I'd go after it. I got it sweet, really sweet.' It was a six, which won the Test. The Aussies had beaten the Proteas with what Healy recalls as a 'lottery shot'. He had become only the seventeenth batsman and the second Australian (after Alan Turner in 1976–77) to win a Test with a six.

> *'I got it sweet, really sweet.'*
> *It was a six, which won the Test.*

Healy's hundredth Test was also against South Africa and perhaps was just as dramatic. There was a personal tragedy off the field and dropped catches, a major controversial decision and frayed tempers culminating in the visiting captain spearing a stump through the door of the umpires' room. It ended in a draw but no one can call it dreary. This was the hotly debated Adelaide Test of January–February 1998. Healy's performance in this landmark Test was lacklustre, scoring one and 10, catching Herschelle Gibbs in the first innings and stumping him in the second.

Healy remembers this Test with affection and sadness. 'Many people, over 50 friends and relatives had specially come from Brisbane to Adelaide to support me in my hundredth Test. But I was not quite focused throughout this Test. It was a sad period for me and the family as my father, Neville, had died a week before. I could concentrate when keeping wicket but not so much when batting. I played shots which I should not have as my mind kept drifting, thinking of Dad.'

How would one rank Healy as a wicketkeeper? Who better than his predecessor, the great Rod Marsh, to assess him: 'I've not seen finer wicketkeeping—standing up to the stumps. He became an integral part of Australian cricket. His understanding of Shane Warne and Tim May behind the wickets had done a lot of good for their careers. He was an outstanding keeper, as good as any.'

When an Australian team of the 20th century was selected, Healy got the job ahead of the legendary Don Tallon, Wally Grout and Rod Marsh.

ANDY FLOWER
Zimbabwe

For a long time, Andy Flower was Zimbabwe's only batsman of Test quality on all conditions. Born on 28 April 1968 in Cape Town, Andy Flower is a left-hand middle order batsman who kept wicket on most occasions.

Flower was behind a magical moment for the young Test-playing nation. Zimbabwe had played 10 Tests that far in three years without winning one. Then came the Harare Test against a strong Pakistani line-up in early 1995. The Test began on a farcical note. Pakistan 'won' the toss but as match referee Jackie Hendricks of the West Indies did not hear the call, he requested a re-spin. Andy Flower, Zimbabwe's captain and wicketkeeper, won the re-toss and elected to bat.

They were soon in trouble, losing 2 for 9 and 3 for 42 when Andy, aged 26, joined his younger brother Grant. They remained unbeaten until the end of the day, adding 247 runs in Zimbabwe's 3 for 289. Andy, the lucky captain, batted as if there was no tomorrow and was unbeaten on 142. They had resisted some testing overs from Wasim Akram whose seven overs after lunch were maidens. The following day, the brothers added 22 more runs before Andy was caught for a chanceless 156. Their partnership of 269 was not only a record for Zimbabwe (since then broken by Andy Flower and Murray Goodwin in March 1998), but also a fraternal record.

The Flowers had overtaken Ian and Greg Chappell's record partnership of 264 runs between brothers (vs New Zealand at Wellington in 1973–74). Andy was the dominant partner, reaching his second Test century in 210 minutes. Andy declared at 4 for 544 as Pakistan's captain, Salim Malik, sorely regretted

Zimbabwe's pride and joy Andy Flower is clean bowled against Sussex in England.

match referee Hendricks' poor hearing on the previous morning. The visitors replied with 322 and 158 as Zimbabweans celebrated their first ever Test triumph and that too by an innings and 64 runs with a day to spare. Apart from contributing 357 runs, the Flower brothers had taken five catches and were adjudged joint Men of the Match.

Three years earlier, they were also made joint Men of the Match. In the Delhi Test against India in March 1993, Grant (96) and Andy (115) had added 192 runs for the fourth wicket. Andy had scored Zimbabwe's first overseas century but Zimbabwe collapsed from 3 for 275 to 321 all out. They lost by an innings despite Andy's defiant 62 not out in the second innings.

The inaugural Test against England was remarkable and ended in bitter controversy. Played at Bulawayo in December 1996, it ended in a draw despite both teams aggregating 610 runs in the match. With Andy scoring his third Test century (112), Zimbabwe totalled 376. England led by 30 runs and on the final day were set 205 runs to win from 37 overs. That is when the drama began and 'a gently smouldering match burst into full flame on the last afternoon', to quote *Wisden* (1998).

England batsmen were frustrated by Zimbabwe's alleged negative bowling. The match see-sawed and in the end England needed five runs to win from the last three balls but could only manage four. As all the wickets had not fallen, the match was not considered a tie but a draw. The English team was incensed as the umpires did not call 'wide' when Heath Streak bowled off-line in the final pulsating over.

Flower hit five successive fifties in limited-overs internationals against Kenya in 1998 and in all made four centuries and 55 fifties. His best innings was his unbeaten 115 in the 1992 World Cup against Sri Lanka in New Plymouth. With namesake Andy Waller, he added 145 dazzling runs in the last 13 overs as Zimbabwe totalled 4 for 312 at 6.24 runs an over, but still lost.

Another match to remember for Andy Flower was his unbeaten 139 off 149 balls (23 fours and a six) against Queensland at Maryborough in December 1994. On this short tour to Australia, Andy was the captain but did not keep wicket. Normally a sound wicketkeeper, he was far from being brilliant.

Zimbabwe lost an acrimonious Test series in Sri Lanka in 1997–98. The second Test in Colombo was fairly explosive. Andy scored an unbeaten 105 in the second innings. Set 326 runs to win, Sri Lanka reached the target with five wickets in hand but the visitors were unhappy with decisions given in favour of the home batsmen. Zimbabwe's coach, David Houghton, was reported as saying, 'I feel the umpires raped us'.

The Test against Pakistan at Bulawayo in March 1998 was a Flower brothers' match, as Grant scored 156 in the first innings (adding 77 runs for the fourth wicket with Andy) and Andy hitting an unbeaten 100 in the second. Andy added 277 for the unbroken fifth wicket with Murray Goodwin (166 not out). Zimbabwe also beat India in the Harare Test seven months later—their second victory in 31 Tests—and Andy became the first Zimbabwean to reach 2000 runs at Test level.

Then in the World Cup in England in 1999, Zimbabwe recorded some shock wins. In a thriller, they defeated India by three runs after Zimbabwe had totalled 252, mainly through Andy's unbeaten 68. Zimbabwe went on to defeat the mighty South Africans and entered Super Six.

Andy dominated the series against Sri Lanka at home in late 1999. He scored 86 and 15 not out in the first Test at Bulawayo; 74 (after coming in at 3 down for 0 after Nuwan Zoysa had completed a hat-trick) and 129 in the second Test at Harare and 14 and 70 not out in the final Test, also in Harare. Thus he had totalled 388 runs at 97.00 in the three drawn Tests.

In the Port-of-Spain Test of March 2000 against the West Indies, Andy scored 113 not out, his seventh Test hundred. This enabled Zimbabwe to a

Wicketkeeping Test All-Rounders

49-run first innings lead. However, when set an easy win target of 99, they collapsed for a pitiful 63, succumbing to the ageing but re-charged Windies pace attack.

Andy recorded five more Test centuries and his place as a batsman of world class is assured. He was at his prolific best when he scored 142 and an unbeaten 199 in the Harare Test against a strong South African attack in September 2001 and was soon after ranked as no.1 batsman in the world by the official PwC international rating system. *Wisden* also honoured him as one of the Five Cricketers of the Year in 2002.

There is no doubt about his standing in international cricket as a batsman, becoming the first wicketkeeper to hit two centuries in one Test. In 63 Tests he amassed 4794 runs at 51.54 with 12 centuries (highest score 232 not out) and 27 fifties. But his wicketkeeping suffered from the added strain of captaincy. He made 160 dismissals in 63 Tests (151 caught and nine stumped, 142 of these catches were taken as a wicketkeeper), as shown in the Table below:

Player	Tests	Runs	Average	HS	100s	50s	Caught	st
As a wicketkeeper	55	4404	53.70	232*	12	23	142	9
Not as a wicketkeeper	8	390	35.45	92	0	4	9	0
Total	63	4794	51.54	232*	12	27	151	9

HS = Highest score; st = Stumped; * = not out

These figures show that he performed better with the bat when he kept wicket.

Off the field, Andy is a keen student of Zimbabwean history. And he himself became a part of his country's history when he and team-mate Henry Olonga protested against the political regime in Zimbabwe, calling it the 'death

Flower power during a Tsunami Relief match at Lord's.

of democracy'. This was on the eve of the 2003 World Cup and brought to an end Andy's international career. In 213 one-day internationals he had amassed 6786 runs at 35.34 with four hundreds and 55 fifties and effected 173 dismissals (141 caught and 32 stumped). As in Test matches, some of his catches were taken when he did not keep wickets.

He played first-class cricket with Essex from 2002 to 2004 and had a stint in the Pura Cup with South Australia in 2003–04. In 223 first-class matches for teams in three continents, he scored 16,379 runs at 54.05 with 49 centuries (an unbeaten 271 being his highest) and made 382 dismissals (361 caught and 21 stumped). Injury forced him to retire in 2007 and he became England's assistant coach.

The down and out Zimbabweans are praying for a new flower to blossom to take them out of their misery.

ADAM GILCHRIST

Australia

Of all the players featured in this chapter, Adam Gilchrist is the most scintillating and spectacular, an excitement machine. You expect fireworks every time he reaches the middle, twirling his bat. No settling down period for the gregarious left-hander with outstanding talent and ears.

If the first ball he receives is a half volley or a full toss, he gives it the full treatment, driving it to the fence for a four. If it is short-pitched, he hooks or pulls it over the ropes for a six. And before you have finished the second plastic glass of beer, he is acknowledging his fifty off forty balls! He has played more match-winning innings than any other wicketkeeper.

And he is the uncrowned Six Sultan, having clobbered an astounding 100 sixes in 96 Tests at a striking rate of 1.04 six per Test. He reached this unique 'century' of sixes in the Hobart Test against Sri Lanka on 17 November 2007 off the bowling of Muttiah Muralitharan. The West Indies legend Brian Lara comes next with 88 in 131 Tests but as he is retired he is no threat to Gilchrist. Gilchrist has also smashed 149 sixes in 287 one-day internationals (ODIs).

Nicknamed 'Gilly' and 'Churchy', Adam Craig Gilchrist was born on 14 November 1971 in Bellingen, New South Wales. He could not break into the New South Wales team as a wicketkeeper as Phil Emery was the regular keeper and had to move over to Western Australia to play first-class cricket.

When you think of 'Gilly' you think of quicksilver innings. But he has proved himself a match-winner as a keeper too with 416 dismissals (379 caught, 37 stumped) in 96 Tests and 472 dismissals (417 catches and 55 stumpings) in 287 ODIs. Only Mark Boucher of South Africa has made more dismissals in

*Adam Gilchrist (left) is airborne while taking
a catch during the 2007 World Cup.*

Test history but Gilchrist's 472 dismissals in ODIs is a record.

Despite his impressive figures as a keeper, 'Gilly' will be remembered as a top flight and exciting batsman. There are times when he loses his concentration behind the wickets and drops a catch. As a batsman also he has his off days but mostly he makes us look up, following the trajectory of his tall hitting. He scored 5570 runs in Test matches (with 17 centuries, top score 204 not out and 26 fifties) at an average of 47.60 and a strike-rate of 81.95.

In 287 ODIs he belted 9619 exhilarating runs (16 centuries, highest score 172, and 55 fifties) at 35.89 and a strike-rate of 96.94, that is almost a run a ball. These adventurous run-rates at international levels would make 'Viv Richards and Gilbert Jessop look like stick-in-the-muds', according to *Cricinfo*. Until rested in 2001 in Hobart, he had played 105 ODIs in a row, a world record.

Going in at no. 7 in whites or as an opener in green and gold, Gilchrist was the nucleus of Australian 'invincibles' from 1996 till now. You expect fireworks when he is at the crease. He received universal accolade (except from skipper Ricky Ponting) when he 'walked' when given not out by the umpire in the 2003 World Cup semi-final. And when sitting on a 'pair' during the Perth Test against England in December 2006, he hammered the second ball he received for a six. His philosophy is: 'Just hit the ball and enjoy' and he rarely strays from it.

Everything is different about 'Gilly'. Gripping the bat handle high, he steers good length deliveries into gaps for singles and smashes others with head straight and wrists soft. An easygoing bloke when you meet him on the street; at the wicket he creates masterpieces spectators remember forever. One can write a book on him and yet leave out someone's favourite innings. So I'll select only some of his magic moments.

In his Test debut against Pakistan in Brisbane in November 1999 he scored

81 runs including five fours in an over from leg-spinner Mushtaq Ahmed. Among Australian keepers only Arthur Jarvis had scored more runs on his Test debut, 82 vs England in Melbourne way back in 1885. Gilchrist's second Test in Hobart was even more memorable. He took four catches, scored 6 and 149 not out, guiding Australia to an unexpected victory with a do-or-die sixth wicket stand with Justin Langer (127). Challenged to score 369 runs for a win, Australia was in trouble at 5 for 126 when the Langer–Gilchrist partnership enabled Australia to triumph against all odds. Gilly's 149 had come off 163 balls and contained 13 glorious fours and a six.

After this innings he said, 'I just tried to survive initially, but maybe my natural instinct in trying to survive was being aggressive. I try to keep my natural game going but it all depends on what the team wants. It's such a varying situation batting at number 7. Someday it's not going to work. Hopefully most times it will.' It certainly has.

Mike Coward was moved to write in *The Australian* after the Hobart masterpiece: 'He [Gilchrist] is what the 21st century elite cricketer should be: an unconditional pro who can adapt to any form of the game. In other words, a complete cricketer; the genuine article.' Peter Roebuck added in the *Sydney Morning Herald*, '... there is no side to him, no trickery, only a commitment to playing well and winning matches'.

Gilchrist reached new heights and lows during the tour to India in February–March 2001. His high was in the Mumbai Test when he reached the crease with Australia 5 down for 99. He hit a spectacular 122, adding 197 runs with Matthew Hayden. Despite the crisis, Gilchrist reached his 100 off 84 balls, the then third fastest Test hundred after Jack Gregory's 100 off 67 balls (Australia vs South Africa, Johannesburg, 1921–22) and Viv Richards's 100 off 56 balls (West Indies vs England, St John's, 1985–86). Gilchrist also snapped up five catches and was the popular Man of the Match. Just then

'Gilly' celebrates his majestic century in the
2007 World Cup final against Sri Lanka.

wheels started falling off both for Australia and Gilchrist. Australia lost an 'un-losable' Test in Kolkata and a thriller in Chennai and Gilchrist made scores of 0, 0, 1 and 1. His scores resembled the prefix for an international phone number!

He was at his effervescent best when scoring an unbeaten double century against South Africa in Johannesburg in February 2002. His 204 off 213 deliveries included 19 fours and eight towering sixes. When 169 he took a pot shot at an advertising hoarding more than 9 metres in the air and well behind the boundary, a carry of at least 100 metres. So sure that no one could hit it, the sponsor—a local gold mine—had offered a bar of gold worth £80,000 for a direct hit. He missed the hoarding and £80,000 by a couple of feet but broke the opponents' spirit and Australia won by an innings and 360 runs. 'Missed it by that much', one can imagine Maxwell Smart moaning in the old sitcom *Get Smart*!

In the next Test in Durban he smashed an unbeaten 138, as he reached his 100 off 91 balls and his last 38 off 17. *Wisden* 2003 described it as 'feverish butchery'. In the final Test he scored 91 and 16 to finish the 3-Test series hammering 473 runs at 157.66 and took 13 catches and stumped one as well.

Gilchrist was at his belligerent best in the Ashes Test in Perth in December 2006. After making a duck in the first Test in Brisbane, 64 in Adelaide and a nought in the first innings in Perth, it appeared that his batting prowess was wilting. And then *it* happened and cricket-lovers remember where they were when 'Gilly' thrashed the Pom attack with a vengeance. He walked in at 5 for 365, being a 'Monty' Panesar victim for a blob in the first innings.

After reaching 50 off 40 balls, he accelerated to notch the next 50 off 17 to reach his frenetic ton in 57 deliveries. Only Master Blaster Viv Richards had scored a century faster—by one ball! 'Gilly' was unbeaten on 102, striking 12 fours and four sixes, when Ricky Ponting declared. Australia won the Test to regain the Ashes they had lost in England 15 months ago. This outcome delighted Gilchrist more than his hurricane hundred.

Australia won the 2007 World Cup in the West Indies for a record fourth time and for the third time in a row. Gilchrist was adjudged Man of the Final on 28 April 2007 after his scintillating 149 off 104 balls with 13 fours and eight sixes (his century coming off 72 balls). And he introduced an innovation, placing a squash ball in his batting gloves to keep his wrist steady. He became the only player to score a century and make three dismissals in a World Cup final.

He was vice-captain under Steve Waugh and led Australia when Waugh was injured. However, he found the extra burden tiring and was happy for Ricky Ponting to take over when Waugh retired. But when Ponting was injured, he led Australia to their first series win in India in 35 years in 2004, crossing the final frontier. In 2007 he was voted the best one-day cricketer among Australians.

Adam Gilchrist is a world-class batsman who can keep rather than a wicketkeeper who can bat like his predecessors Ian Healy and Rod Marsh. According to experts 'Gilly' lacks Marsh's acrobatics and Healy's finesse. Yet his record behind the stumps is most impressive. His dismissals-per-Test ratio of 4.25 is superior to Adam Boucher's of 3.80, Marsh's of 3.70 and Healy's of 3.32. And Gilchrist did not concede a bye when England compiled an imposing 6 declared for 551 in the Adelaide Test of December 2006.

As Robert Drane wrote in *Inside Sport*, 'His [Gilchrist's] batting is as effortlessly potent as Pavarotti's singing.' On his retirement in January 2008, Cricket Australia Chairman said, 'Adam has been a great adornment to the game and his statistics with the bat and gloves speak for themselves. His influence on the game has gone well beyond statistics both in terms of the dignity with which he has played the game and his respect for the tradition and the spirit of cricket.'

South Africa

Mark Boucher holds quite a few Test records; he reached 100 dismissals in Test cricket in the shortest time, made the highest score by a 'nightwatchman' (since broken by Australia's Jason Gillespie in 2006) and did not concede a bye in most innings. But there is more!

In 2007 Boucher became the first cricketer to make 400 dismissals in Test annals, overtaking Ian Healy's record of 395 dismissals. Currently he has scored 4098 runs at 29.91 with four centuries and has taken 406 catches (another record, next best is Adam Gilchrist with 379) and made 19 stumpings in 111 Tests. So he is the second cricketer after Gilchrist to achieve the double of 4000 runs and 400 dismissals and the only one to accept 400 catches in Test annals.

He announced himself as a quality batsman in his second Test. Against Pakistan in Johannesburg in February 1998, he came to the crease at 8 for 166, faced the chin music of Shoaib Akhtar and Waqar Younis and the spin of Mushtaq Ahmed and Saqlain Mushtaq and scored 78, adding a record 195 runs for the ninth wicket with no. 10 batsman Pat Symcox (108). In this 3-Test series Boucher took 17 catches and stumped one.

He had made his Test debut against Pakistan in Sheikhupura, Pakistan in October 1997 when the regular keeper Dave Richardson was injured and he was flown in as a replacement. He took over the gloves for his country when Richardson retired soon after.

He started hesitatingly, especially in the 1999 World Cup in England, but went on to play 75 Tests in a row.

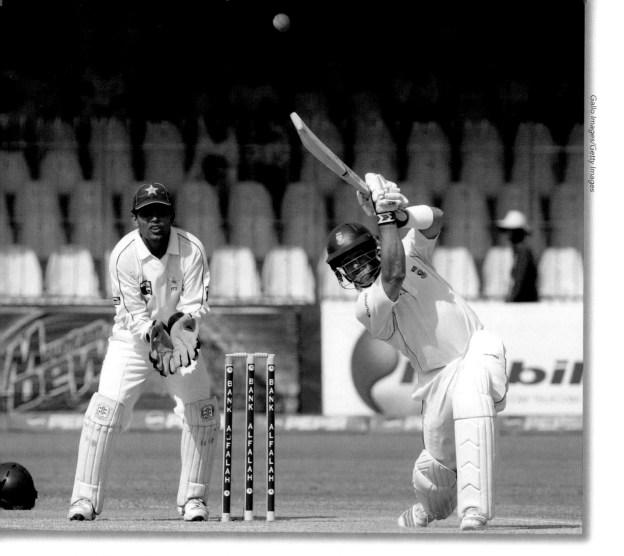

Mark Boucher having a go at the Pakistan attack in the 2007 Lahore Test.

An unproven 'accusation of match-fixing' made the selectors cautious and left him out of the tour to India in 2004. Since then he has been a permanent fixture in the South African team at both Test and one-day international (ODI) levels. In 263 ODIs, he has compiled 4203 runs at 28.98, scored a century (147 not out), accepted 368 catches and stumped 18.

The ODI between South Africa and Australia at Johannesburg on 12 March 2006 was a classic, 'a freak that'll never be repeated', to quote Chris Broad, the match referee. Australia amassed a record and what appeared an unsurpassable total of 4 for 434 in 50 overs, skipper Ricky Ponting stroking

164 off 105 balls and belting 13 fours and nine sixes. Incredibly, South Africa scored 9 for 438 off 49.5 overs to win this fascinating duel by one wicket and with a ball to spare. Herschelle Gibbs hit a superlative 175 off 111 balls, smacking 21 fours and seven sixes. The tail was held together by Boucher as his team collapsed from 4 for 327 to 9 for 433. With two balls remaining and one run to win Boucher hit Brett Lee for a four 'to complete one of the finest fifties—and the most phenomenal of games', according to *Wisden* 2007.

In the Test series to follow, he demonstrated immaculate skill behind the stumps. Like his captain Graeme Smith, Boucher loved combat with Australians and hit two gritty fifties. After being South Africa's highest scorer in Champion's Trophy in India in 2006, he hit two timely fifties against India in South Africa, enabling his country to win a see-sawing 3-Test series 2–1.

Born on 3 December 1976 in Cape Province, Mark Verdon Boucher was in and out as South Africa's captain but it is as a wicketkeeper-batsman that he will be judged.

Golden age is always in the past but in Gilchrist and Boucher we have high quality wicketkeeper-batsmen in this decade. Below are their figures at Test and one-day international (ODI) levels (as at 21 March 2008).

Player	Tests	Runs	Av.	100s	ct.	st.	ODIs	Runs	Av.	100s	ct.	st.
Adam Gilchrist	96	5570	47.60	17	379	37	287	9619	35.89	16	417	55
Mark Boucher	111	4098	29.91	4	406	19	263	4203	28.98	1	368	18

ct. = caught; st. = stumped.

Their statistics raise an interesting question. If a World XI of 2000s is to be selected who would keep wickets? Gilchrist would be an automatic choice in ODIs for his ferocious batting as an opener but in Tests it would be really hard to pick the gloveman.

KUMAR SANGAKKARA
Sri Lanka

A versatile all-rounder, there are few things left-handed Kumar Sangakkara cannot do. He is an elegant stroke player, a stylish wicketkeeper and a deep thinker of the game whose ambition is to become a lawyer when he hangs up his gloves.

He arrived on the international scene with a bang against South Africa and Pakistan in the 2000 Triangular Singer series in Sri Lanka. Sri Lanka was in trouble at 3 for 35 in Galle when the 22-year-old showed maturity beyond his years when rescuing his team with a stroke-filled 85 from 115 balls, hitting 11 fours. Sri Lanka won narrowly and Sangakkara was made Man of the Match. He had to struggle to become the regular keeper for his country as the hard-hitting Romesh Kaluwitherana was established in the team as a wicketkeeper. But once in the Test team, Sangakkara was hard to shift. His batting oozed class and, according to Charlie Austin, 'he possessed the grace of David Gower with the attitude of an Australian'.

He can sledge when provoked, capable of upsetting the most unflappable characters. Indeed a barrister in the making! The selectors reasoned that wicketkeeping was interfering with his batting and relieved him of glove duties in one-day internationals after the 2003 World Cup. This improved his batting average but left the team unbalanced and he was brought back as the keeper in one-dayers.

A charismatic character, Sangakkara is tipped as a future captain. His attitude, aptitude and flamboyance earned him a spot in the International Cricket Council (ICC) World XI for the Super Series one-day matches in Melbourne in October 2005.

And a sixer climbs the sky. Sri Lankan Kumar Sangakkara hits a towering six during the 2007 World Cup in Port-of-Spain.

Wicketkeeping Test All-Rounders

In July 2006 he made headlines by scoring 287 against South Africa in Colombo and was engaged in a third wicket partnership of 624 runs with Mahela Jayawardene (374). It remains the highest partnership for any wicket and the only stand of over 600 runs, not only in Test but in all first-class matches. More important is the fact that this record was not set when the match was 'dead'. His 287 had come off 457 balls and contained 35 fours. Incidentally, he had not kept wicket in this series.

He followed this double hundred with back-to-back unbeaten centuries when touring New Zealand in December 2006. In the first Test in Christchurch he scored an unbeaten 100 out of Sri Lanka's 170, which was 56 per cent of the team's total as the visitors lost by six wickets. But Sri Lanka levelled the series one-all, as Sangakkara stroked 156 not out. In the 2-Test series, he had made 291 runs at 145.50 but again he was not keeping.

Born in Matale, Sri Lanka, on 27 October 1977, Sangakkara was a bright academic student and was awarded the Ryde Gold medal at Trinity College. He was drawn to tennis but switched back to cricket after watching top Sri Lankan and overseas cricketers. Just as well as he has scored 6032 runs at an impressive average of 56.37, hitting 16 centuries and 24 fifties in 71 Tests. He kept wickets in 47 of these Tests and his statistics when he kept wicket and when he did not are as under:

Kumar Sangakkara	Tests	Runs	Average	HS	100s	50s	Caught	Stumped
As a wicketkeeper	47	3093	41.24	230	7	11	124	20
Not as a wicketkeeper	24	2939	91.84	287	9	13	25	0
Total	71	6032	56.37	287	16	24	149	20

This shows that his batting was affected when he kept wickets, his batting average escalating from 41.24 to 91.84, more than double. Thus like Adam Gilchrist he was a batsman who kept wicket than a keeper in the Ames, Marsh, Healy and Boucher mould.

Injury kept him out of the first Test against Australia in Brisbane in November 2007 but he gave a sterling display in the second and final Test in Hobart a week later. Against Australia's daunting total of 5 declared for 542, Sri Lanka replied with 246 (Sangakkara 57, skipper Mahela Jayawardene 104). Then when set an astronomical 507 runs to win, Sangakkara played a magnificent innings of 192 (including 27 fours and a six) and was ninth out at 364. He was given out caught in the slips but the ball was nowhere near his bat or glove. It had touched his shoulder. Later umpire Rudi Koertzen apologised to Sangakkara for his error. The way Sangakkara was batting, it appeared that a win target of 507 was not an impossibility.

He carried on brilliantly against England in the Kandy Test of December 2007 when he scored 92 out of Sri Lanka's total of 188 and 152 in the second innings as his country won by 88 runs. He was all smiles as he received the Man of the Match award. And why not? He became only the ninth batsman to register centuries against all nine Test-playing nations. He is the only batsman to have recorded 150 runs or more in four consecutive Tests. Here are his scores from 3 July to 5 December, 2007: 200 not out vs Bangladesh in Colombo, 222 not out vs Bangladesh in Kandy, 57 and 192 vs Australia in Hobart and 92 and 152 vs England in Kandy. This is more than Bradmanesque as even Don Bradman could not achieve this. In four successive Tests, the smiling Sri Lankan amassed 915 runs at an incredible average of 228.75.

Apart from centuries, catches and stumpings, he is also interested in deep and meaningful literature. In Australia in November 2007, he was seen scouring second-hand bookshops for classics by Lucretius and Shakespeare.

One-day International All-Rounders

As Test all-rounders have dwindled in this age of specialisation, some have emerged in the shorter version of the game. It has also thrown in interesting characters. For instance, Michael Bevan was more of a cat burglar than a bank robber, not armed with machine guns but with enough oil on him to foil the cleverest cop.

Classy Test all-rounder Wasim Akram also holds many records in one-day internationals (ODIs) including in World Cup matches. He is the only bowler to capture 500 wickets in ODIs (502 in 356 matches). Other modern Test all-rounders, Ian Botham, Richard Hadlee, Imran Khan, Kapil Dev, Chris Cairns, Jacques Kallis, Shaun Pollock, Andrew Flintoff… have done equally well in ODIs. Their performances in these matches have been mentioned in Chapter 1 along with their excellence with bat and ball at Test level.

Thanks to limited-overs revolution even a tail-ender is expected to score runs when chasing a target. Hence 'rabbits' are fast becoming an endangered species, with centuries scored by lesser batsmen Jason Gillespie, Chaminda Vaas and Anil Kumble even at Test level.

The ODI specialist all-rounders featured in this Chapter are Steve Waugh, Michael Bevan and Andrew Symonds of Australia, Sanath Jayasuriya of Sri Lanka, Chris Gayle of West Indies, Chris Harris of New Zealand, Lance Klusener of South Africa and Abdul Razzaq and Shahid Afridi from Pakistan. Many more will emerge in the next decade.

STEVE WAUGH

Australia

Steve Rodger Waugh was a cricketing maestro, shining out at both Test and ODI levels as a player, thinker, motivator and leader. But whereas in Test cricket he concentrated mostly on his batting, in ODIs he was a genuine all-rounder, his tight medium paced bowling at the 'death' (in over numbers 45 to 50) contributed to many wins for Australia.

Australian cricket was at a low ebb in the late 1970s and 1980s. First the World Series Cricket, the simultaneous retirements of Greg Chappell, Dennis Lillee and Rod Marsh, and finally the rebel tours to South Africa had clipped Australia's wings. By 1989 Australia had lost to just about every country. So low was Australia's morale that few expected them to make the semi-final of the 1987 World Cup in the Indian subcontinent, let alone winning it. Channel 9 ignored the event, considering Australia as rank outsiders.

However, just one victory, by one run, over India in Bombay (now Mumbai), in the World Cup opener, changed their mindset. The man behind this morale-booster was Steve Waugh. In reply to Australia's 270, India needed only 15 runs to win in the last four overs with four wickets in hand. However, two were run out. In the heart-stopping final over, India needed six runs to win with the last man Maninder Singh on strike. The bowler chosen for the last over was 'Ice Man' Waugh. He conceded four runs and bowled the bearded Maninder off the fifth ball. This one run victory was a confidence booster for Australia.

Their next match against New Zealand in Indore was almost an action replay of the Mumbai thriller. Steve bowled another pressure-cooker final

Steve Waugh bowling against India in his final Test in Sydney in January 2004.

over when the Kiwis needed seven runs with four wickets intact. Steve had their master batsman Martin Crowe (who was in top form with 58 runs off 46 deliveries) caught, bowled Ian Smith the next ball and ran out Martin Snedden, and Australia won their second cliffhanger by three runs.

In the semi-final at Lahore against Pakistan Steve scored 32 not out including 18 in one over from Saleem Jaffer and Australia won. Now to the final in Calcutta (now Kolkata) watched by about 90,000 against old enemy England. With David Boon top scoring, Australia totalled 253. England started confidently but Steve ran out a well-set Bill Athey and bowled free-scoring Allan Lamb in the 47th over. Steve conceded only two runs in the 49th over and had danger man Philip De Freitas caught. That left England 17 runs in the final pulsating over but Craig McDermott allowed only nine and Australia won another thriller and, with it, their first World Cup.

In bowling, batting and fielding, Steve was one of the chief contributors to Australia's surprising and well-merited win. He scored 167 runs at 55.66 and took 11 crucial wickets at 26.67. 'I like to bowl the last few overs', he said. 'Bowling-wise I never feel under too much pressure. I am not the world's greatest bowler but if it gets down to the last couple of overs, I'll back myself against any batsman.'

According to Greg Matthews, 'Steve carried the Australian side during the 1987 World Cup. The resurgence of the team as a one-day side dates back to him.'

If Steve Waugh shone out as a bowler in the 1987 World Cup it was as a batsman—and captain—that he won for Australia the 1999 World Cup in England. The two matches against South Africa which enabled Australia to enter the semi-final and final of the 1999 World Cup were among the most heart-pounding, hair-raising thrillers I have witnessed. At Leeds on 13 June, Steve Waugh scored a priceless 120 off 110 balls, coming in at 3 for 48, chasing 272 and was adjudged Man of the Match. This enabled Australia

Final hurrah for Steve Waugh in his Test farewell, 2004 in Sydney.

to enter the semi-final where their opponents were South Africa again. He scored a valuable 56 after his team was tottering at 4 for 68 and the match ended in a tie. The Aussies entered the final because they had finished higher on the Super Six table. In a tame final, Australia annihilated Pakistan. It was a golden hour for the new captain Steve Waugh who came out of his predecessor Mark Taylor's shadow after this World Cup triumph.

In 325 ODIs, Steve scored 7569 runs at 32.90, hitting three centuries (highest 120 not out) and 45 fifties. He also took 195 wickets at 34.67 (best 4 for 33) and 111 catches. Thus he narrowly fell short of a one-day triple of 2000 runs, 200 wickets and 100 catches. He would have achieved this but for his bad back which almost forced him to give up his bowling in the new millennium. His best match as an ODI all-rounder was against Pakistan in Perth on 2 January 1987 when he followed his 82 runs with a 4 for 48 haul.

Sadly, he was unceremoniously dropped from the ODI side after Australia's poor showing in the 2000–01 VB Series. The tenacious Steve protested against this sacking but could not change the selectors' minds. He went out on his own terms at Test level after a series of tall scores—especially on the Sydney Cricket Ground—but his ambition to play in the 2003 World Cup in South Africa remained unfulfilled. However, the Waugh years will be remembered as much as the Bradman years when Australia reached the invincible status.

Noted journalist Phil Wilkins wrote in the *Sydney Morning Herald*, 'In the environment of limited-overs cricket, Steve Waugh is more than a batsman. He is an all-rounder whose confidence in his medium-paced bowling extends to an enjoyment of competing against the destructive force that is Ian Botham.' Greg Baum, the former editor of *Wisden Australia*, described Steve as 'the ultimate evolved cricketer'.

MICHAEL BEVAN

Australia

Many experts rank Bevan as the finest one-day batsman, not so much for his elegance or slogging but the way he farmed the strike, for his cool temperament and taking a run practically every ball with superb placements.

When Australia's greatest One-Day International XI from 1971 to 2007 was selected in February 2007, the names of Ian Chappell and Allan Border were missing and Greg Chappell could make it only as the 12th man. However, left-handed Michael Bevan was selected as a batting all-rounder, his left-arm spin bowling supplementing his peerless batting at number 6. His batting average of 53.58 in 232 ODIs confirms his standing. He is way ahead of the giants of one-day cricket; Viv Richards (batting average of 47.00), Sachin Tendulkar (44.33) and Brian Lara (40.48). And that too after coming in to bat during the 'slam-bang slog overs' during most of his career. Bevan's batting average remained a world record till 2006 when his namesake and fellow Australian, Michael Hussey, eclipsed him, averaging 55.60 with the bat in 85 ODIs.

Bevan did not indulge in six-hitting sprees like Viv Richards did or the current hurricane-hitters Adam Gilchrist, Sanath Jayasuriya, Andrew Symonds and Shahid Afridi do. Slowly but surely he squeezed life out of his frustrated opponents.

But was he an all-rounder? Does a bowling average of 45.97 (36 wickets in 232 ODIs) put him in the all-rounder category? However, he once did take 10 wickets (4 for 31 and 6 for 82) in a Test against the West Indies in Adelaide in January 1997. Also his left-arm Chinaman type of bowling was often compared with Ernie Toshack's in the 1940s and 1950s and the great Garry Sobers's in 1960s and 1970s. And there was his lissome fielding, 69 catches in ODIs and countless saves near the boundary ropes.

Bevan hit six centuries and 46 fifties in ODIs, either rescuing Australia from certain defeat or guiding them to a surprise victory. Every cricketer has his favourite innings. Bevan's is the one-dayer against the West Indies in Sydney on the New Year of 1996. Chasing the opponents' total of 172, Australia was in a precarious position at 6 for 34 when Ian Healy joined Bevan. It became 7 for 74 when Healy left. Bevan thrives in crises and this was a mega crisis. With Paul Reiffel he added 83 runs but when Reiffel and Shane Warne fell in quick succession, Australia were 9 for 167, five runs to win in the last over with only 'prize rabbit' Glenn McGrath to give him support.

It came down to the final ball from Roger Harper with four runs needed for an epic win. Cool man Bevan lofted it for a four to win by the narrowest of margin, by one wicket off the final ball! 'I reckon my arms were in the air in triumph before the ball reached the boundary', recalls Bevan in his autobiography *The Best of Bevan*. He had scored an unbeaten 78 from 89 balls.

Bob Simpson who had watched most ODIs as a commentator and coach, called this Bevan masterpiece as the 'best chasing innings I've seen'. *Wisden* 1997 described this match as 'the most thrilling game yet'.

While other batsmen resort to slogging at number 6 or 7 in the final overs, Bevan placed a single here, a brace there, a dot ball in between and a spanking cover-drive to the ropes to break the monotony and averaged six runs an over without sweat or a wrinkle. 'He has been, and remains, peerless', concluded Rob Smyth in *Inside Edge* of 2004.

Bevan was more of a cat burglar than a bank robber, not armed with machine guns but with enough oil on him to foil the cleverest cop. He was smooth the way he batted, bowled, fielded, ran between the wickets, or sang on the national television show *It Takes Two*.

Australia's best one-day all-rounder Michael Bevan hitting out in a Pura Cup match in 2005.

LANCE KLUSENER

South Africa

Mention the name Lance Klusener to 10 cricket lovers and nine will remember the 1999 World Cup semi-final between South Africa and Australia. The one person who would like to forget it would be Klusener himself—especially the final tragic over for all South Africans.

Let's recall that heart-stopping over on 17 June 1999 at Birmingham. Australia totalled 213 and South Africa (SA) were 9 for 205 when Australia's fast bowler Damien Fleming bowled the final over. Nine runs were needed for victory for SA in six balls with the in-form batsman Klusener on strike. He was in magnificent form in this World Cup and was then averaging an incredible 136.50 with the bat. He smashed the first two deliveries from Fleming for fours. The score was level and SA needed only one run in four balls. That's when nerves got the better of both Klusener and Allan Donald, the last man in. Donald was almost run out off the third ball.

Now to the fourth fateful ball: Klusener drove straight and charged. Donald was looking at the ball when he realised that Klusener was running towards his end. In a daze, Donald grounded his bat, dropped it and finally started running. Mark Waugh, at mid-on, flicked the ball to Fleming who rolled it to the wicketkeeper Adam Gilchrist who broke the stumps and the South African hearts. It was a nerve-racking tie, both teams all out for an identical score. *Wisden* 2000 described this match as the best one-day international of the 1483 played that far. But as Australia had finished higher on the Super Six table, they were declared winners. They went on to beat Pakistan in a disappointing final to lift the World Cup.

Bang bang all-rounder Lance 'Zulu' Klusener driving with power and poise against the Windies in Centurion in 2004.

One-day International All-Rounders

Klusener later commented, 'In hindsight, there were ten other ways we could have done it, but when you are out there it's not easy. You forget that you have not quite finished the job. We thought we had won it. Maybe, we should have communicated more.'

But for this final-over debacle, it was a grand World Cup for him. He had scored 281 runs at a phenomenal average of 140.50 at a strike-rate of 122.17 and had taken 18 wickets as well with 5 for 21 against Kenya as his best. It was a splendid all-round performance and he was adjudged the Player of the 1999 World Cup.

In 14 World Cup matches in 1999 and 2003, he aggregated 372 runs at an average of 124.00 and at a strike-rate of 121.17. Both are records in international matches.

Lance 'Zulu' Klusener was born in Durban on 4 September 1971 and grew up in his parents' sugarcane farm. All his friends were black farm workers with whom he spoke in Zulu. That is the reason behind his nickname. When practising at provincial nets in Natal, he was spotted by the West Indian great fast bowler Malcolm Marshall. Lance flourished under Marshall's mentorship.

Two years later he made his Test debut against India in Kolkata in November 1996 and started with a bang one would associate with a Zulu warrior. He took 8 for 64 in the second innings on a flat tract. In his fourth Test, also against India but at home in Cape Town, he came in at no. 9 and scored a quickfire 102 off 100 balls with 13 fours and two sixes. He became the 11th player to take eight wickets in an innings and hit a century. Amazingly, Lance had achieved this feat within five weeks.

His Test career was up and down but he excelled in one-dayers with both bat and ball. Fearless Lance hit a six off the last ball from New Zealand's Dion Nash to win a one-dayer in Napier in March 1999. He hit 35 runs off 19 balls and was made Man of the Match.

Ambidextrous Klusener started off as a right-arm fast-medium bowler and a tail-end left-hand batsman. He believes that he turned into an all-rounder when he was told not to bowl for several months following ankle surgery. So he focused on his batting and provided entertainment for the spectators. During the 1999 World Cup his batting assumed Bothamesque proportions.

He was perhaps the most committed and aggressive South African player of them all. In 171 one-day internationals he stroked 3576 runs at 41.10 at an impressive strike-rate of almost 90, hitting two centuries and 19 fifties and captured 192 scalps at 29.95 (taking 5 wickets in an innings six times). His best match as an all-rounder was against Sri Lanka at Lahore in November 1997 for the Wills Golden Jubilee Tournament when he slammed 54 runs off 41 balls and captured 6 for 49, his career-best bowling figures in an ODI. Two days later in the final, also against Sri Lanka, he scored 99 runs (embellished with 11 fours and two sixes) off 96 balls, took two spectacular catches and was made Man of the Tournament.

An erratic genius, Lance Klusener was among the most entertaining players in the game and one of the most intelligent and adaptable.

CHRIS HARRIS
New Zealand

The first New Zealander to capture 200 ODI wickets, he remained the highest wicket-taker for his country until overtaken by Daniel Vettori in 2007. Harris was around NZ cricket from 1990 to 2004 but remained in the shadow of his namesake and sizzling Test all-rounder Chris Cairns. Spectacular Harris was not. Regarded as a one-day specialist, he was at one stage his country's most capped player in the shorter version of the game.

Alec Bannerman had played 28 Tests for Australia in late 19th century. When coaching, he had advised one of his pupils, 'Son, if you are not a cricketer, at least look like one'.

Chris Harris was a genuine one-day international all-rounder achieving the double of 4000 runs and 200 wickets but somehow did not look like a cricketer—especially when he took off his cap to bowl, showing his shiny scalp.

His bowling was ideally suited to the one-day game, a gentle medium pace with late swing which forced the batsmen to do all the hard work. He was a reliable fielder and his batting was effective in the 'death overs'. At one stage in 1997–98 he scored 310 runs against Zimbabwe and Australia without getting out and averaged 320.00 with the bat.

Born on 20 November 1969 in Christchurch, Canterbury, Chris Zinzan Harris was an ambidextrous cricketer, batting left-handed and bowling right-arm medium fast. He scored 4379 runs at 29.00 with a century and 16 fifties, took 203 wickets at 37.50 with 5 for 42 as his best and 96 catches

An ecstatic Chris Harris celebrates after taking a wicket against England at Old Trafford in 1999.

in 250 ODIs. Until recently ovetaken by Damiel Vettori in 2007, he was New Zealand's highest wicket-taker in one-dayers. His father, P.G. Zinzan Harris, had played nine Tests for New Zealand from 1955 to 1964.

Chris's highest ODI score of 130 was recorded in the 1996 World Cup match against Australia at Chennai. And his top score in a first-class match was 251 not out for Canterbury against Central Districts at Ranjiora in January 1997. It included 29 fours and he was adjudged Man of the Match.

One-day International All-Rounders

Chris took his 200th ODI wicket in the NatWest Series final against the West Indies at Lord's on 10 July 2004, his 244th match. Not only was he the first New Zealander to reach 200 ODI scalps, he was the second in the world after Sri Lanka's Sanath Jayasuriya to attain the ODI double of 4000 runs and 200 wickets. He was happier because his country had won the final to lift the Cup.

Of his 203 wickets, 29 were caught by him which was a record then. His best bowling, 5 for 42, was against Pakistan at Sialkot on 6 December 1996 when he wrecked the opponents' strong middle order.

Apart from his lone century, his successful batting sequence was in Zimbabwe in October 1997. In three consecutive matches he scored 77, 29 and 18 without getting dismissed. His unbeaten 77 was at Bulawayo (when the Kiwis needed 30 runs from the last two overs and 15 in the final over) enabled New Zealand to tie the match. Then when New Zealand was struggling at 6 for 45 against Australia in Melbourne two months later, he scored an unbeaten 62.

In first-class cricket he averaged 45.75 with the bat (highest score an unbeaten 251) and 36.03 with the ball. His leisurely right-arm deliveries have teased and at times bemused some of the world's best batsmen, particularly on New Zealand wickets. On slow dry pitches his mystery leg cutters were most effective.

SANATH JAYASURIYA

Sri Lanka

Jayasuriya's brutal bat-wielding is complemented with effective and clever left-arm spinning where his stock leg-stump attack is mixed with subtle variations of pace. His statistics are staggering, being the only cricketer to achieve the ODI triple of 12,000 runs, 300 wickets and 100 catches.

Dizzily dangerous, Sanath Jayasuriya is one of world's most uncompromising hitters of the ball at Test, one-day international (ODI), World Cup, first-class and Twenty20 levels. In ODIs, the short, balding, left-handed Jayasuriya remains cricket's Mr Adventure—an all-rounder and a match-winner, even at 38. Sanath Teran Jayasuriya was born on 30 June 1969 in Matara, Sri Lanka. The first cricketer to play 400 ODIs, he has scored 12,310 runs at an average of 32.30 at an attractive strike-rate of 90.39, hitting 25 centuries (highest score 189) and 64 fifties; taken 308 wickets at 36.39 with 5 wickets in an innings four times (best 6 for 29) and 116 catches in 411 ODIs.

His run aggregate of 12,310 is second only to Indian champion batsman Sachin Tendulkar's 16,361 in 417 ODIs. Jayasuriya's 25 centuries are third highest after Tendulkar's 42 and Australia's Ricky Ponting with 26 in 298 ODIs. Jayasuriya's 249 sixes is a record in ODIs. The next best is Pakistan's 'Mad Max' Shahid Afridi (245 sixes in 253 ODIs). No one else has hit 200 sixes in this form of cricket.

Jayasuriya's top ODI score of 189 came off only 161 balls and was against India at Sharjah in the Coca-Cola Champions Trophy final on 29 October 2000. This knock included 21 fours and four spectacular sixes, his last 89 runs had come off only 43 balls and he was adjudged Man of the Match (MoM) and Man of the Series. His 189 remains the joint second highest score in ODI history after Pakistan's Saeed Anwar stroked 194 against India at Chennai in 1996–97 and the West Indies legend Viv Richards smashed 189 not out against England at Manchester in 1984.

Jayasuriya's best bowling spell was against England at Moratuwa, Sri Lanka on 20 March 1993 when he captured 6 for 29. His best 'double' was against Australia in Sydney on 9 January 2003 when he hit 122, took 4 for 39 and captained his country to a 79 run surprise victory in the VB Series. His century came off only 87 balls for which he was cheered by a crowd of almost 34,000 and deserved the MoM award. Five days later on the same venue, but against England, he smashed a dynamic 106, led Sri Lanka to another win and was adjudged MoM again.

He established himself as a world class batsman and an innovator of 'pinch-hitting' during the 1996 World Cup in the Indian subcontinent. Against India in Delhi on 2 March 1996, opening batsmen Jayasuriya and Romesh Kaluwitharana smashed 42 runs in the first three overs and shot past 50 runs in five overs. Jayasuriya charged to 79 off 76 deliveries with 9 fours and two sixes but the latter part of his innings appeared sedate after the initial rampage.

The attacking Sri Lankan duo changed the way ODIs were played. Instead of settling for 60 to 70 runs from the first 15 overs when fielding restrictions applied, the 'Jaya-Kalu' pair attempted to reach 100 in those first 15 overs; smashing 90 against Zimbabwe, 117 vs India, 123 vs Kenya and 121 vs England. And the term 'pinch-hitter' was coined for openers going for quick runs from the first ball, no 'playing yourself in' or 'first watch the ball' theory. They were the trendsetters of this type of instant attack.

Against England at Faisalabad on 9 March 1996, Jayasuriya—later to be named the Most Valued Player of the 1996 World Cup—clobbered 82 off 44 balls

And that's a four! Sanath Jayasuriya, Sri Lanka's aggressive opening batsman, pulls one against England in Colombo in 2007

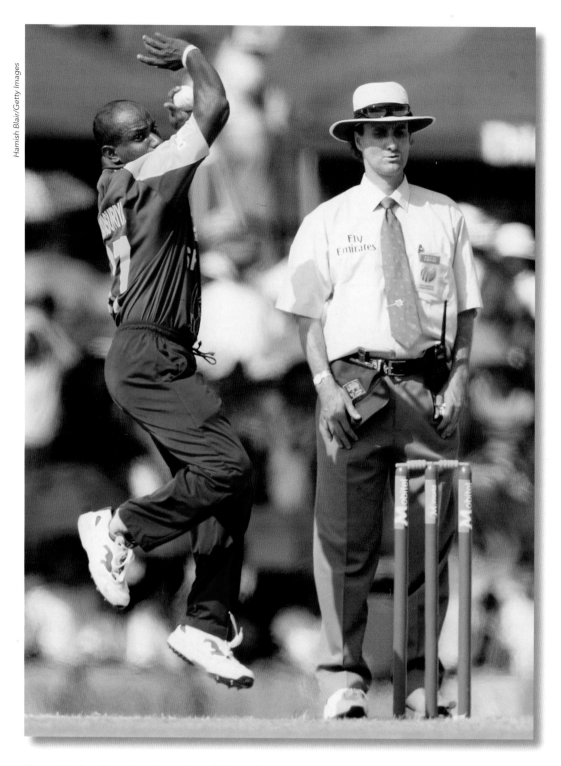

*Jayasuriya bowls against Australia in 2004 under
the watchful eye of umpire 'Billie' Bowden.*

at a thundering strike-rate of 186. While belting 13 fours and three sixes, he was most particularly savage on the left-arm spin of Richard Illingworth who he smacked for four fours in a row and on the seam of Phillip DeFreitas. Off the latter's second over he took 22 runs. 'Jayasuriya's assault on England's bowling in the quarter final at Faisalabad was authentic, aggressive batting without insult to the coaching manual', commented *Wisden* 1997.

Sri Lanka shocked the world by winning the 1996 World Cup, beating Australia by seven wickets in the final at Lahore.

However, Jayasuriya was not just a one-day wonder. In Tests his figures are equally impressive, 6973 runs at 40.07 with 14 centuries (top score 340) and 31 fifties and 98 wickets at 34.31 with two hauls of five wickets per innings (best 5 for 34) and 78 catches in 110 matches. His masterpiece of 340 runs was recorded against India in the Colombo Test of August 1997. He went in as an opener and added 576 runs for the second wicket with Roshan Mahanama (225 runs). It was then the highest partnership for any wicket at Test level and fell only one run short of the first-class record held by India's Vijay Hazare and Gul Mahomed for Baroda against Holkar at Baroda in 1946–47. Jayasuriya had played for 799 minutes, faced 578 balls and hit 36 fours and two sixes. Sri Lanka declared at 6 for 952, which is a Test record. His 340 was then the fourth highest Test score and now is the seventh highest.

His batting records are so awe-inspiring that one tends to forget his useful left-arm spin bowling which enabled him to bag 308 scalps in one-dayers. He was also an excellent close-in fielder. But it was his majestic and daredevil batting that enthralled millions. When Sanath Jayasuriya, 38, announced his retirement from Test cricket on 5 December 2007 after scoring 78 in his final Test innings (against England at Kandy), team mate Kumar Sangakkara said, 'That World Cup win [in 1996] probably not just inspired me, but a whole generation of young cricketers to try and play for Sri Lanka. He changed the face of world cricket, especially in the one-day arena.'

SHAHID AFRIDI
Pakistan

A flamboyant all-rounder, 'never afraid' Afridi holds the record for the best strike-rate (110.95) in ODIs, which is more than a run every ball he faced in 253 matches. But there is more! He has scored the fastest century in ODIs. His century against Sri Lanka at Nairobi on 4 October 1996 came off 37 balls and included 11 sixes and 6 fours.

Shahid Afridi, Adam Gilchrist and Sanath Jayasuriya are the 'Three Musketeers' of current one-day internationals. They are not quite the 'one for all and all for one' type but rather are 'all for sixes', brandishing their bats as swords to flay their opponents into submission. Between them, the six-o-maniacs have hammered 643 sixes in 951 ODIs and 209 sixes in 232 Tests. Jayasuriya and Afridi also share the record of hitting most sixes in an ODI innings, 11 each in 1996. Afridi's 102 against Sri Lanka in Nairobi on 4 October 1996 included 11 sixes and six fours and his strike-rate was an astounding 255.00.

Imagination boggles had the three played in the same team, a total of 450 runs in a 50-over match would have become the norm rather than an impossibility.

At Test level he was just as slam-bang, smashing a Test century off 78 balls against the West Indies at Bridgetown in 2005. To prove that this was not a fluke 'Mad Max' Afridi repeated this feat, his century against India at Lahore also came off 78 deliveries in 2005–06.

Born in Khyber, Pakistan, on 1 March 1980, Shahid Afridi made his debut in an ODI as a 16-year-old leg-spinner. He surprised every one but himself by

Tom Shaw/Getty Images

*Pakistan's dynamic batsman Shahid Afridi smacks
one against England in the 2006 Lord's Test.*

265

slamming the fastest century in his maiden innings, off 37 balls, as mentioned earlier. In 253 ODIs, he has scored 5369 runs at 23.75 with four centuries (highest score 109) and 29 fifties and taken 217 wickets at 36.02 with his mixture of leg-breaks, googlies and medium pacers (best figures being 5 for 11) and 89 catches. His best match was against England in Lahore on 27 October 2000 when he followed his 5 for 40 (his skidding quicker deliveries causing havoc) with a match-winning 61 off 69 balls as swarms of flies attracted by the humidity and floodlights, descended on the ground.

Handsome Afridi's compulsive hitting kept him in and out of Test arena but a combination of maturity on and off the field, and advice from coach Bob Woolmer—alas no more—saw him blossom into one of modern cricket's most dangerous players. He went berserk against India and hit his Test best of 156 from only 128 balls at Faisalabad in January 2006.

Expect the unexpected when Shahid Afridi is in the middle.

An agile fielder with a strong arm, his versatile spin bowling has improved in recent years and on occasions he gets turn as well as drift, and when least expected he delivers a vicious faster ball and an off-spinner. Expect the unexpected when Shahid Afridi is in the middle.

ABDUL RAZZAQ
Pakistan

Abdul Razzaq may lack the charisma and the 'six appeal' of team-mate Shahid Afridi but remains a useful player with both bat and ball. He appeared laid-back but was determined and supremely gifted. Early in his career he promised to be Pakistan's most gifted all-rounder since Imran Khan and although he has not quite lived up to that promise, he remained Pakistan's utility man.

He showed the full range of his versatility in Australia in 2000 when he was adjudged the Player of the Carlton & United Tournament with 225 runs and 14 wickets. I vividly remember Razzaq smacking Australian great Glenn McGrath for five fours in one over in Sydney on 19 January.

He scored 4465 runs at 29.96 (belting 103 sixes) with two centuries (highest score 112) and 22 fifties in 231 ODIs. Capable of bowling skiddy seamers at a lively pace, he took 246 wickets at 31.13, grabbing 5 wickets in an innings three times with 6 for 35 (against Bangladesh in Dhaka on 25 January 2002 as his best) and 31 catches. His bowling is characterized by a galloping approach, accuracy and reverse-swing.

Unfortunately, he was given no fixed batting order and batted from top of the order to the bottom. 'He boasts of a prodigious array of strokes and is particularly strong driving through the cover and mid-off from both front and back foot', observed Osman Samiuddin in *Cricinfo*. 'He has two gears: block and blast.' He once scored four painfully slow runs against Australia and yet hammered England's bowlers for 51 runs off 22 balls at Karachi on 15 December 2005.

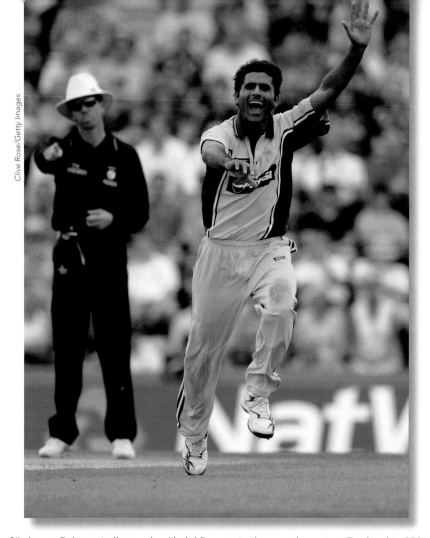

"Howzatt?" shouts Pakistani all-rounder Abdul Razzaq in the match against England in 2006.

Born on 2 December 1979 in Lahore, Abdul (also known as Abdur) Razzaq played two outstanding ODIs in Australia. Against India at Hobart on 21 January 2000, 20-year-old Razzaq scored an unbeaten 70 (with four fours and two sixes) off 52 balls and snared 5 for 48. Then against the mighty Aussies in Perth on 30 January 2005, he followed his 4 for 53 with 63 not out off 61 balls, enriched with two fours and two sixes, and Pakistan won by three wickets.

Like Afridi, Abdul Razzaq was not consistent but always posed a threat with the bat and the ball. They typified the Pakistani norm of being terrific one day and terrible the next.

Pakistan's all-rounder Abdul Razzaq is hitting out against India in the Peshawar international in 2004.

CHRIS GAYLE

West Indies

Gayle is a pugnacious left-handed opening batsman who shows opposing bowlers little respect and no mercy. His fiery batting is supplemented by his brisk right-arm off-spin. As a batsman Gayle attacks from the first ball and loves to hit through the covers off front or back foot. Although spanking square cuts and cover-drives are his strong points, he seldom hesitates to hook or pull a bouncer.

Described as 'Invincibles' in 1980s, the West Indies team is sliding down to become the third most 'vincible' after Zimbabwe and Bangladesh. With the retirement of Brian Lara after the 2007 World Cup and the ageing of Shivnarine Chanderpaul, the future of Windies cricket rests with their ambidextrous all-rounder Chris Gayle.

He made his ODI debut when ten days short of his 20th birthday and his Test debut six months later. The highlight of his Test career has been his 317 against South Africa at St John's, Antigua in May 2005. He started this innings by hammering Shaun Pollock for 14 runs in the opening over, reached his 50 off 34 balls, 100 off 96 and went on and on as the West Indies piled on 747 and all 11 South Africans (including wicketkeeper Mark Boucher) bowled.

In ODIs he is considered an all-rounder scoring 6244 runs at 39.02 with 15 centuries (an unbeaten 153 being his highest) and 34 fifties, 142 wickets at 32.52 (5 for 46 being his best) and 81 catches in 176 matches. His proud moment has been hitting England's fast bowler Matthew Hoggard for 24 runs (six fours) in an over against England at The Oval in 2004.

The West Indies' cavalier Chris Gayle hits out against
England in the Old Trafford Test of June 2007.

One-day International All-Rounders

Apart from Sanath Jayasuriya, Gayle is the only one to achieve the double of a century and three wickets in the same ODI on three occasions:

- *He smacked an unbeaten 112 off 75 balls and took 4 for 24 off 10 overs against Zimbabwe at Harare on 30 November 2003*
- *made a match-winning 132 not out and took 3 for 57 against England at Lord's on 6 July 2004 and*
- *hit 101 and bagged 3 for 31 against England at Ahmedabad, India, in the Champions Trophy 2006. He was the Player of the Champions Trophy 2006 where he hit three centuries, including a 106-ball hundred against South Africa in the semi-final.*

Gayle is also the second cricketer after Jayasuriya to score 50 or more runs and take three or more wickets in the same ODI six times, and the only one to perform the double of 50 runs and four wickets in the same match three times. He is currently the captain of the West Indies.

Born in Kingston, Jamaica on 21 September 1979, Chris Henry Gayle is image conscious and often wears silver-frame sun glasses, even when bowling.

Summed up *Wisden* 2007, 'His deceptively languid off-spin—slow, slow, quick—made him a genuine all-rounder in the one-day game [in 2006], and his left-handed brand of stand and deliver were one of the few reasons to keep watching the West Indies. If Gayle could only convert his cameos into concrete, there would have been even more.'

ANDREW SYMONDS

Australia

Dreadlocks, zinc-painted lips, lordly swagger when going in to bat or about to bowl, diving horizontal to save a four. That's Andrew 'Roy' Symonds in a nutshell. He exudes excitement and embodies cricket's 50 over games and Twenty20 matches. In Tests he is just making his mark but in one-day internationals he is the complete package.

Symonds is a devastating batsman with a penchant for sixes, a versatile and underrated two-in-one bowler (who can mix up medium-pace with off-spin) and an extraordinary fielder in the Jonty Rhodes mould who dives to take a catch a millimetre from grass and converts a sure four into a brilliant run-out. Birmingham-born, Queensland-raised and of West Indian origin, Symonds is a multinational who made his mark when playing county cricket for Gloucestershire.

Against Glamorgan at Abergavenny in August 1995, the 20-year-old Symonds hit an unbeaten 254 off 206 balls with 16 sixes and in the second innings 76 runs with four sixes. Both 16 sixes in an innings and 20 sixes in a match are records in first-class cricket. Against Sussex at Hove in June that year, his fierce hits struck the same spectator, a woman from Bristol, *twice* when he scored 83. Having been struck in the face by a four, she returned from treatment only to be hit on the leg by a six from the rampaging Symonds. Ouch! And it was back to the first-aid room for the bandaged lady.

After this season he was elected the Young Cricketer of the Year and selected for England 'A' team to tour Pakistan in 1995–96. After a lot

A big hit by Australia's Andrew Symonds during a one day international in Nagpur, India, in 2007. M.S. Dhoni is behind the wickets.

of deliberation he declined the offer and opted to play for Queensland in domestic tournaments.

Born on 9 June 1975 in Birmingham, England, he announced himself as a promising free-hitting batsman in December1992. The 17-year-old shared in a record first-wicket stand of 446 with Matthew Mott in a 50-over match for Gold Coast Dolphins against Souths at Wynnum, Brisbane. Symonds's swashbuckling 270 had come off 99 balls and included 27 fours and 14 sixes.

He has been in and out of Test cricket but has made his position secure in late 2007 with consisteht batting performances. The 32-year-old has scored 1031 runs at 41.24 and taken 22 wickets at 34.81 and 14 catches in 19 Tests. An entertaining batsman, he has smacked 21 sixes, that is a six every Test. His innings of 156 came in a crisis. In the fourth Ashes Test in Melbourne in December 2006, Australia was in trouble at 5 for 84 when he joined Matthew Hayden. They added match-winning 279 runs for the sixth wicket, Symond's spectacular innings included 15 fours and a six.

On the same ground a year earlier, they had added 124 electrifying runs against South Africa. For an hour on 29 December 2005 it rained sixes, Hayden (137 with two sixes) and Symonds (72 off 54 balls with six sixes). In this match Symonds had also taken five wickets (3 for 50 and 2 for 6).

Nicknamed Roy, Symond's record in the shorter version of the game is

He has hammered 99 sixes so far and his strike-rate is 92.72.

even more impressive. He has scored 4845 runs at 39.71 with six centuries (top score 156) and 27 fifties and taken 125 wickets at 38.36 with the best figures of 5 for 18 (against Bangladesh in Manchester on 25 June 2005) and 79 catches in 190 ODIs. He has hammered 99 sixes so far and his strike-rate is 92.72.

One-day International All-Rounders

His top score in ODIs was against New Zealand at Wellington in the second Chappell-Hadlee Trophy match on 7 December 2005 where his 156 came off just 127 balls—the last 56 in only 18 deliveries—and included 12 fours and eight sixes. As Australia won by only two runs, Man of the Match Symond's hurricane hitting was as crucial as it was entertaining. After the innings, which included three consecutive sixes off Chris Cairns as Symonds galloped from 100 to his dismissal in 18 deliveries, Ricky Ponting said 'nobody else could bat like that.'

'Roy' Symonds is an entertainment machine but a coach's nightmare. His previous coach Toot Byron lamented, 'I used to hate watching him bat. He wasn't in control of his shot selection… He'd get 24 off an over and then go [get] out on the last ball of the over.'

'Roy' is anything but conventional. There is a story that he once turned up barefoot and wearing a cowboy hat for a contract meeting with Cricket Australia's then Chief Executive Malcolm Speed. No wonder he is labelled as a dreadlocked Queensland larrikin!

Also during a one-day international against Bangladesh at Cardiff on 18 June 2005 he turned up drunk on the morning of the match. For this he copped a two match ban. He was the One-Day International Player of the Year in January 2005 at the Allan Border Medal Night and would have retained this title the next year but graciously ruled himself ineligible because of turning up drunk before the match against Bangladesh in Cardiff.

This is the story of Symond's life, up with the stars one day, down in the dog house the next. A surprise selection for the 2003 World Cup in South Africa, he was an important contributor in Australia regaining the Cup. He played the innings of his life against Pakistan on 11 February at Johannesburg. In this opening game, Australia was struggling at 4 for 86 (losing Adam Gilchrist for one, Damien Martyn for nought, Jimmy Maher for nine and Hayden for

27) when Symonds smashed an unbeaten 143 off 125 balls to carry his team to a comfortable 82 runs victory.

Australia was again in trouble at 3 for 51 against Sri Lanka at Port Elizabeth in the semi-final on 18 March when rescued by Symonds who made a patient 91 (by his standard!) off 118 balls and Australia won by 48 runs. He did not get a chance to bat in the final against India five days later as Australia plundered 2 for 359 but took 2 for 7 and Australia triumphed by 125 runs.

Before the 2003 World Cup he had managed only 762 runs in ODIs at a disappointing average of 23. Since then he has averaged over 48 with the bat in subsequent ODIs and has become a folk hero. By the end of 2007, he averaged 40.99 with the bat. Statistically, he appears a batsman rather than an all-rounder but his steady bowling and stupendous fielding make him an important member of the champion Aussie side of the 2000s.

His steady bowling and stupendous fielding make him an important member of the champion Aussie side of the 2000s.

As to how much he means to the Australian one-day team was put in perspective when he ripped the tendon from his arm in an ODI against England in Sydney on 2 February 2007. And suddenly, Australia seemed to lose its air of invincibility by getting beaten in five matches in a row; two to England in the Commonwealth Bank Tri-series final in Australia and three to New Zealand in the Chappell–Hadlee Trophy in New Zealand in February 2007. This was the worst losing streak for Australia in a decade.

Symonds made headlines when Australia toured India in September–October 2007. In seven ODIs he topped batting aggregate and averages from both sides by scoring 365 runs at an average of 73.00 and a brilliant strike-rate of 110.60. A model of consistency, he scored 87, 89, 75 and 107, clobbering

12 sixes and was the undisputed Player of the Series. Yet he was treated shamefully by sections of the crowd at some venues. They hackled him with monkey chants when fielding in the deep. He later made it clear that he had not lodged complaints about this treatment. 'Over the past couple of weeks I have felt as though I have been put in a situation that is not of my making', he said in the *Sydney Morning Herald*.

This crowd reaction was surprising as he has been popular wherever he has played. His six-appeal and acrobatic fielding have won him a legion of admirers.

Symond's top score of 162 not out came in the acrimonious Sydney Test against India in January 2008. This innings was behind Australia's 122 run win which gave them their record-equalling 16th consecutive Test victory and the Border-Gavaskar Trophy. He was adjudged Man of the Match but was also involved in a bitter on-field controversy involving India's off-spinner Harbhajan Singh. Allegations of racial taunts were floated but unproven and the controversy was resolved. Many issues were raised but it is beyond the scope of this book to go into the details.

Symond's contributions as a spectacular batsman, a marvellous fielder and a two-in-one bowler make him an all-rounder to fear, especially in one-day internationals. More is to come from this extraordinary cricketer.

In a rare self-analytical mood, Symonds revealed, 'In the past I was a man without a map when I went out to bat'. Now he understands his role perfectly, thanks to the 'Street Directory' loaned to him by the former wild character and now his captain Ricky Ponting.

Snippets

Trott's Tragedy

For all sad words of tongue or pen, the saddest are these: Albert Trott. In his Test debut for Australia against England in Adelaide in January 1895, tall, moustached and confident 'Alberto' Trott went in to bat at no.10 and scored 38 not out and 72 not out against a strong attack of Tom Richardson, Bill Lockwood, Bobby Peel and Johnny Briggs. In the second innings he captured 8 for 43, becoming the first bowler to take eight wickets in an innings on Test debut. In the second Test in Sydney he made an unbeaten 85, thus recording 195 runs in his first two Tests without being dismissed.

In three Tests he had marvellous all round figures of 205 runs at 102.50 and nine wickets at 21.33. His reward? The 23-year-old was dropped from the Australian squad to England, captained by his elder brother Harry in 1896. Disappointed, he migrated to England and representing Middlesex he achieved the double of 1000 runs and 200 wickets twice, in 1899 and 1900. He hit some memorable sixes off Fred Tate and Monty Noble. But these spectacular sixes went to his head and he turned into a slogger. He also took all 10 wickets in an innings against Somerset in Taunton in 1900.

Selected to represent England against South Africa in 1898–99, he took 4 for 61 and 5 for 49 in the first Test in Johannesburg and 4 for 69 and 4 for 19 in the second and final Test in Cape Town. Surprisingly, this turned out to be 26-year-old Trott's final Test match. Why, he must have asked then, as we ask the same question a century later.

In five Tests for Australia and England he had scored 228 runs at 38.00 and taken 26 wickets at 15.00. To be discarded after such impressive figures by two countries must have been heart-breaking for him.

After 1904 he put on weight and in 1907, in his benefit match for Middlesex against Somerset at Lord's, he took four wickets in four balls and then finished off the match by taking another hat-trick in the same innings. Thus he deprived himself of a full day's gate money and his wry comment was that he had bowled himself into the penury. He became a first-class umpire from 1911 to 1913 but his health deteriorated. Plagued by ill health, loss of form and acute financial problems, he shot himself through the head at his lodgings at Willesden Green. He was only 41. It was a tragic end to a brilliant but erratic career.

What a swan song for Jason!

Australia's Jason Gillespie cannot be qualified as an all-rounder but in 2006 he had his big moment. Call it a fairy story which should start with 'Once upon a time' and end with 'And then there were none!' In the 2-Test series against Bangladesh in Bangladesh in March 2006, fast bowler Gillespie averaged 231.00 with the bat and 11.25 with the ball. In the second Test in Chittagong he surprised every one, including himself, by scoring an unbeaten 201 as a nightwatchman and taking 3 for 11 in the first innings. For this grand all-round performance he was made Man of the Match and Man of the Series. And, look at the irony, the 31-year-old was never picked for Australia again.

One and only for Hirst and Parks

In 1906, Yorkshire legend George Hirst became the only cricketer to score 2000 runs (2385) and take 200 wickets (208) in one first-class season. And in 1937 James

H. Parks became the only one to score 3000 runs (3003) and take 100 wickets (101) in a season for Sussex. Another Yorkshire legend, Wilfred Rhodes, achieved the first-class double of 1000 runs and 100 wickets most times (16).

Lindsay's prolific Test series

South Africa's wicketkeeper batsman Denis Lindsay had a prolific Test series against Australia in 1966–67, hitting 606 runs at 86.57 (more than anyone else on either side, and it was the highest aggregate by any wicketkeeper in a Test rubber). He also held 24 catches as his country beat Australia for the first time on home soil at the 22nd attempt and after a 64 year wait. His batting sequence in the Test series was remarkable: 69 and 182 (including five sixes) in Johannesburg, five and 81 in Cape Town, 137 in Durban and 131 in Johannesburg again. In the first Test in Johannesburg he also took six catches in an innings becoming the first keeper to score a century and snap six catches in one Test. His victims included Australia's top order batsmen Bill Lawry, Ian Redpath, Bob Cowper, Keith Stackpole and Ian Chappell and also Brian Taber. He took two more catches in the second innings, Cowper and Chappell.

His overall Test figures were impressive, 1130 runs at 37.66 (with three centuries and five fifties) and 59 dismissals (57 caught and two stumped) in 19 Tests.

The Murray Quartet

Of the seven Murrays to play Test cricket, four were wicketkeeper-batsmen, John from England and Deryck, David and Junior from the West Indies. Here are the statistics of the unrelated Murray quartet:

Snippets

Murray	Test span	Tests	Runs	Ave	HS	100s	50s	ct	st	D/T
John T. (Eng)	1952–75	21	506	22.00	112	1	2	52	3	2.62
Deryck (WI)	1960–81	62	1993	22.90	91	0	11	181	8	3.05
David (WI)	1970–84	19	601	21.46	84	0	3	57	5	3.26
Junior (WI)	1987–01	33	918	22.39	101*	1	3	99	3	3.09

HS = Highest Score; * = not out; ct. = caught; st. = stumped; D/T = Dismissals per Test.

All four Murrays had batting averages in early 20s (from 21 to 23) and made about three dismissals (2.6 to 3.3) per Test.

Franklyn's fireworks

Born in Barbados, Franklyn Stephenson played 219 first-class matches for Barbados, Gloucestershire, Nottinghamshire, Sussex, Orange Free State and Tasmania. His around-the-world safari enabled him to collect 8622 runs at 27.99 with 12 centuries (highest score 166) and 792 wickets at 24.26. The globetrotter missed out on Test selection because he toured South Africa in 1980s and incurred a ban. He was a fearsome opening bowler mixing up pace and swing. He was also a useful batsman. For Nottinghamshire against Yorkshire in Nottingham in September1988, he put up an extraordinary all-round performance, slamming 111 and 117 and taking 4 for 105 and 7 for 117. It was the last match of the season and he reached both his 1000th run and his 100th wicket in this epic game. After retirement from cricket he took up golf, which he played to professional standard in Barbados.

Double internationals

Let me conclude with the ultimate all-rounders—the double internationals; those who have represented their country in two sports. Although it is beyond the scope of this book to give a complete and authentic list of cricketers who were double internationals in team sports, here is an interesting selection.

Test cricketers who played Football (Soccer) at international level

England: C.B. Fry, Arthur Milton, Andy Ducat, R.E. 'Tip' Foster, Harry Makepeace, Hon. Alfred Lyttelton, Leslie Gay, Harold 'Wally' Hardinge, Albert Knight, Jack Arnold, William Gunn, Jack Sharp, Sir Charles Aubrey Smith and Willie Watson represented England in soccer. Foster captained England in both cricket and soccer. Watson represented England in the 1950 Soccer World Cup. Sir Charles Aubrey Smith later made a name for himself as a stage and movie actor.

South Africa: Gordon White, John 'Mick' Commaille and Sid O'Lynn represented South Africa in soccer.

New Zealand: Ken Hough represented New Zealand and Australia in soccer.

Test cricketers who played rugby at international level

England: Albert 'Monkey' Hornby, Andrew Stoddart, M.J.K. Smith, Reggie Spooner and George Vernon represented England in rugby. Hornby and Stoddart captained England in both cricket and rugby. Maurice Turnbull played rugby and hockey for Wales. Gregor McGregor played rugby for Scotland.

England and Australia: Sammy Woods represented England in rugby.

England and South Africa: Frank Mitchell represented England in rugby.

South Africa: Tony Harris, John 'Biddy' Anderson, Percy Twentyman-Jones, Albert Powell and Alfred Richards represented South Africa in rugby. James Sinclair played rugby for South Africa and England. Reggie Schwarz, Harold 'Tuppy' Owen-Smith, Reginald Hands, Sir William Milton and Clive van Ryneveld played rugby for England. Michael Elgie played rugby for Scotland.

Australia: Otto Nothling represented Australia in rugby.

New Zealand: Eric Tindill, George Dickinson and M.L. 'Curley' Page represented New Zealand in rugby. Martin Donnelly represented England in rugby.

Then there were players who represented their country *in one-day internationals (ODIs) in cricket* and in rugby. Here are three instances, according to Martin Williamson in *Cricinfo*.

A throwback to an early era where dual internationals were more commonplace, New Zealander Jeff Wilson started as a cricketer, playing four ODIs as a 19-year-old all-rounder of considerable promise, before turning his attention to rugby where he became an All Black legend with 44 tries in 60 appearances. On retiring he returned to playing cricket, and after a 12-year gap he played two more ODIs and a one-off Twenty20 for New Zealand against Australia in February and March 2005.

Another New Zealander Brian McKechnie was the unwilling participant in controversies in both cricket and rugby. In 1981 he was the batsman on the receiving end of Trevor Chappell's infamous underarm delivery at the end of the third final of the Benson & Hedges World Series between New Zealand and Australia at the MCG. Three years earlier he kicked the penalty that gave the All Blacks a hotly disputed 13–12 victory over Wales at Cardiff. The result secured New Zealand's rugby players a 'grand slam' of victories against all four countries.

Rudi van Vuuren is unique in that he represented Namibia at the 2003 cricket World Cup in South Africa and at the rugby World Cup in Australia later that year. His five matches in cricket were mixed affairs; he was hammered for a then-record 28 in one over by Darren Lehmann but a week earlier he had taken 5 for 43 against England. A decent fly-half, he was injured for much of Namibia's rugby campaign, including their 142–0 defeat against the defending champions Australia.

Test cricketers who played hockey at international level

Australia: Brian Booth played hockey for Australia in the 1956 Melbourne Olympics. Trevor Laughlin represented Australia in hockey.

South Africa: 'Jonty' Rhodes and Russell Endean represented South Africa in hockey.

England and India: Nawab of Pataudi Sr. played hockey for India.

England: Maurice Turnbull played hockey and rugby for Wales.

India: M.J. Gopalan played hockey for India.

New Zealand: Edwin McLeod and Keith Thomson played hockey for New Zealand.

Zimbabwe: David Houghton played hockey for Zimbabwe.

Test cricketer who played tennis at international level

India: Cotar Ramaswami played Davis Cup for India.

Test cricketers who played baseball at international level

Australia: Vic Richardson and Bruce Dooland played baseball for Australia.

Richardson, the grandfather of Ian, Greg and Trevor Chappell, besides shining for Australia in cricket and baseball also represented South Australia in golf and tennis. He was prominent at lacrosse and basketball and was a first-rate swimmer.

Although not an international, as a versatile sportsman the daddy of them all was extrovert Bill Alley from New South Wales and Somerset. He was a blacksmith's striker, boilermaker, deep-sea fisherman, dance-hall bouncer, professional boxer, an aggressive left-handed batsman who scored 3019 runs for Somerset in 1961 aged 42 and went on to umpire 10 Test matches. In 400 first-class matches for NSW, Somerset and Commonwealth XI from 1945 to 1968, he hit 19,612 runs at 31.88 with 31 centuries (221 not out being his top score) and 92 fifties. He also captured 768 wickets at 22.68 (taking 5 wickets in an innings 30 times, best being 8 for 65 and 10 wickets in a match once) and 293 catches.

Now with cricket going on almost 12 months a year, there has not been a cricketer who has represented his country in another sport in decades. England's Arthur Milton was probably the last of the cricket–football internationals.

The list of dual internationals presented above is not complete, only an appetising entrée for perhaps a future publication.

Statistics

All figures are as at 21 March 2008.
(Compiled with the help of Rajesh Kumar)

Also added are the impressive all-round figures of Shane Warne, Anil Kumble and Chaminda Vaas (bowlers who could bat), and of Carl Hooper (an elegant batsman who bowled off-spin). These four, although not featured in this book, are among 14 cricketers to have achieved the rare double of 2000 runs and 200 wickets in Test cricket and thus could not be bypassed here.

Statistics

At Test Level

Statistics of Test All-Rounders Featured in Chapter 1

All-Rounders	Tests	Runs	Bat Ave	100s	Wkts	Bowl Ave	5w/i	100 & 5w/i	Catches
George **Giffen** (Aus)	31	1238	23.35	1	103	27.09	7	0	24
'Monty' Noble (Aus)	42	1997	30.25	1	121	25.00	9	0	26
Aubrey Faulkner (SA)	25	1754	40.79	4	82	26.58	4	0	20
Jack Gregory (Aus)	24	1146	36.96	2	85	31.15	4	1	37
Maurice Tate (Eng)	39	1198	25.48	1	155	26.16	7	0	11
Wally Hammond (Eng)	85	7249	58.45	22	83	37.80	2	0	110
Keith Miller (Aus)	55	2958	36.97	7	170	22.97	7	1	38
'Vinoo' Mankad (Ind)	44	2109	31.47	5	162	32.32	8	1	33
Trevor Bailey (Eng)	61	2290	29.74	1	132	29.21	5	0	32
Richie Benaud (Aus)	63	2201	24.45	3	248	27.03	16	1	65
Alan Davidson (Aus)	44	1328	24.59	0	186	20.53	14	0	42
John Reid (NZ)	58	3428	33.28	6	85	33.35	1	0	43 +1 st

All-Rounders	Tests	Runs	Bat Ave	100s	Wkts	Bowl Ave	5w/i	100 & 5w/i	Catches
Trevor Goddard (SA)	41	2516	34.46	1	123	26.22	5	0	48
Garry Sobers (WI)	93	8032	57.78	26	235	34.03	6	2	109
Tony Greig (Eng)	58	3599	40.43	8	141	32.20	6	1	87
Ian Botham (Eng)	102	5200	33.54	14	383	28.40	27	5	120
Imran Khan (Pak)	88	3807	37.69	6	362	22.81	23	1	28
Kapil Dev (Ind)	131	5248	31.05	8	434	29.64	23	0	64
Richard Hadlee (NZ)	86	3124	27.16	2	431	22.29	36	0	39
Wasim Akram (Pak)	104	2898	22.64	3	414	23.62	25	1	44
Chris Cairns (NZ)	62	3320	33.53	5	218	29.40	13	0	14
Shaun Pollock (SA)	108	3781	32.31	2	421	23.11	16	0	72
Jacques Kallis (SA)	116	9477	57.78	29	229	30.91	5	2	121
Daniel Vettori (NZ)	79	2627	27.36	2	241	34.51	13	0	37
Andrew Flintoff (Eng)	67	3381	32.50	5	197	32.02	2	0	44

Statistics

All-Rounders	Tests	Runs	Bat Ave	100s	Wkts	Bowl Ave	5w/i	100 & 5w/i	Catches
Carl Hooper (WI)	102	5762	36.46	13	114	49.42	4	0	115
Shane Warne (Aus)	145	3154	17.32	0	708	25.41	37	0	125
Anil Kumble (Ind)	125	2419	18.60	1	604	28.85	35	0	56
Chaminda Vaas (SL)	102	2815	23.85	1	331	29.43	11	0	30

Av. = average; Wkts. = wickets; 5w/i = 5 wickets per innings; st = stumped;
100 & 5w/i = a century and 5 wickets per innings in the same Test.

Note: *Sobers and Kallis are the only ones to achieve the Test triple of 8000 runs,
200 wickets and 100 catches.*

Sobers, Botham, Hooper, Kallis and Warne are the only ones to achieve the Test triple of 3000 runs, 100 wickets and 100 catches.

Warne is the only one to reach the Test triple of 3000 runs, 500 wickets and 100 catches.

Kapil Dev is the only one to perform the Test double of 5000 runs and 400 wickets.

Botham is the only one to score a century in an innings and take 5 wickets in an innings in the same Test five times. No-one else has achieved it three times.

Test Double of 2000 Runs and 150 Wickets

All-Rounder	Country	Tests	Runs	Wickets	Catches
Garry Sobers	WI	93	8032	235	109
Richard Hadlee	NZ	86	3124	431	39
Ian Botham	Eng	102	5200	383	120
Kapil Dev	Ind	131	5248	434	64
Imran Khan	Pak	88	3807	362	28
Wasim Akram	Pak	104	2898	414	44
Jacques Kallis	SA	116	9477	229	121
Shaun Pollock	SA	108	3781	421	72
Chris Cairns	NZ	62	3320	218	14
Richie Benaud	Aus	63	2201	248	65
Keith Miller	Aus	55	2958	170	38
Andrew Flintoff	Eng	67	3381	197	44
Vinoo Mankad	Ind	44	2109	162	33
Ravi Shastri	Ind	80	3830	151	36
Shane Warne	Aus	145	3154	708	125
Chaminda Vaas	SL	102	2815	331	30
Anil Kumble	Ind.	125	2419	604	56
Daniel Vettori	NZ	79	2627	241	37

All-Rounders' Tests

(A fifty, a century and 5 wickets/innings in the same Test)

Player	Performances	For	Against	Venue	Year
Aubrey Faulkner	78, 123, 5–120	SA	Eng	Johannesburg	1909–10
'Vinoo' Mankad	72, 184, 5–196	Ind	Eng	Lord's	1952
'Polly' Umrigar	56, 172*, 5–107	Ind	WI	Port-of-Spain	1961–62
Garry Sobers	104, 50, 5–63	WI	Ind	Kingston	1961–62
Mushtaq Mohammad	121, 56, 5–28	Pak	WI	Port-of-Spain	1976–77
Ian Botham	50, 149*, 6–95	Eng	Aus	Leeds	1981
Wasim Akram	52, 123, 5–100	Pak	Aus	Adelaide	1989–90
Jacques Kallis	110, 88*, 5–90	SA	WI	Cape Town	1998–99

* = not out

Century and Five Wickets in a Test Innings

Country	Player	100	5 w/i	Against	Venue	Year
Australia	Charles Kelleway	114	5–33	SA	Manchester	1912
	Jack Gregory	100	7–69	Eng	Melbourne	1920–21
	Keith Miller	109	6–107	WI	Kingston	1954–55
	Richie Benaud	100	5–84	SA	Johannesburg	1957–58
England	Tony Greig	148	6–164	WI	Bridgetown	1973–74
	Ian Botham	103	5–73	NZ	Christchurch	1977–78
	Ian Botham	108	8–34	Pak	Lord's	1978
	Ian Botham	114	6–58, 7–48	Ind	Bombay	1979–80
	Ian Botham	149*	6–95	Aus	Leeds	1981
	Ian Botham	138	5–59	NZ	Wellington	1983–84
South Africa	James Sinclair	106	6–26	Eng	Cape Town	1898–99
	Aubrey Faulkner	123	5–120	Eng	Johannesburg	1909–10
	Jacques Kallis	110	5–90	WI	Cape Town	1998–99
	Jacques Kallis	139*	5–21	Ban	Potchefstroom	2002–03
West Indies	Denis Atkinson	219	5–56	Aus	Bridgetown	1954–55
	'Collie' Smith	100	5–90	Ind	Delhi	1958–59
	Garry Sobers	104	5–63	Ind	Kingston	1961–62
	Garry Sobers	174	5–41	Eng	Leeds	1966
New Zealand	Bruce Taylor **	105	5–86	Ind	Calcutta	1964–65

Statistics

Country	Player	100	5 w/i	Against	Venue	Year
India	'Vinoo' Mankad	184	5–196	Eng	Lord's	1952
	'Polly' Umrigar	172*	5–107	WI	Port-of-Spain	1961–62
Pakistan	Mushtaq Mohammad	201	5–49	NZ	Dunedin	1972–73
	Mushtaq Mohammad	121	5–28	WI	Port-of-Spain	1976–77
	Imran Khan	117	6–98, 5–82	Ind	Faisalabad	1982–83
	Wasim Akram	123	5–100	Aus	Adelaide	1989–90
Zimbabwe	Paul Strang	106*	5–212	Pak	Sheikhupura	1996–97

* = not out; ** = on debut; 5w/i = 5 wickets in an innings

Note: *The following three scored 100+ runs and took 10+ wickets in one Test:*

Alan Davidson (Aus) scored 44 and 80 and took 5–135 and 6-87 vs WI, Brisbane, 1960–61.

Ian Botham (Eng) scored 114 and took 6–58 and 7–48 vs Ind, Bombay, 1979–80.

Imran Khan (Pak) scored 117 and took 6–98 and 5–82 vs Ind, Faisalabad, 1982–83.

Wicketkeepers Scoring a Century and Making Five Dismissals in a Test Innings

Player	Runs	Dismissals	For	Against	Venue	Year
Denis Lindsay	182	6 ct	SA	Aus	Johannesburg	1966–67
Ian Smith	113*	4 ct, 1 st	NZ	Eng	Auckland	1983–84
Sampathawaduge Silva	111	5 ct	SL	Ind	Colombo (PSS)	1985–86
Adam Gilchrist	133	4 ct, 1 st	Aus	Eng	Sydney	2002–03

* = not out; ct = caught; st = stumped

Wicketkeepers Scoring 2000 runs and Making 200 Dismissals in Test Cricket

Players	Tests	Runs	Ave	100s	ct	st	Total Dismissals
Mark Boucher (SA)	111	4098	29.91	4	406	19	425
Adam Gilchrist (Aus)	96	5570	47.60	17	379	37	416
Ian Healy (Aus)	119	4356	27.39	4	366	29	395
Rod Marsh (Aus)	96	3633	26.51	3	343	12	355
Jeff Dujon (WI) #	79	3146	31.46	5	265	5	270
Alan Knott (Eng)	95	4389	32.75	5	250	19	269
Alec Stewart (Eng) #	82	4540	34.92	6	227	14	241
Godfrey Evans (Eng)	91	2439	20.49	2	173	46	219
Ridley Jacobs (WI)	65	2577	28.31	3	207	12	219
Adam Parore (NZ) #	67	2479	26.94	2	194	7	201

Below are presented the statistics of those players featured in Chapter 2 who did **not** achieve the Test double of 2000 runs and 200 dismissals

Players	Tests	Runs	Ave	100s	HS	ct	st	Total Dismissals
Syed Kirmani (Ind)	88	2759	27.04	2	102	160	38	198
Andy Flower (Zim) #	55	4404	53.70	12	232*	142	9	151
Kumar Sangakkara (SL) #	47	3093	41.24	7	230	124	20	144
Les Ames (Eng) #	44	2387	43.40	8	149	72	23	95
Farokh Engineer (Ind)	46	2611	31.08	2	121	66	16	82
John Waite (SA)	49	2336	30.33	4	134	124	17	141
Jim Parks (Eng) #	43	1876	32.34	2	108*	101	11	112

HS = Highest score, * = not out, ct = caught, st = stumped

Note: *In the above two Tables, the figures given are only when the players kept wicket. The runs scored and catches taken when they did not keep wickets are excluded.*

 # The record for Dujon excludes 176 runs and two catches taken in two Tests when not keeping wicket; Stewart's record likewise excludes 3923 runs and 36 catches in 51 Tests, Parore's 386 runs and three catches in 11 Tests, Parks's 86 runs and two catches in three Tests, Flower's 390 runs and nine catches in eight Tests, Sangakkara's 2939 runs and 25 catches in 24 Tests, Ames's 47 runs and two catches in three Tests and Waite's 69 runs in one Test.

At First-Class (FC) Level

Memorable All-Round FC Matches

Players	Batting	Bowling	For	Against	Venue	Year
Vyell E. Walker	20*, 108	10–74, 4–17	England	Surrey	The Oval	1859
W.G. Grace	104	2–60, 10–49	MCC	Oxford Uni	Oxford	1886
George Giffen	271	9–96, 7–70	S. Australia	Victoria	Adelaide	1891–92
Bernard Bosanquet	103, 100*	3–75, 8–53	Middlesex	Sussex	Lord's	1905
George Hirst	111, 117*	6–70, 5–45	Yorkshire	Somerset	Bath	1906
Franklyn Stephenson	111, 117	4–105, 7–117	Notts	Yorkshire	Nottingham	1988

* = not out; Stephenson was born in Barbados, WI.

Century and Hat-Trick in the Same FC Match

Players	For	Against	Venue	Year
George Giffen	Australians	Lancashire	Manchester	1884
William Roller	Surrey	Sussex	The Oval	1885
William Burns	Worcestershire	Gloucestershire	Worcester	1913
Vallance Jupp	Sussex	Essex	Colchester	1921
Robert Wyatt	MCC	Ceylonese	Colombo	1926–27
Learie Constantine	West Indians	Northamptonshire	Northampton	1928
D. Emrys Davies	Glamorgan	Leicestershire	Leicester	1937
Vijay Merchant	Pereira's XI	Mehta's XI	Bombay	1946–47
Mike Procter	Gloucestershire	Essex	Westcliff-on-Sea	1972
Mike Procter	Gloucestershire	Leicestershire	Bristol	1979
Kevan James	Hampshire	Indians	Southampton	1996

Unique instances: Roller scored a double century and took a hat-trick.

James scored a century and took 4 wickets in 4 balls.

1000 Runs and 100 Wickets in a Season (8 times or more)

Wilfred Rhodes (16 times), George Hirst (14), Vallance Jupp (10), W. Ewart Astill (9), Trevor Bailey, W.G. Grace, Morris Nichols, Albert Relf, Frank Tarrant, Maurice Tate, Fred Titmus and Frank Woolley (8 times each).

All these players are from England and they achieved this double of 1000 runs and 100 wickets during English first-class seasons except Tate who once achieved it during MCC's tour of India in 1926–27.

The best seasons were for Hirst who scored 2385 runs and took 208 wickets in 1906 and James H. Parks who amassed 3003 runs and took 101 wickets in 1937.

This first-class double (1000 runs and 100 wickets in a season) became exceptionally rare after the reduction of County Championship matches in 1969. Richard Hadlee in 1984 and Franklyn Stephenson in 1988—both overseas imports—are the only players to achieve this double since 1969.

Bailey in 1959 was the last player to perform the double of 2000 runs and 100 wickets in a season and Tate in 1925 was the last to reach the double of 1000 runs and 200 wickets.

Wicketkeeper's Double of 1000 Runs and 100 Dismissals in a Season

In 1928 and 1929, Les Ames performed the double of 1000 runs and 100 dismissals. In 1932 he went one better, scoring 2000 runs and making 100 dismissals.

John T. Murray is the only other wicketkeeper to achieve the 1000 run/100 dismissal double in 1957.

At One-day International (ODI) Level

2000 Runs and 200 Wickets

Player	ODIs	Runs	Bat Ave	HS	Wickets	Bowl Ave	BB
Kapil Dev (Ind)	225	3783	23.79	175*	253	27.45	5–43
Wasim Akram (Pak)	356	3717	16.52	86	502	23.52	5–15
Chris Cairns (NZ)	215	4950	29.46	115	201	32.80	5–42
Sanath Jayasuriya (SL)	411	12,310	32.30	189	308	36.39	6–29
Chris Harris (NZ)	250	4379	29.00	130	203	37.50	5–42
Shaun Pollock (SA)	303	3519	26.45	130	393	24.50	6–35
Heath Streak (Zim)	189	2943	28.29	79*	239	29.82	5–32
Jacques Kallis (SA)	274	9541	45.21	139	239	31.53	5–30
Abdul Razzaq (Pak)	231	4465	29.96	112	246	31.13	6–35
Shahid Afridi (Pak)	253	5369	23.75	109	217	36.02	5–11

Near misses: Steve Waugh (Aus) scored 7569 runs and took 195 wickets in 325 ODIs, Carl Hooper (WI) 5761 runs and 193 wickets in 227, Lance Klusener (SA) 3576 runs and 192 wickets in 171 and Chaminda Vaas (SL) 1953 runs and 392 wickets in 312.

* = not out; BB = Best Bowling performance

50 Runs and 5 Wickets in an ODI

Players	Performances	Against	Venue	Date
Viv Richards (WI)	119 and 5–41	NZ	Dunedin	18–3–1987
Krish Srikkanth (Ind)	70 and 5–27	NZ	Visakhapatnam	10–12–1988
Mark Waugh (Aus)	57 and 5–24	WI	Melbourne	15–12–1992
Lance Klusener (SA)	54 and 6–49	SL	Lahore	6–11–1997
Abdul Razzaq (Pak)	70* and 5–48	Ind	Hobart	21–1–2000
Graeme Hick (Eng)	80 and 5–33	Zim	Harare	20–2–2000
Shahid Afridi (Pak)	61 and 5–40	Eng	Lahore	27–10–2000
Sourav Ganguly (Ind)	71* and 5–34	Zim	Kanpur	11–12–2000
Scott Styris (NZ)	63* and 6–25	WI	Port-of-Spain	12–6–2002
Ronnie Irani (Eng)	53 and 5–26	Ind	The Oval	9–7–2002
Chris Gayle (WI)	60 and 5–46	Aus	St George's	1–6–2003
Paul Collingwood (Eng)	112* and 6–31	Ban	Nottingham	21–6–2005

* = not out

Abbreviations for Countries

Aus for Australia, Eng for England, SA for South Africa, WI for West Indies, NZ for New Zealand, Ind for India, Pak for Pakistan, SL for Sri Lanka, Ban for Bangladesh and Zim for Zimbabwe.

Name Changes

Cities in India where important matches were played have gone through name changes in the last two decades. To avoid confusion, they are as follows: Bombay to Mumbai, Calcutta to Kolkata, Madras to Chennai, Mysore to Karnataka.

Bibliography

Books

Arlott, John (editor), *Cricket: the Great All-Rounders*, Pelham Books, UK, UK, 1969.

Arlott, John, *Rothman's Jubilee History of Cricket* 1890–1965, Arthur Barker, UK, 1965.

Bailey, Trevor, *Sir Gary*, William Collins Sons & Co., Glasgow, 1976.

Benaud, Richie, *Willow Patterns*, Hodder & Stoughton, UK, 1969.

Benaud, Richie, *On Reflection*, Willow Books (Collins), Aus., 1984.

Benaud, Richie, *Anything but an Autobiography*, Hodder & Stoughton, Aus., 1998.

Bose, Mihir, *Keith Miller, A Cricketing Biography*, George Allen & Unwin, London, 1979.

Brayshaw, Ian, *Caught Marsh Bowled Lillee*, ABC Books, Aus., 1983.

Brodribb, Gerald, *Maurice Tate, A Biography*, London Magazine Edition, UK, 1976.

Browning, Mark, *Richie Benaud—Cricketer*, Captain, Guru, Kangaroo Press, Aus., 1996.

Cairns, Lance, *Give It a Heave, Lance Cairns*, Moa Publications, NZ, 1984.

Cashman, Richard, Franks, Warwick, Maxwell, Jim, Stoddart, Brian, Weaver, Amanda and Webster, Ray (editors), *The Oxford Companion to Australian Cricket*, Oxford University Press, Melbourne, 1996.

Davidson, Alan, *Fifteen Paces*, Souvenir Press, London, 1963.

Eagar, Patrick (photography), *Botham*. (Essays by John Arlott, Text by Graeme Wright), The Kingswood Press, Surrey, 1985.

Fiddian Marc, *Australian All-Rounders: from Giffen to Gilmour*, Pakenham Gazette, Aus., 1992.

Frindall, Bill (compiled), *The Wisden Book of Test Cricket*, 1876-77 to 1977-78, Macdonald & Jane's, London, 1979.

Frindall, Bill (compiled), *The Wisden Book of Test Cricket*, Vol. II, 1977- 1994, Headline Book Publishing, London, 1995.

Frindall, Bill (compiled), *The Wisden Book of Cricket Records*, Macdonald Queen Anne Press, UK, 1986.

Green, Benny (compiled), *The Wisden Book of Cricketers' Lives*, Queen Anne Press, UK, 1986.

Gupta, Sujoy, *Seventeen Ninety Two—A History of The Calcutta Cricket & Football Club*, Calcutta Cricket & Football Club, India, 2002.

Hadlee, Richard and Brittenden, Dick, *Hadlee*, A.H. & A.W. Reed, Wellington, NZ, 1981.

Healy, Ian, *Hands and Heals: The Autobiography*, HarperSports, Sydney, 2000.

Howat, Gerald, *Walter Hammond*, George, Allen & Unwin, London, 1984.

Imran Khan (with Patrick Murphy), *Imran: The Autobiography of Imran Khan*, Pelham Books, London, 1983.

Lodge, Derek, *The Test Match Career of Walter Hammond*, The Nutshell Publishing Co., Kent, 1990.

Martin-Jenkins Christopher, *World Cricketers—A Biographical Dictionary*, Oxford University Press, Oxford, 1996.

Meher-Homji, Kersi, *The Waugh Twins*, Kangaroo Press / Simon & Schuster, Aus., 1998.

Meher-Homji, Kersi, *Famous Cricketing Families*, Kangaroo Press / Simon & Schuster, Aus., 2000.

Meher-Homji, Kersi, *Heroes of 100 Tests*, Rosenberg Publishing, Aus., 2003.

Moyes, A.G., *A Century of Cricketers*, Angus & Robertson, Aus. 1950.

Moyes, A.G., *Australian Batsmen—From Charles Bannerman to Neil Harvey*, George G. Harrap & Co., Aus., 1954.

Pollard, Jack, *Australian Cricket: The Game and the Players*, Hodder & Stoughton with ABC, Aus., 1982.

Robinson, Ray, *On Top Down Under: Australia's Cricket Captains*, Cassell, Aus., 1975.

Sobers, Gary (with Cozier, Tony), *Gary Sobers' Most Memorable Matches*, Stanley Paul, UK, 1984.

Sobers, Garry (with Harris, Bob), *Gary Sobers, My Autobiography*, Headline Book Publishing, London, 2002.

Tate, Maurice, *My Cricketing Reminiscence*, Stanley Paul, UK, 1934.

Wisden Cricketers' Almanack (Many editions, latest by John *Wisden* & Co. Ltd., UK).

Website

cricinfo.com

Magazines/Dailies

ABC Cricket Book (Aus.)
Australian Cricketer
Inside Cricket (Aus.)
Inside Edge (Aus.)
Inside Sport (Aus.)
Mid Day (Ind.)
Sportsweek (Ind.)
The Australian
The Cricketer (UK)
The Indian Down Under (Aus.)
The Sun-Herald (Aus.)
The Sydney Morning Herald
The Wisden Cricketer (South Africa)
The Wisden Cricketer (UK)
Wisden Cricket Monthly (UK)
World of Cricket Monthly (Aus)

Index

Afridi, Shahid, 164, 243, 249, 259, 264–6, 268, 301, 302

Agnew, Jonathan, 156, 158

Ahmed, Mushtaq, 231, 235

Akhtar, Shoaib, 126, 235

Akram, Wasim, 14, 16, 19, 22, 25, 125, 140–7, 151, 166, 222, 289, 291–2, 294, 301

Akram's Test, 18

Alabaster, John, 97

Alam, Intikhab, 123

Alderman, Terry, 211

all-rounders
    criteria, 16–20, 24, 180–1, 249
    definition, 25, 87
    one-day international all-rounders, 242–78, 301–2
    top test all-rounders, 25–179, 288–97
    wicketkeeping test all-rounders, 180–241, 295–7

Allan Border Medal presentation, 20, 30, 276

Allen, David, 90

Allen, 'Gubby', 184

Alley, Bill, 286

Allom, Maurice J.C., 144

Alston, Rex, 63

Altham, Harry, 28, 30

Ambrose, Curtly, 21, 126, 140, 144, 158, 165, 209, 218

Ames, Les, 181, 182–5, 202, 241, 297, 300

Anderson, Peter, 218

Andrews, Tommy, 49

Anwar, Saeed, 260

Arlott, John, 19, 52, 73

Armstrong, Warwick, 25, 29, 35, 38, 92

Astle, Nathan, 150

Atapattu, Marvan, 164

Atherton, Michael, 195

Athey, Bill, 246

Austin, Charlie, 238

Azharuddin, Mohammad, 53

Bacher, Adam, 157

Bailey, Trevor, 15, 19, 22, 25, 74–7, 102, 163, 188, 288, 300

Bannerman, Alec, 256

Barbour, Eric, 31

Bardsley, Warren, 38, 50

Barlow, Eddie, 25, 101

Barnes, Syd, 50, 52

Baum, Greg, 248

Beck, John, 96

Bedi, Bishan, 126, 191, 207

Bedser, Alec, 18, 52, 53, 71, 74, 80, 188

Benaud, John, 220

Benaud, Lou, 78, 80

Benaud, Ritchie, 14, 15, 16, 22, 25, 78–86, 89, 90, 92, 93, 106, 112, 136, 181, 288, 291, 293

Benaud's Test, 18, 85

Berry, Scyld, 143

Bert Oldfield Sports Shop, 53

Bevan, Michael, 15, 217, 242, 243, 249–51

BHIK quartet, 21–3

Bichel, Andy, 17

Binney, Roger, 130

Bishop, Ian, 144

Blewett, Greg, 171

bodyline, 48, 51

Boon, David, 246

Booth, Lawrence, 195

Border, Allan, 21, 220, 249

Border-Gavaskar Trophy, 278

Bose, Mihir, 61, 64

Botham, (Sir) Ian, 14, 16, 17, 18, 19, 21–3, 25, 31, 61, 62, 86, 92, 114–19, 125, 126, 136, 147, 168, 173, 177, 179, 181, 243, 248, 289–94

Botham's Tests, 18, 23, 116–19

Boucher, Adam, 234

Boucher, Mark, 165, 166, 181, 198, 200, 209, 217, 228, 235–7, 241, 270, 296

Bowden, 'Billie', 262

Bowley, Ted, 47

Boycott, Geoff, 163, 199, 214

Bracewell, Brendon, 152

Bradman, (Sir Donald) Don, 21, 43, 51, 52, 54, 57, 58, 61, 65, 66, 68, 70, 88, 89, 103, 106, 107, 164, 184, 187, 218, 241, 248

Bradman's 1948 Invincibles, 21

Braund, Len, 45

Brayshaw, Ian, 212

Brearley, Mike, 112, 117, 179

Briggs, Johnny, 279

Brodribb, Gerald, 18, 47, 48, 52, 64

Brown, Bill, 67, 70

Brown, Vaughan, 138

Browning, Mark, 86

Butcher, Basil, 105

Byron, Toot, 276

Caddick, Andy, 148

Cairns, Chris, 14, 19, 25, 148–54, 155, 172, 173, 243, 256, 276, 289, 291, 301

Cairns, Lance, 150, 152

Index

Cairns, Louise, 153
Cameron, Don, 96, 98, 136
Campbell, Sherwin, 148
Cardus, Neville, 57, 66
Caught Marsh Bowled Lillee, 212
Chanderpaul, Shivnarine, 270
Chandler, 'Chubby', 176
Chandrasekhar, Bhagwat, 126, 207
Chappell, Greg, 16, 21, 43, 53, 135, 212, 215, 219, 220, 222, 244,
    249, 286
Chappell, Ian, 43, 112, 119, 135, 202, 212, 218, 222, 249, 281, 286
Chappell, Trevor, 215, 284, 286
Chapple, Murray, 97
Chapple-Hadlee Trophy, 276, 277
Chettle, Geoffrey, 96
Clifton, 'Paddy', 89
Collinge, Richard, 135, 136, 207
Collingwood, Francis, 35
Collingwood, Paul, 302
Collins, Herbert (Herbie), 42, 49–50
Compton, Denis, 66, 74, 75, 96, 173, 187
Compton-Miller Medal, 177
Constantine, Learie, 25, 125, 299
Coward, Mike, 231
Cowdrey, Colin, 43, 51, 66, 74, 82, 188, 191, 197
Cowper, Bob, 281
Coy, S.C., 35
Cozier, Tony, 211
Craig, Ian, 83
Cricinfo, 99, 125, 166, 195, 203, 230, 267, 284
Cricketer, The, 35, 41
Cronje, Hansie, 158, 165, 220
Crowe, Dave, 153
Crowe, Martin, 246
Cullinan, Daryll, 165

Darling, Joe, 30
Davidson, Alan, 14, 15–16, 19, 22, 25, 85, 87–93, 108, 122, 180,
    181, 184, 288, 294
Davidson's Test, 18
DeFreitas, Phillip, 246, 263
Dev, Kapil, 9, 16, 17, 19, 18, 21, 22, 23, 25, 31, 68, 86, 125,
    126–32, 136, 155, 181, 207, 208, 243, 289–91, 301
Dexter, Ted, 84, 85
Dhoni, M.S., 274
Dilley, Graham, 118
Docker, Cyril, 42
Donald, Allan, 157, 252
double internationals, 283–6
Dowling, Graham, 97
Drane, Robert, 234

Dravid, Rahul, 159, 174
Duckworth, George, 185
Dujon, Jeffrey, 144, 209–11, 296, 297
Dyson, John, 118

Earle, Guy, 50
Edgar, Bruce, 142
Edrich, Bill, 65, 66, 191
Emery, Phil, 228
Engineer, Farokh 'Rooky', 189–92, 205, 297
Evans, Godfrey, 181, 184, 186–8, 189, 192, 202, 217, 296
Fairbrother, Neil, 176

Fairfax, Alan, 51
Farewell to Cricket, 70
Faulkner, Aubrey, 14, 19, 20, 24, 25, 37–9, 113, 288, 292–3
Faulkner's Test, 18
Ferguson, Bill, 35 , 43–4
Ferguson, Ellen, 35
Fleming, Damien, 252
Fleming, Stephen, 171, 172
Fletcher, Duncan, 176
Fletcher, Keith, 110
Flintoff, Andrew 'Freddie', 14, 15–16, 17, 18, 19, 25, 31, 62, 155,
    166, 168, 173–9, 243, 289, 291
Flintoff, Colin, 173
Flower, Andy, 222–7, 297
Flower, Grant, 222, 224, 225
football (soccer) double internationals, 283, 286
Franks, Warwick, 40
Freeman, 'Tich', 182, 184–5
Frith, David, 41, 62, 65
Fry, C.B., 34, 61

Gabba, 217
Garner, Joel, 21, 140, 209
Gavaskar, Sunil, 21, 104–5, 114, 126, 128, 130, 191
Gayle, Chris, 243, 270–2, 302
George Giffen Stand, 30
Ghavri, Karsan, 207
Gibbs, Herschelle, 221, 237
Gibbs, Lance, 190
Giffen, George, 14–15, 19, 20, 24, 25, 26–30, 44, 288, 298–9
Gilchrist, Adam, 16, 61, 125, 140, 153, 169, 173, 181, 196, 209,
    215, 217, 228–34, 235, 237, 241, 249, 252, 264, 276, 295–6
Gillespie, Jason, 17, 235, 243, 280
Gilligan, Arthur, 45, 47, 48, 49, 60
Gilmour, Gary, 15, 16
Goddard, Trevor, 14, 22, 25, 99–101, 289

Goldsmith, Jemima, 125
Gomes, 'Larry', 211
Gooch, Graham, 132
Goodwin, Murray, 222, 225
Gower, David, 21, 53, 238
Grace, W.G., 25, 28, 57, 60, 88, 114, 298, 299
Graveney, Tom, 74, 75, 191
Greenidge, Gordon, 21, 197, 210, 211
Gregory, Arthur, 40
Gregory, Charlie, 40
Gregory, Dave, 40
Gregory, Edward Jnr (Ned), 40
Gregory, Edward William, 40
Gregory, Jack, 23, 40–4, 231, 288, 293
Gregory, John, 43
Gregory, Syd, 29, 40
Greig, Sandy, 113
Greig, Tony, 14, 19, 20, 109–13, 289, 293
Griffith, Adrian, 148
Griffith, Charlie, 140, 190
Grigg, May, 30
Grimmett, Clarrie, 65, 80
Grout, Wally, 184, 207, 216, 221
Gupta, Sujoy, 50

Hadlee, Barry, 136
Hadlee, Dayle, 135, 136
Hadlee, Karen, 136
Hadlee, (Sir) Richard, 14, 16, 17, 19, 21, 22–3, 25, 86, 94, 125,
    126, 133–9, 152, 155, 168, 171, 172, 181, 243, 289, 291, 300
Hadlee, Walter, 136, 137
Hadlee's Test, 18, 23
Hall, Wes, 80, 92, 126, 140, 189, 190
Hammond, Wally (Walter), 21, 24, 25, 42–3, 53–60, 61, 65, 68,
    151, 180, 184, 288
Harmison, Steve, 177
Harper, Roger, 250
Harris, Chris, 243, 256–8, 301
Harris, P.G. Zinzan, 257
Harvey, Ian, 15
Harvey, Neil, 83, 90, 173, 188, 198
Hayden, Matthew, 231, 275, 276
Hayes, Desmond, 130
Hazare, Vijay, 126, 263
Headley, George, 184
Healy, Ian, 16, 20, 181, 209, 215, 217–21, 234, 235, 241, 250, 296
Healy, Neville, 221
Hemmings, Eddie, 132
Hendricks, Jackie, 222, 224
Hill, Clem, 30, 38
Hirst, George, 280–1, 298, 299

Hirwani, Naren, 132
Hobbs, Jack, 21, 96
hockey double internationals, 285
Hogg, Rodney, 49
Hoggard, Matthew, 270
Holding, Michael, 21, 122, 140, 209
Holford, David, 106
Holt, Jack, 75
Hooper, Carl, 14, 25, 287, 290, 301
Houghton, David, 225
Howat, Gerald, 60
Howell, Bill, 28
Hue, Sang, 111
Hughes, Kim, 118
Hughes, Merv, 26, 114, 175
Hunte, Conrad, 193
Hussey, Michael, 249
Hutton, Len, 57–8, 66, 72, 74, 75, 96, 105

Illingworth, Ray, 25
Illingworth, Richard, 263
Imran see Khan, Imran
Iredale, Frank, 29

Jackson, Archie, 33, 51
Jaffer, Saleem, 246
Jameson, John, 190
Jardine, Douglas, 48, 51, 185
Jarvis, Arthur, 231
Jayasuriya, Sanath, 164, 243, 249, 258, 259–63, 264, 272, 301
Jayawardene, Mahela, 240–1
Jessop, Gilbert, 56, 230
Johnson, Ian, 52, 81
Johnston, Brian, 60
Julien, Bernard, 111

Kallicharran, Alvin, 111
Kallis, Jacques, 14, 17, 18, 19, 20, 25, 103, 113, 116, 125,
    145, 155, 160–7, 180, 243, 289–93, 301
Kallis's Test, 18, 165
Kaluwitherana, Romesh, 238, 260
Kanhai, Rohan, 106, 207
Kapil see Dev, Kapil
Kasprowicz, Michael, 17
Kelly, Jim, 34
Kennedy, Albert, 48
Kenyon, Don, 75
Khan, Ayub, 86
Khan, Imran, 17, 19, 21, 22, 23, 25, 62, 86, 92, 120–5, 126, 143,

Index

144, 147, 168, 173, 181, 243, 267, 289, 291, 294
Kippax, Alan, 49
Kirby, Prue, 108
Kirmani, Syed, 130, 205–8, 217, 297
Kirsten, Gary, 165
Klusener, Lance, 148, 243, 252–5, 301, 302
Knott, Alan, 184, 186, 191, 201–4, 296
Koertzen, Rudi, 241
Kumble, Anil, 22, 24, 243, 287, 290–1
Kunderan, Budhi, 189

Lal, Madan, 130
Lamb, Allan, 147, 246
Langer, Justin, 171, 231
Lara, Brian, 153, 158, 167, 173, 228, 249, 270
Larwood, Harold, 41, 42, 43, 51, 140, 182
Law, Stuart, 175
Lawry, Bill, 86, 216, 281
Lawson, Geoff, 138
Lee, Brett, 17, 126, 166, 216, 237
Lehmann, Darren, 15, 285
Lewis, Chris, 119, 147
Leyland, Maurice, 51, 183
Lillee, Dennis, 16, 21, 104, 111, 118, 122, 133, 136, 137, 140, 184, 202, 212, 244
Lindsay, Denis, 207, 281, 295
Lindwall, Ray, 61, 70, 92, 140
Lister, Dorothy, 59
Lloyd, Clive, 21, 211
Lockwood, Bill, 279
Lodge, Derek, 56, 60
Long, Ted, 42

Macartney, Charlie, 38, 49, 50
MacGill, Stuart, 215
MacLean, John, 218
McCabe, Stan, 51, 51, 58
McCullum, Brendon, 171
McDermott, Craig, 246
McDonald, Ted, 42, 52
McGlew, Jackie, 99, 101, 199
McGrath, Glenn, 17, 22, 52, 145, 216, 250, 267
McKenzie, Graham 'Garth', 90
Mahanama, Roshan, 263
Maher, Jimmy, 276
Mahindu, Anju, 108
Mahmood, Fazal, 52
Mahomed, Gul, 260
Mailey, Arthur, 49
Malcolm, Devon, 139

Malik, Aamer, 131
Malik, Salim, 222
Mallett, Ashley, 111
Mankad, Ashok, 73
Mankad, Vinoo, 14, 18, 19, 22, 24, 25, 31, 63, 68–73, 126, 136, 288, 291–2, 294
Mankad's Test, 18, 68, 72
Manthorp, Neil, 99
Marsh, Rod, 16, 104, 124, 181, 184, 209, 212–16, 218, 219, 221, 234, 241, 244, 296
Marshall, Howard, 58
Marshall, Malcolm, 21, 126, 140, 144, 254
Martin-Jenkins, Christopher, 62, 75, 109, 112, 201
Martyn, Damien, 171, 276
Mason, Ronald, 54
Massie, Bob, 201
Matthews, Greg, 114, 246
Matthews, Jimmy, 144
May, Peter, 66, 74, 85
May, Tim, 221
MCG, 33, 44, 65, 66
Mead, Philip, 47, 48
Miandad, Javed, 21, 114, 123, 124, 131, 142, 197
Milburne, Colin, 129
Miller, Keith, 14, 15, 16, 18, 19, 22, 25, 42, 61–7, 70, 75, 81, 86, 92, 109, 125, 140, 168, 173, 181, 288, 291, 293
Miller's Test, 18
Milton, Arthur, 286
Mitchell, Glenn, 67
Mohammad, Khan, 142
Mohammad, Mushtaq, 25, 116, 143, 292, 294
Mohammad, Sadiq, 126, 128
Mohammad, Shoaib, 131
Mohan, R., 131
Monty Noble's Benefit Match, 35
Morris, Arthur, 80, 96
Mosey, Don, 23, 133, 137
Moss, Stephen, 175
Mott, Matthew, 275
Moyes, A.G. 'Johnnie', 41, 78, 85, 86, 106
Muralitharan, Muttiah, 22, 23, 163, 172, 228
Murray, David, 281–2
Murray, Deryck, 281–2
Murray, John T., 182, 193, 207, 281–2, 300
Murray, Junior, 281–2
Musharraf, President Pervez, 125
Mushtaq, Saqlain, 145, 235

Nadkarni, Bapoo, 25
Naqqash, Tahir, 142
Nash, Dion, 254

Nash, Malcolm, 107
Nawaz, Sarfraz, 120
Nees-Harvey, Sybil, 59
Nicholson, Matthew, 17
Noble, Montague Alfred (Monty), 14–15, 19, 24, 25, 31–6, 136, 279, 288
Noffke, Ashley, 17

O'Neill, Norm, 92
O'Reilly, Bill, 43, 81
Old, Chris, 118, 144
Oldfield, Bert, 42, 50, 53, 184, 217
Olonga, Henry, 226
On Top Down Under, 26, 29, 31, 86
one-day international all-rounders, 242–78, 301–2
one-day Internationals (ODIs), 144, 150, 155, 158, 160, 164, 177, 228, 230, 236–7, 243, 244, 248, 249, 250, 255, 257–60, 264, 266–8, 270, 272, 275–7, 284, 301–2

Packer, Kerry, 109, 112, 204, 205, 216
Parker, R.A., 73
Parks, James H., 193, 280–1, 297, 299
Parks, James M., 193–4, 199
Parore, Adam, 150, 296, 297
Peebles, Ian, 39
Peel, Bobby, 279
Pollard, Jack, 29
Pollock, Anthony, 155, 289
Pollock, Graeme, 17, 155
Pollock, Peter, 17, 155, 156, 157, 158
Pollock, Shaun, 14, 17, 19, 21–2, 25, 31, 125, 155–9, 243, 291, 301
Ponsford, Bill, 49, 51
Ponting, Ricky, 21, 166, 178, 216, 230, 233, 234, 236,
Prasanna, Erapalli, 126, 207
Pringle, Derek, 119
Proctor, Mike, 25, 123, 157, 299

Quested, David, 148

Ranatunga, Arjuna, 218
Randall, Derek, 114
Ranjitsinhji, Kumar Shri, 21, 33, 51
Razzaq, Abdul, 243, 267–9, 301, 302
Redpath, Ian, 281
Reid, John, 14, 25, 94–8, 142, 288
Reiffel, Paul, 250
Rhodes, Jonty, 273, 285
Rhodes, Wilfred, 25, 68, 73, 281, 299

Richards, (Sir Vivian) Viv, 21, 53, 114, 130, 158, 173, 210, 211, 230, 231, 233, 249, 260, 302
Richardson, Dave, 51, 200, 235
Richardson, Tom, 279
Richardson, Vic, 286
Ring, Doug, 81
Rixon, Steve, 220
Roberts, Andy, 21, 116, 140, 209
Robinson, Ray, 26, 29, 31, 41, 86
Roebuck, Peter, 140, 147, 231
Row, Subba, 85
Rowan, Eric, 200
Rowan, Lou, 93
Rowe, Lawrence, 211
Roy, Pankaj, 72
rugby double internationals, 283–5
Russell, R.C. 'Jack', 195

Saeed, Shahid, 131
Salisbury, Ian, 144
Samiuddin, Osman, 167, 267
Sangakkara, Kumar, 181, 238–41, 263, 297
SCG, 35, 42, 66, 122, 172, 248
Schwarz, Reggie, 37, 38
Selvey, Mike, 209
Shastri, Ravi, 25, 207, 291
Simpson, Bob, 43, 84, 85, 93, 102, 175, 250
Singh, Harbhajan, 278
Singh, Maninder, 244
Sir Garry Sobers Trophy, 19
Sir Gary biography, 15, 19, 76, 102
Smith, Alan, 93
Smith, Collie, 103, 293
Smith, Graeme, 165, 237
Smith, Ian, 246, 295
Smith, Michael J.K., 102, 193, 199, 283
Smith, Mike, 60
Smyth, Rob, 250
Snedden, Martin, 246
Snow, John, 123
Sobers, Daniel, 108
Sobers, (Sir Garfield) Garry, 14, 15, 16, 18, 19, 20, 22, 25, 54, 75, 86, 92, 93, 103–8, 113, 116, 125, 158, 160, 163, 181, 190, 289–93
Sobers, Genevieve, 108
Sobers, Matthew, 108
Soulez, Geoff, 205
Speed, Malcolm, 276
Srikkanth, Krish, 130, 302
Stackpole, Keith, 281
Statham, Brian, 74, 140
Stanworth, 173

Index

statistics, 287–303
Stephenson, Franklyn, 282, 298, 300
Stewart, Alec, 195–7, 296, 297
Stewart, Micky, 144
Stollmeyer, Jeff, 75
Strauss, Andrew, 177, 179
Streak, Heath, 224, 301
Surti, Rusi, 25
Sutcliffe, Herbert 'Bert', 49, 57, 96
Swanton, E.W., 72
Sydney Cricket Ground see SCG
Symonds, Andrew 'Roy', 15, 16, 97, 243, 249, 273–8
Taber, Brian, 212, 281
Tallon, Don, 221
Tate, Fred, 45, 46, 47, 51, 279
Tate, Maurice, 19, 25, 45–52, 288, 299
Tate, Maurice Jr, 49
Tate's Test, 18
Tattersall, Roy, 80
Taylor, Bob, 116–17, 201
Taylor, Mark, 21, 53, 220
Taylor, Peter, 219
Tendulkar, Sachin, 53, 126, 168, 177, 249, 259
tennis double internationals, 285
Thicknesse, John, 203
Thomson, A.A., 80, 81, 83
Thomson, Jeff, 21, 111, 122, 126, 137, 140, 202
Thorpe, Graham, 195
Titmus, Fred, 76, 299
top test all-rounders, 25–179, 288–97
Toshack, Ernie, 250
Trott, Albert, 48, 279–80
Trott, Harry, 279
Trueman, 'Fiery' Fred, 18, 42, 62, 71, 74, 80, 84, 140
Trumble, Hugh, 144
Trumper, Vic, 21, 32, 38, 57, 61, 92
Turner, Alan, 220
Turner, Charles 'Terror', 28
Turner, Glenn, 135
Tyson, Frank 'Typhoon', 42, 74, 80, 99, 126, 140

Umrigar, Polly, 25, 192, 292, 294
Umrigar's Test, 18
Underwood, Derek, 201, 204

Vaas, Chaminda, 24, 145, 243, 287, 290–1, 301
van der Merwe, Peter, 102
Vaughan, Michael, 176, 177, 178, 179
Vengsarkar, Dilip, 129
Verity, Hedley, 73, 184

Vettori, Daniel, 25, 168–72, 256, 257, 289, 291
Viswanath, Gundappa, 21
Voce, Bill, 140, 182
Vogler, Bert, 37, 38

Wadekar, Ajit, 191
Wagner, Margaret 'Peggy', 66
Waite, John, 198–200, 297
Walcott, Clyde, 193
Wall, Tim, 28
Waller, Andy, 224
Walsh, Courtney, 22, 126, 140, 144, 217, 218
Wardle, Johnny, 80
Warne, Shane, 15, 22, 24, 114, 125, 151, 155, 163, 168, 170, 172, 177, 215, 220, 221, 250, 287, 290–1
Warner, G.F., 29
Warner, (Sir) Pelham, 29, 41, 59
Washbrook, Cyril, 65
Watkins, John, 219
Watson, Shane, 15, 16
Watson, Willie, 75, 283
Waugh, Mark, 53, 157, 171, 252, 302
Waugh, Steve, 15, 21, 148, 158, 168, 171, 218, 220, 234, 243, 244–8, 301
Weekes, Everton, 75
wicketkeeping test all-rounders, 180–241, 295–7
White, Louis, 17
Whitington, RS, 63
Wilde, Simon, 179
Wilkins, Phil, 150, 248
Willis, Bob, 118
Willow Patterns, 80
Woodcock, John, 119
Woolley, Frank, 25, 299
Woolmer, Bob, 158, 266
World Cricketers, 75, 109, 112
World Series Cricket (WSC), 86, 109, 112, 122–3, 136, 204, 205
Worrell, (Sir) Frank, 85, 92, 106, 173, 192
Wright, John, 142
Wyatt, Bob, 195

Yardley, Norman, 63
You'll Keep, 216
Younis, Waqar, 123, 140, 143–4, 235

Zoysa, Nuwan, 225